BALTIMORE

LIFE IN THE CITY

Introduction by

BARRY LEVINSON

Art Direction by
KAREN GEARY

Sponsored by
THE GREATER BALTIMORE ALLIANCE

URBAN TAPESTRY SERIES

TOWERY
PUBLISHING, INC.

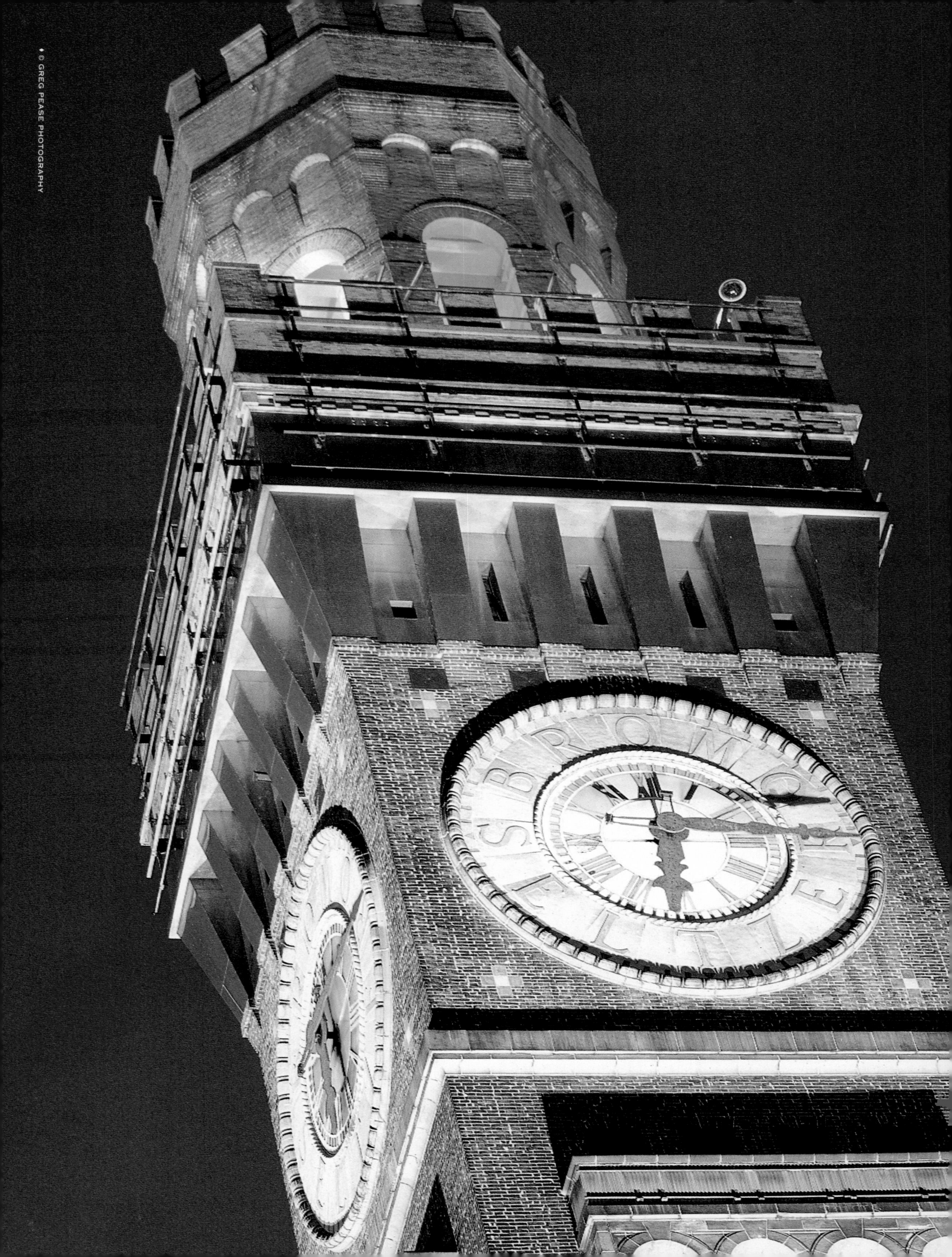

CONTENTS

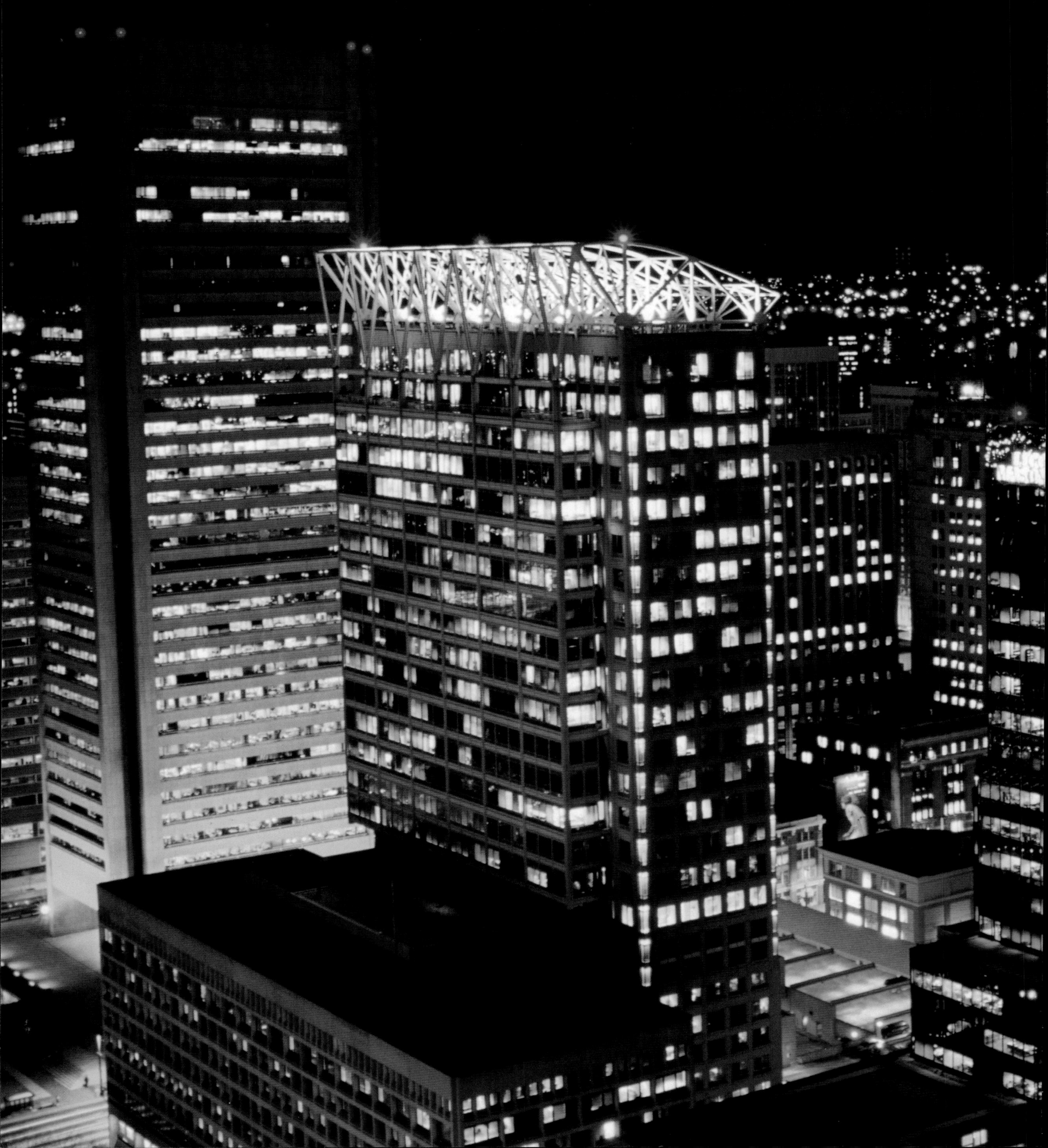

by Barry Levinson

Titles for movies sneak up on you. When I was writing what would become the third Baltimore film, I was stuck for a title . . . stuck. I was well into filming, and still nothing came to mind. And then, the way many ideas happen— they just arrive unexpectedly—Avalon. The title of the film would be *Avalon*. I didn't know why Avalon, or what Avalon meant. It just felt right. There was an Avalon theater in my neighborhood, but that wasn't what I had in mind. I looked up the definition of the word Avalon and found it came from the Arthurian legend. Avalon was the home of the heart, and for me, that's what Baltimore is all about. No matter how long I've been away, it resonates deep inside, beyond something I can articulate. It is not just remembrances, but sights and sounds, rhythm and light, seasons full of humidity and frost, back creeks and the Chesapeake Bay, row houses that go on forever and rolling horse farms. "They keep Native Dancer here," we'd say every time we drove into the country-

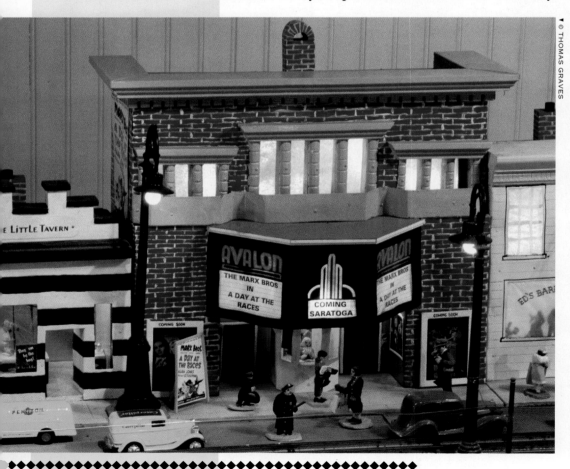

© THOMAS GRAVES

side, never sure if in fact the once-famous horse actually was kept there. But it thrilled us to think the horse might be boarded in our area. You couldn't drive by St. Mary's without checking the ball field in back. Babe Ruth played ball there as a kid. The Babe went on to fame in New York, but as a kid he rounded the bases in Baltimore. We were proud. We had the horse and the king of home runs. ▶

Growing up in Baltimore during the 1950s was a time of miracles, or so it seemed to us young kids. We got a major-league baseball team, the Orioles, and a national football team, the Colts. The city had arrived! We were Big League. Baltimore was the seventh-largest city in the United States, and we checked the yearly list, hoping to move up. We wanted to be big time in every way. As a teenager, it was "cool" to be from a large city, not a small town . . . and cool was very important. The reality is that Baltimore was neither a big city nor a small town. It lacked that definition, which would be its fate. By today's standards, that seems perfectly fine, but in the "bigger is better" era, we never got there. ▶

Its lack of definition would always be the Baltimore dilemma. It was bad enough that northerners thought we were from the south, and southerners thought of us as northerners. We were actually both. During the Civil War, the area was divided between North and South sympathizers. Families were divided, sometimes brother against brother . . . or so we were taught. The Mason-Dixon line divided the city, or was somewhere nearby. To be honest, we never truly understood where the line was, but we were definitely divided!

In 1958, the unthinkable happened: The Baltimore Colts became the National Football League champions. Led by John Unitas (bottom and opposite), they beat the New York Giants in sudden death overtime. "The greatest game ever played!" And the ultimate irony—defeating a New York team! And then again, in 1959, twice defeating the Empire

State . . . oh, sweet revenge. Although it was never clear why we wanted revenge, other than that we, as a city, suffered an inferiority complex. Nevertheless, it was sweet revenge! We were on top of the world, but in retrospect we had peaked going into the 1960s.

It is not easy to see a city decline. You don't notice the first telltale signs of a downhill slide. One day, the city seems wonderful; the next day, the entire downtown has collapsed, a vacated wasteland. The movie palaces gone. The great department stores empty, boarded up. It was the end of an era. The impact of suburbia had altered lifestyles—redefined how we did business or dealt with leisure time. Once upon a time, we thought of going downtown as a special event: "You're going downtown?" We dressed up for it. If you took a date downtown, she had to be special. There were movie palaces that could seat 2,000 people, with hard tickets, which meant you had a reserved seat. It didn't get any fancier than that! Suddenly, it was passé. It was of another time. Everything new was better . . . and suburbia was king. ▶

Randy Newman wrote a song about Baltimore, and although the melody was pretty, the lyrics didn't paint a pleasant picture:

> Hooker on the corner
>
> Waitin' for a train
>
> Drunk lyin' on the sidewalk
>
> Sleepin' in the rain
>
> And they hide their faces
>
> And they hide their eyes
>
> 'Cause the city's dyin'
>
> And they don't know why

Baltimore declined until it bottomed out in 1983, when the beloved Colts were moved out of town on a snowy night. Moving vans packed up all of the Colts' equipment and reputation and moved to another city. The team that slew the Giants was a bygone

memory. Memorial Stadium, home of the Colts—"the outdoor insane asylum"—would now lie quiet on fall Sundays, and the city mourned. But an odd thing happened, which reflects character . . . for in the end, a city is about its people first and foremost. And above all else, Baltimore is about character and characters. No one outside Baltimore cared whether or not the city got a new football team . . . no one. The city stood alone against the football world, and its defiance was defined by the Baltimore Colts marching band. The band that played at every game and many public functions did not disband. They continued to play. Even though they didn't have a football team, the Baltimore Colts marching band played on! It doesn't get much crazier than that! Year after year, they played on, practiced, worked out their moves—a marching band without a team. They didn't stop until 1995, when Baltimore got the Cleveland team and renamed them the Ravens, after an Edgar Allan Poe poem. Poe didn't grow up in Baltimore, but he did die drunk in the gutter there. Baltimore will take its heroes any way it can get them.

The Baltimore marching band was about pride. Pride. The city has that in abundance, and with it a renewed sense of purpose. A new downtown has grown up—not where the old one was, but along the harbor. Miles of shops and restaurants and other amusements line the old harbor that once was a busy port in decline.

Social and economic problems still prevail, but there is a sense that the city is once again moving in the right direction. A new millennium is upon us, and Baltimore struggles with its past and its future—a work in progress, but with a sense of optimism. Nearly 400 years ago in Newfoundland, the first Lord Baltimore founded a colony he called Avalon. His son, the second Lord Baltimore, went on to colonize Maryland and, ultimately, lend his name to the city.

Avalon has gone, but the city of Baltimore remains.

◆◆◆

HIGH ABOVE CHARLES STREET, atop a 228-step pedestal, the Washington Monument welcomes visitors to downtown Baltimore. The statue—the first permanent public tribute to George Washington—was designed by Robert Mills, who would later design the District of Columbia's Washington Monument.

FROM CITY HALL (LEFT) TO the Washington Monument (OPPOSITE), the circular form punctuates Baltimore's skyline. A 227-foot-high marble dome caps the $2.3 million City Hall, which features historical and art exhibits.

LIGHTING THE WAY: THE EMERSON Bromo-Seltzer Tower clocks continue to cast their trademark blue light over the city, as they have since the tower's completion in 1911. The Bank of America Building (OPPOSITE), erected in 1929, shines by day and at night: In 1994, a coating of gold leaf was applied to the structure's roof, restoring the original luster to this architectural crown jewel.

PROVIDING DIFFERENT SLANTS on Baltimore, Charles Center (LEFT) and the Phoenix Shot Tower (OPPOSITE) are perennially popular sight-seeing destinations. Charles Center intersperses plazas, parks, and shops with apartment and office buildings. The Phoenix Shot Tower—one of just four of its kind still standing—manufactured lead shot from 1828 through 1892, and was designated a National Historic Landmark in 1972.

As part of the Baltimore-Washington corridor's network of information technology development, Baltimore is becoming increasingly attractive to new high-tech firms. The city's efforts to capitalize on this trend include 7 million square feet of new office space—with the potential for creating more than 30,000 new jobs in the Baltimore area.

Although rush hour is inevitable, Baltimore's highways—including Interstates 83, 95, 695, and 895—generally keep traffic moving at the speed of light.

THERE'S SELDOM A NEED TO mark time when traveling the Baltimore region's section of the Maryland Mass Transit Adminis- tration (MTA). The MTA keeps com- muters on track with its Maryland Rail Commuter service (MARC), Metro Subway, and Light Rail.

BALTIMORE

THE GRACEFUL GRANDEUR of Baltimore's neoclassical Pennsylvania Station (LEFT AND OPPOSITE TOP) ties together the past and present of the region's railroads. Amtrak now runs more than 45 trains daily from the station to Washington, D.C. and New York, and the station also services MARC travelers. At the Locust Point train yard (OPPOSITE BOTTOM), freight trains transport goods inland from South Baltimore's docks.

A MURAL AT BALTIMORE/ Washington International Airport (BWI) paints a clear picture of the facility's escalating importance to both cities. Just eight miles from Baltimore and 30 miles from Washington, D.C., BWI is one of the fastest-growing airports in the nation, employing some 10,000 people and bringing more than $5 billion in revenue to Central Maryland each year.

LIFE IN THE CITY

BALTIMORE

© THOMAS GRAVES

THE PORT OF BALTIMORE HAS long played a key role in keeping the city's economy afloat. In the constant wake of increasing cargo business, the westernmost port on the eastern seaboard remains one of the busiest in the United States for both commerce and recreation.

From the dawn's early light to the waning glow of dusk, the cannons at Fort McHenry National Monument and Historic Shrine stand as a tangible link to Baltimore's past. As the fort protected the city from British attack in September 1814, a young lawyer and poet named Francis Scott Key watched from the British ship where he was a prisoner. Inspired by the American forces' defense, Key jotted down a few lines that would eventually become part of "The Star-Spangled Banner."

Baltimore teems with tributes to its participation in the nation's development. Visitors to Fort McHenry (ABOVE) can view tactical demonstrations and reenactments of the bombardment of the fort—including fireworks that mimic the British troops' ship-to-shore attack. The three-masted USS *Constellation* (OPPOSITE), a sloop of war, was first launched in 1854 and served the Union Army, defending merchant ships against Confederate raids.

46

48

HOORAY FOR THE RED, WHITE, and blue: From stars-and-stripes hats perched on the heads of Fourth of July parade spectators, to the stone eagles guarding the U.S. Appraisers Stores Building at Lombard and Gay streets, Baltimore takes pride in its patriotism.

I N June 2000, an armada of tall ships bore down upon Baltimore's Inner Harbor (PAGES 50-53). Operation Sail (OpSail) 2000, heralded as the largest tall-ship event in history, also made stops in more than a half dozen other U.S. cities. During the seven-day festival, a fleet of more than 1.5 million visitors thronged Baltimore to view and tour the ships. In all, OpSail funneled some $110 million in tourism dollars into the region's coffers.

B A L T I M O R E

FOR THOSE WILLING TO INVEST some time and stamina in exploring the Inner Harbor, a paddleboat may be the way to go. These small rental craft allow passen- gers to get up close and personal with the USS *Constellation* or the *Torsk*, a submarine docked near the National Aquarium.

When visitors to the Inner Harbor need to get back on terra firma, many of them make their way to the Power Plant, adjacent to the National Aquarium. An ESPN Zone restaurant and a Hard Rock Café are just two of the many attractions that generate business at the enormous entertainment complex.

EVEN AFTER 15 YEARS OF SERVING meals to hungry patrons, the Captain James restaurant (LEFT) in historic Fells Point remains shipshape. The lightship *Chesapeake* (OPPOSITE) fed a different need during her tenure guiding mariners to safety from the entrances to the Chesapeake and Delaware bays. A National Historic Landmark, the *Chesapeake* became a permanent floating exhibit at the Baltimore Maritime Museum in 1988.

Baltimore offers oppor-tunities and equipment galore for tackling fishing expeditions or for simply enjoying the sight and sound of weather and water.

S CIENTISTS KEEPING TRACK of the size of baby crabs help fisherfolk like Jimmy Iman (OPPOSITE) get a line on the strength of the following year's harvest. As of 2000, Iman was the youngest licensed commercial crabber in Maryland.

THE MARYLAND BLUE CRAB
is an acknowledged delicacy
among seafood lovers, who
annually shell out more money for
crabs than for any other crustacean.
Some aficionados even go so far as to
wear their appreciation emblazoned
across their chests.

BALTIMORE

OR THOSE WHO PREFER THE fishy business of watching sea creatures to that of eating them, the National Aquarium in Baltimore invites visitors to watch whales and white sharks, seals and sea turtles, and puffins and parrot fish. Some 10,000 animals represent more than 600 species at the aquarium, which has entertained more than 23 million guests and garnered several awards over the past two decades.

Kids and their families aren't the only ones to leap with joy over the National Aquarium in Baltimore. The facility caused a splash as the first in the Mid-Atlantic region to be designated a Coastal America Ecosystem Learning Center, and its unique, community-service-based programs and exhibitions have garnered a National Award of Museum Service.

72

TO KEEP A HOT DAY FROM becoming unbearable, Baltimoreans of all species seek out the nearest available sources of cool water.

BALTIMORE

THERE'S NO PLACE LIKE HOME at the Baltimore Zoo, where residents and visitors observe each other with equal aplomb. Zoo employees, who work to maintain authenticity in their charges' habitats, maintain offices in the historic Mansion House, built in 1801.

BALTIMORE

Feast your eyes: Nestled in the Guilford section of North Baltimore, stately Sherwood Gardens (pages 77-79) erupts in a riot of color each spring—ablaze with azaleas, flowering trees, and more than 80,000 tulips. Cylburn Mansion (opposite) was completed in 1888 and now houses the administrative offices of Cylburn Arboretum, a 176-acre nature preserve. Bird-watchers and budding horticulturists flock to the northwest Baltimore site, which welcomes more than 55,000 visitors annually.

LIFE IN THE CITY

78

Apillar of Baltimore's tourism industry, Evergreen House began as a modest home in 1858 and underwent a series of modifications and expansions between 1878 and 1942. The 48-room Italianate mansion and its lushly wooded grounds are now the property of the Johns Hopkins University, and house extensive collections of books and art, as well as a private theater.

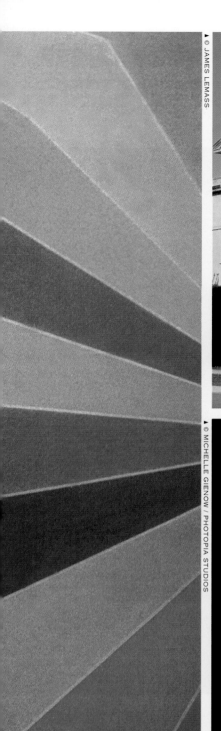

THE BALTIMORE MUSEUM OF Art (BMA), Maryland's largest such facility, sits regally enthroned in North Baltimore. With more than 85,000 works in its permanent collection, ranging from the ancient to the avant-garde and from sculptures to mosaics, the BMA is a treasure trove of international art. Museum guard William Landrum (OPPOSITE) demonstrates his professional dedication by keeping a close watch on Frank Stella's *Abra Variation III.*

ATTENDEES AT THE BALTIMORE Book Festival (ABOVE), an annual event since 1996, generally don't judge books by their covers. That specialty is the province of Will Noel (OPPOSITE), curator of the Walters Art Gallery's Manuscripts and Rare Books collection. The Walters' ever expanding archives represent a history of art from the third century B.C. to the present.

Baltimore native and noted composer Philip Glass entered the Peabody Conservatory of Music at age eight, and remained a student there until he was 15. In May 2000, he returned to the Conservatory to receive its highest honor—the George Peabody Medal for Outstanding Contributions to Music in America. Glass' minimalist compositions stand in stark contrast to the elaborate cast-iron balconies of the George Peabody Library. Part of the Special Collections Department of the Johns Hopkins University's Milton S. Eisenhower Library, the Peabody serves as a repository for more than 300,000 reference books.

DURING THE WINTER HOLIDAYS, Baltimore blooms with elaborate light displays and traditional train gardens. Some of these microcosmic cityscapes, like Jacques Kelly's (ABOVE), have grown so large and complex that they now maintain a head of steam all year round.

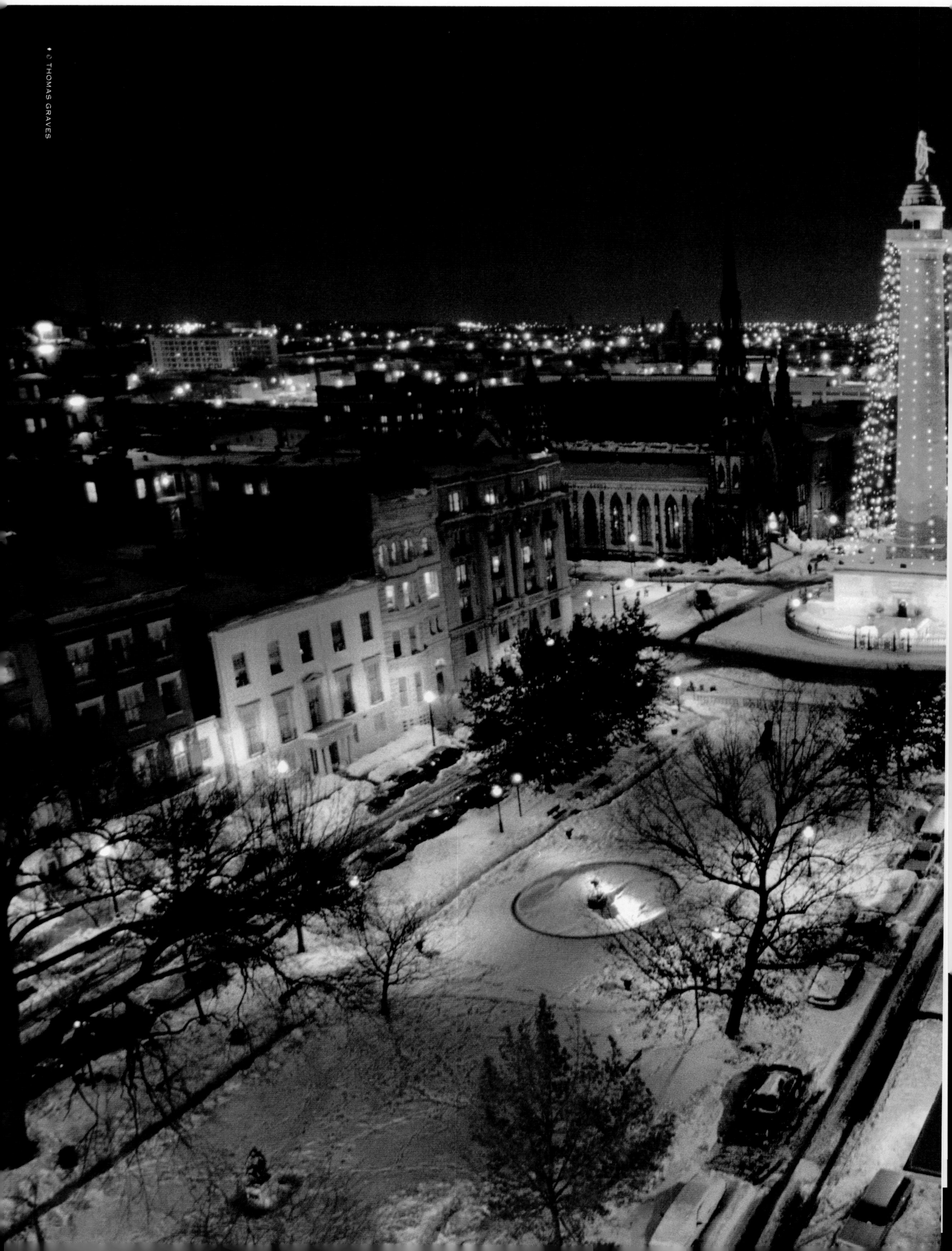

© THOMAS GRAVES

BALTIMORE'S WASHINGTON Monument glistens proudly beneath a double mantle of snow and colorful strands of light. The ceremonial decoration of the monument has been a popular holiday spectacle for several decades.

BALTIMORE

SNOWED UNDER: SHROUDED beneath a heavy snowfall, Baltimore takes on a hushed, eerie beauty. Storms of this magnitude are a relative rarity. As a rule, the city weathers the winter months with an average accumulation of just two feet of snow.

B ALTIMORE'S LANDSCAPES provide a blizzard of choices for savoring the flap caused by wintry weather. The Patterson Park Pagoda proves a breathtaking backdrop for sleighing or sledding (PAGES 114 AND 115), and views of downtown figure prominently at the Inner Harbor Ice Rink at Rash Field (BOTTOM), the city's only such outdoor establishment.

BALTIMORE

Flocking together: Both William Hall (TOP) and Harvey Smith (BOTTOM) raise and train racing pigeons. More than a fly-by-night fad, pigeon racing as a sport has roosted in Baltimore since the early days of the 20th century.

Baltimore Orioles fans are easily identified by their bright plumage and the interesting rituals they observe during baseball season. The American League team's popularity has been assured since its 1954 Baltimore debut, and the Orioles have earned that loyalty by winning three World Series titles.

BALTIMORE

O RIOLE PARK AT CAMDEN YARDS started life as a diamond in the rough. The baseball-only stadium, completed in April 1992 at a cost of approximately $110 million, has a 48,876-person capacity, and was built on the site of a former rail yard. From its position beyond the right-field wall, the 1,000-foot-long B&O Warehouse reminds fans of the location's railroading history.

BALTIMORE

THERE'S NO SUCH THING AS A wasted ball in Oriole country. In the hands of an adoring fan, even a foul ball can be a grand slam, as the packed stands at Oriole Park attest.

WOODEN BAT, LEATHER glove, Iron Man: During the 2000 season, Orioles third baseman Cal Ripken became the seventh player in Major League Baseball history to reach the rarefied realm of 3,000 hits and 400 home runs. Although Ripken stands 6'4", Number Eight's stature and status in Baltimore and in baseball have reached legendary proportions.

© 1931 LEROY MARRIKEN / THE BALTIMORE SUN

© LEE FOSTER

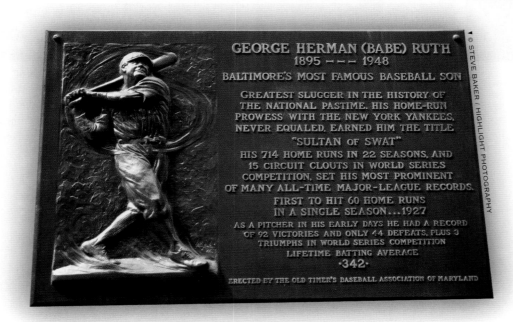

© STEVE BAKER / HIGHLIGHT PHOTOGRAPHY

GEORGE HERMAN (BABE) RUTH
1895 — 1948
BALTIMORE'S MOST FAMOUS BASEBALL SON

GREATEST SLUGGER IN THE HISTORY OF
THE NATIONAL PASTIME. HIS HOME-RUN
PROWESS WITH THE NEW YORK YANKEES,
NEVER EQUALED, EARNED HIM THE TITLE
"SULTAN OF SWAT"
HIS 714 HOME RUNS IN 22 SEASONS, AND
15 CIRCUIT CLOUTS IN WORLD SERIES
COMPETITION, SET HIS MOST PROMINENT
OF MANY ALL-TIME MAJOR-LEAGUE RECORDS.
FIRST TO HIT 60 HOME RUNS
IN A SINGLE SEASON...1927
AS A PITCHER IN HIS EARLY DAYS HE HAD A RECORD
OF 92 VICTORIES AND ONLY 44 DEFEATS, PLUS 3
TRIUMPHS IN WORLD SERIES COMPETITION
LIFETIME BATTING AVERAGE
·342·

ERECTED BY THE OLD TIMER'S BASEBALL ASSOCIATION OF MARYLAND

Just two blocks from Oriole Park at Camden Yard stands the Babe Ruth Birthplace and Museum, dedicated to preserving the legacy and iconography of its namesake. Exhibits at the museum— first opened to the public in 1974—make a clean run of the bases and include uniforms, bats, balls, and trophies, as well as vintage baseball programs, baseball cards, and other mementos. The site is also the official curator of the departed Baltimore Colts' archives.

© ROB BROWN

© RICK STEWART / ALLSPORT

© DOUG PENSINGER / ALLSPORT

© MATTHEW STOCKMAN / ALLSPORT

LOCATED WITHIN CHEERING range of Oriole Park, the bluegrass playing surface at PSINet Stadium (PAGES 132 AND 133) has seen a lot of action since the American Football Conference Baltimore Ravens inaugurated the 1.6 million-square-foot venue in 1998. In 2001, Brian Billick (OPPOSITE, BOTTOM RIGHT)—the Ravens' head coach since January 1999—led his team to a 34-7 victory over the New York Giants in Super Bowl XXXV.

B A L T I M O R E

PURPLE HAZE ALL AROUND: The trappings are fanciful, but the expressions are serious during the Ravens' home games. Growing interest in the team has brought an upsurge in revenue and an increase of new blood—royal purple, of course—to the city in recent years. The team's mascots — Edgar, Allan, and Poe—are living reminders of the poem that gave the team its name.

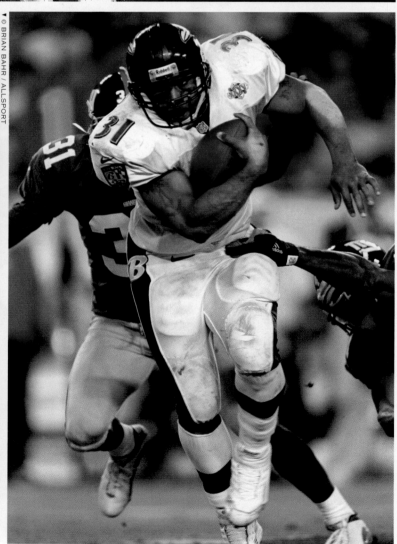

Ravens fans yelled themselves blue in the face during Super Bowl XXXV—and justifiably so. Outrunning personal controversy, Ray Lewis (BOTTOM) became the first middle linebacker ever named most valuable player in a Super Bowl. Brandon Stokley (TOP) caught a 38-yard touchdown pass from quarterback Trent Dilfer (OPPOSITE, BOTTOM LEFT) to begin the scoring onslaught that dwarfed the Giants. Jamal Lewis, rookie running back (OPPOSITE, BOTTOM RIGHT), finished the job in the fourth quarter with a three-yard dive into the end zone.

BALTIMORE

Baltimore was bathed in a purple glow as Ravens fans danced in the streets, honoring the kings of Super Bowl XXXV. After four decades as an NFL team owner, an emotional Art Modell (ABOVE, IN CENTER) took home his first Vince Lombardi trophy, while tight end Shannon Sharpe (OPPOSITE TOP) held aloft his own proof of victory.

B A L T I M O R E

PATTERSON BOWL

Duckpin bowling is right up Patterson Bowl's alley. The facility opened on Eastern Avenue in 1927, and is the oldest of its kind in Baltimore, the sport's birthplace. Longtime players like Margaret Leon (LEFT AND OPPOSITE TOP, ON RIGHT) and Catherine Dollenger (OPPOSITE BOTTOM) still try regularly to pin down that perfect game.

144

CINEMA ALFRESCO: ON FRIDAY nights during the summer, a parking lot in Little Italy is transformed into an open-air film festival. Each movie shown addresses an Italian theme, and old movie trailers and live entertainment round out the evenings.

WITH SWIRLS OF COLOR AND bursts of sound, Baltimore marvels at and celebrates the spectrum of its cultural heritage (PAGES 148-151). The most recent influx of new residents includes Latinos, Koreans, and Indians: Germans, Lithuanians, and other Europeans immigrated to Baltimore in the city's earlier days.

BALTIMORE

LIFE IN THE CITY

BALTIMORE

THERE'S NO CAUSE FOR ALARM with the Baltimore City Fire Department on call. Firefighters in training at the Frank J. Trenner Fire Academy (THIS PAGE AND OPPOSITE TOP) battle simulated fires, and also receive instruction in dealing with hazardous materials and emergency medical services. The department's Marine Division (OPPOSITE BOTTOM), founded in 1890, played a major part in extinguishing the Great Baltimore Fire, which destroyed some 140 acres of the city in 1904.

Portrait of the city as a powerhouse: Southwest Baltimore's long industrial history still asserts itself in the area's skyline (LEFT). Employees at BGE— Baltimore Gas & Electric (ABOVE)— have had a line on the region for nearly two centuries: In 1816, BGE became the first gas utility company in the nation, and one of the pioneering electric services as well. Today, providing 1.1 million customers with electricity and some 580,000 with gas, BGE's range encompasses 2,300 square miles of Central Maryland. Bethlehem Steel in Sparrows Point (PAGES 158 AND 159) has been a major area employer since 1916. Workers at the steel-processing operation have, through the years, produced steel and iron plates vital to aircraft, ships, and buildings.

ON SUGAR MOUNTAIN: Employing some 500 workers, Domino Sugar's Baltimore refinery has been a fixture in the city's Locust Point area since the early 1920s. Upgraded and updated in 2000, the plant is the largest of its kind in the country—and Domino's landmark, basketball-court-sized neon sign casts a steady glow onto the water.

162

UPSCALE, PERFECTLY PREPARED entrées and a romantic atmosphere are the trademarks of the Prime Rib steakhouse, which emulates the setting of a 1940s Manhattan supper club. Baking a name for himself, Joseph Poupon (OPPOSITE)—who with his wife, Ruth, opened Patisserie Poupon in 1986—specializes in creating cakes, pastries, and other delicacies.

BALTIMORE

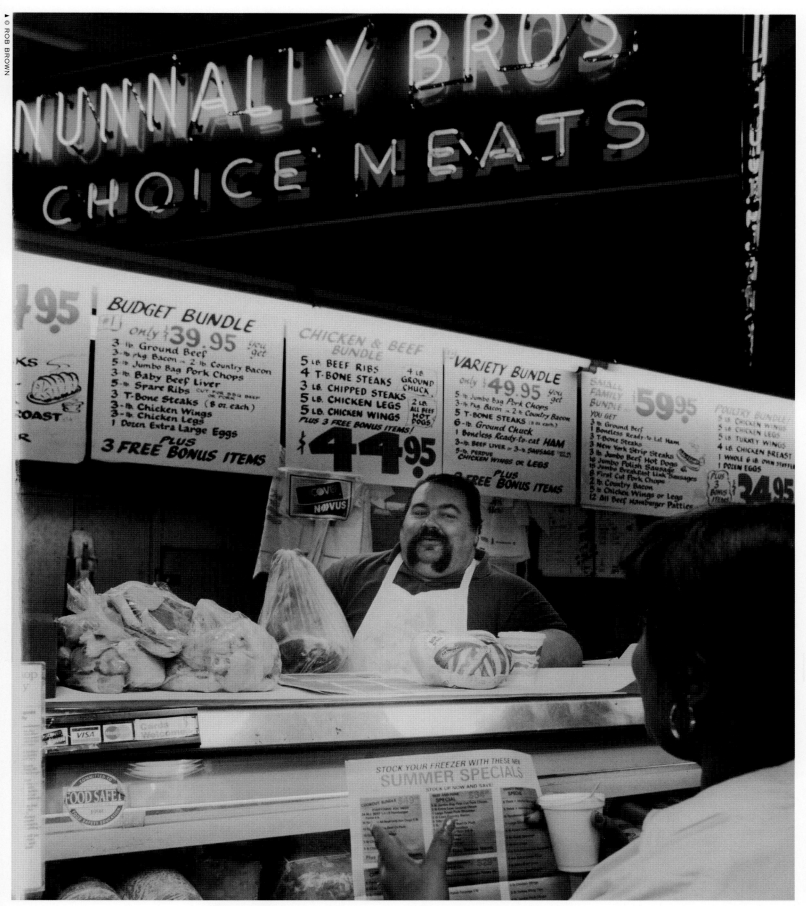

WHERE THE ELITE MEET: For four generations, Nunnally Bros. Choice Meats has provided fresh food for its customers, ably assisted by employees such as Bill Kirby (ABOVE) at the business' stall at the Cross Street Market. Serving up sweet treats at Nick's (OP-POSITE) on Riverside Avenue, Dennis Graves worked at the soda shop as a teenager and now finds himself running the place. The shop retains much of its 1920s hardware and all of its early atmosphere.

Atwater Breads
Organic Grains

L OAFING AS AN END RESULT doesn't negate the hard work that goes into the preparation. Each weekend, locals converge on the various locations of the Baltimore City Farmers Market in search of just-picked fruits and vegetables, newly cut flowers, and fresh bread—or simply to enjoy a sunny day and a lively conversation.

© 1958 RICHARD STACKS / THE BALTIMORE SUN

© 1927 / THE BALTIMORE SUN

Baltimore's Arabbers predate the advent of the supermarket. Still peddling their wares from lavishly decorated horse-drawn carts, these street vendors—once part of a thriving, multigenerational tradition— have become an endangered breed. The Arabber Preservation Society was formed in 1994 in a concerted effort to keep this remnant of the city's past from vanishing entirely.

Hats off to spring: The annual Flower Mart festival first blossomed in Mount Vernon Square in 1911. Activities include booths featuring myriad plants, arts and crafts, and food. Maypole dancing and the program's signature event—a contest to determine which attendee has sprouted the most elegant headgear—cap off the fun.

BALTIMORE

N o Flower Mart would be complete without a heavenly hat and a petaled pooch. Another long-standing tradition, the lemon stick—concocted and consumed by pushing a peppermint stick into a halved lemon, then drinking the tart juice through the candy—has been producing interesting expressions for decades.

Gardening brings out the water sprite in Kate Carus (opposite), who rents a plot in the community gardens at Druid Hill Park. These patches of land provide welcome oases for residents with no backyards of their own.

Baltimore's Dr. Samuel D. Harris National Museum of Dentistry, which opened in 1996 on the University of Maryland Baltimore campus, doesn't just pay lip service to good oral hygiene. For video-oriented visitors, The Tooth Jukebox keeps classic toothpaste and mouthwash commercials playing through word of mouth. The daring young woman on the flying trapeze—situated at the entrance to the museum's permanent exhibit, *32 Terrific Teeth*—demonstrates the benefits of a strong jaw.

32
TERRIFIC
TEETH

Step right up: The American Dime Museum (ABOVE) is the only fun house of its sort in the world. Devoted entirely to novelty entertainment, this two-story show and exhibition hall, founded in 1999, commemorates all that is bizarre in Americana. Cofounder and curator Dick Horne (OPPOSITE) is largely responsible for creating and collecting the museum's menagerie of shrunken heads, mounted mermaids, and sideshow banners and props.

IT'S FULL SPEED AHEAD AT THE B&O Railroad Museum, located at Mount Clare Station. As the Baltimore & Ohio (B&O) line's first station, the roundhouse was also the site of the country's initial passenger train departure—in January 1830. Today, the site includes historic locomotives and buildings, as well as such smaller-scale bits of railroading history as dining-car china and silverware.

F ROM THE NIGHTLIFE TO A
dog's life, Baltimore has it all.
Fells Point is home to a wide
variety of nightclubs (RIGHT) whose
musical offerings run the gamut from
rock to Latin to blues. Still listening
for his master's voice, 1,710-pound
Nipper (OPPOSITE) has had several
homes since he was born in 1954. The
fiberglass canine has guarded the roof
of the Maryland Historical Society's
Heritage Gallery since 1998.

INTERNATIONALLY RENOWNED MUSIC director Yuri Temirkanov leads the noted Baltimore Symphony Orchestra (BSO) at Joseph Meyerhoff Symphony Hall (ABOVE AND OPPOSITE TOP). National Public Radio's *Perfor-* *mance Today* broadcasts many of the BSO's scores of concerts—some of which feature special guests, such as Mayor Martin O'Malley (OPPOSITE BOTTOM).

EVERYONE NEEDS TO RELAX sometimes on the weekends, and Mayor Martin O'Malley (RIGHT)—elected in 1999 with more than 90 percent of the vote—is no exception. Regulars at Kooper's Tavern (OPPOSITE, TOP LEFT) and Bertha's (OPPOSITE, TOP RIGHT) sing the praises of these Fells Point establishments. The Waterfront Hotel and Restaurant (OPPOSITE BOTTOM), also located in Fells Point, frequently served as a set for the television program *Homicide: Life on the Street* until the show was cancelled in 1999.

LIFE IN THE CITY

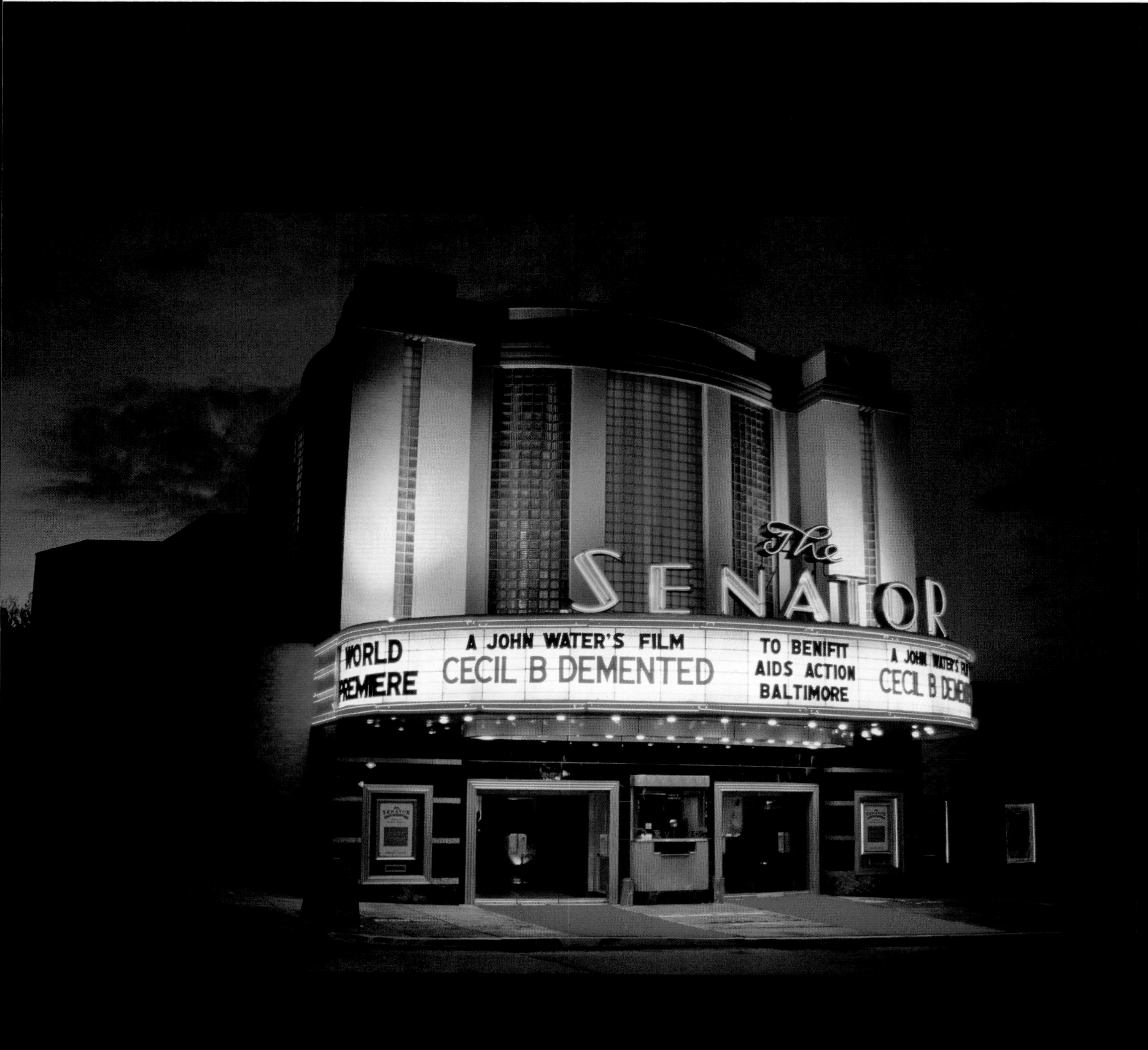

▼ © MARK HAMILTON

Nɴᴏᴛ ᴍᴀɴʏ ʟɪᴠɪɴɢ Bᴀʟᴛɪ-moreans are more famous— or more infamous–than filmmaker John Waters (ᴀʙᴏᴠᴇ), once dubbed The Pope of Trash by writer William S. Burroughs. Waters' deliberate paeans to pop culture and poor taste are all set in his hometown, and a number of them, including *Hairspray* and *Cecil B. Demented*, have premiered at the Senator The-atre (ᴏᴘᴘᴏsɪᴛᴇ). The art deco venue, built in 1939, is a cinematic icon in its own right, featuring some 900 seats and the largest movie screen in the state.

Baltimore's houses of worship represent a wide array of shapes, sizes, and faiths (PAGES 208 AND 209). When Pope John Paul II came to the city in October 1995, he visited many of the area's Catholic institutions, including the Basilica of the Assumption (ABOVE) and the Cathedral of Mary Our Queen (OPPOSITE).

A S SENIOR PASTOR OF BETHEL
A.M.E. Church, the Reverend
Dr. Frank M. Reid III (ABOVE)
ministers to more than 14,500 wor-
shippers. A relatively recent, shining
addition to the Baltimore skyline,
the new home of St. Michael the
Archangel Ukrainian Catholic Church
(OPPOSITE) was completed in 1991.

LOYOLA COLLEGE

Food for thought: Historic institutes of higher learning enrich the Baltimore area. Morgan State University (top), Loyola College (bottom), and the University of Maryland Baltimore (opposite) all contribute to the educational growth of students drawn from across the country.

The
Johns Hopkins Hospital
Children's Center

<figure>ONSISTENTLY RECOGNIZED as one of the top health care centers in the nation, the Johns Hopkins Hospital network includes a number of specialty clinics, such as Hopkins Cancer Center and the Johns Hopkins Children's Center, built around its trademark dome.</figure>

224

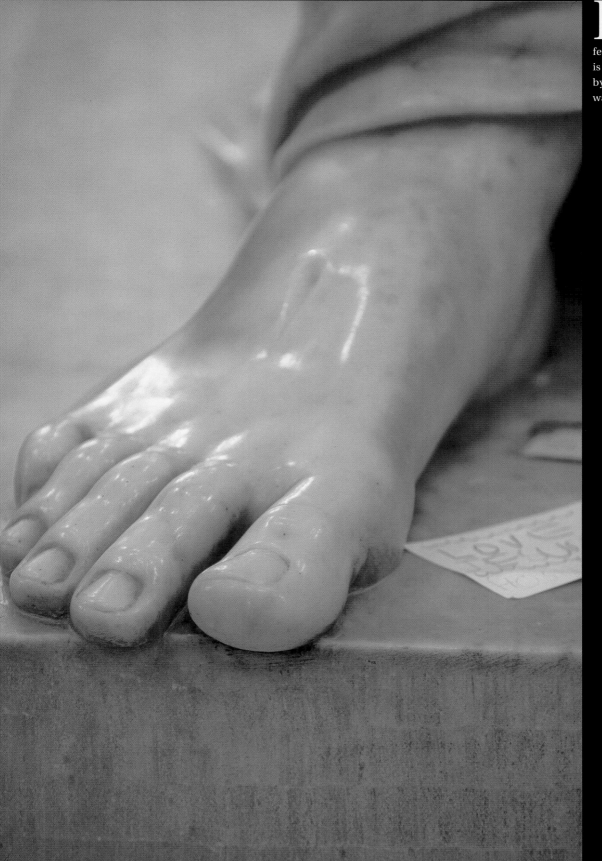

INSIDE THE DOME AT THE JOHNS Hopkins Hospital, family members or friends of patients may seek a few minutes' respite. The statue that is the hall's centerpiece was sculpted by Theo Stein of Copenhagen, and was dedicated in 1896.

BALTIMORE

Elvis never really leaves the building: Each year, Baltimore hosts Night of 100 Elvises, a fund-raiser for Johns Hopkins Hospital's Children's Center and the Lithuanian Hall Association. The ladies of the Ontario, Canada-based Graceliners (ABOVE) tour North America and strut their stuff in homage to the King. Tony Dee (OPPOSITE RIGHT), who has registered the trade name Baltimore's Black Elvis, and Frank Raines (OPPOSITE LEFT)—stockbroker by day, Presley impersonator by night—bow to the pressure of myriad fans.

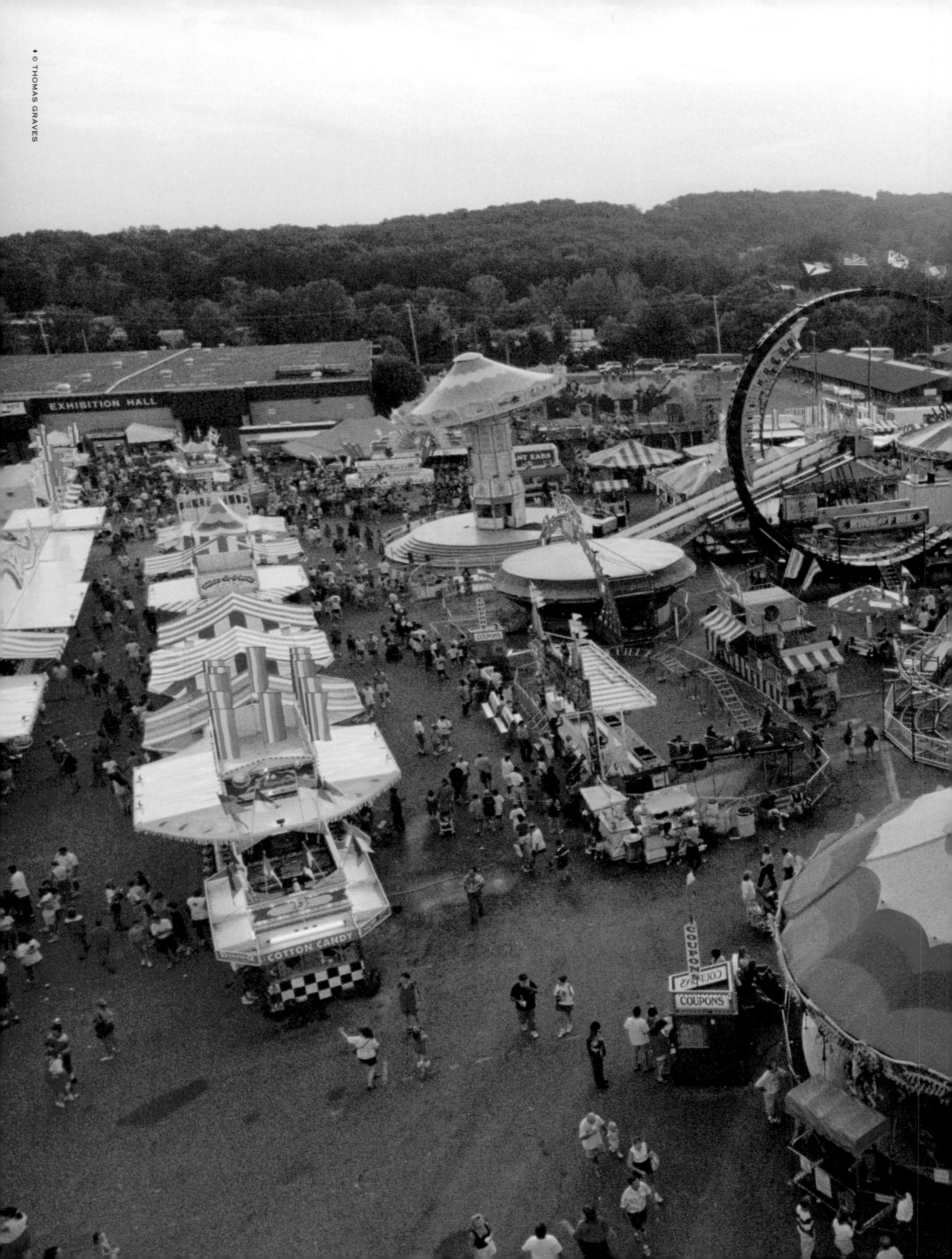

© THOMAS GRAVES

230

The Maryland State Fair (PAGES 228-231) in Timonium—just north of Baltimore—offers up a dizzying display of color during the summer. In 2000, at the 119th annual fair, rides, games, and livestock shows competed for the attention of the event's 427,266 attendees.

THE MANE EVENT: IN 1870, Pimlico Racetrack opened for horse racing and became the second such facility in the nation. The track, nicknamed Old Hilltop, is best known as the home of the Preakness Stakes, the middle gem in the Triple Crown. A number of the horses that compete in races around the country are bred at the area's many equine farms (PAGES 232 AND 233).

I N THE DAYS PRECEDING Pimlico
Racetrack's biggest annual race,
Preakness Week (PAGES 236-239)
draws thousands of visitors to the
area. The festivities include parades
featuring decorated floats and marching bands. Nightly block parties attract
crowds in excess of 15,000, and the
gauzy, gaudy spectacle of a hot-air
balloon race uplifts participants and
onlookers alike.

LIFE IN THE CITY

THE BALTIMORE REGION'S LUSH beauty and quiet, rural areas offer ample opportunities for getting away from it all.

T HE BREATHTAKING VISTAS of the area surrounding Baltimore capture the eye of many a beholder. The region's gently rolling, forested hills are ideal for sight-seeing, whether on foot or by car.

A NNAPOLIS—MARYLAND'S
historic capital—is located
35 miles north of Baltimore
at the confluence of the Chesapeake
Bay and the Severn River. Home of
the United States Naval Academy, the
city was founded in 1649 and enjoys
strong ties to its roots.

252

H onor, Courage, Commit-ment: Since 1845, more than 60,000 men and women have graduated from the United States Naval Academy in Annapolis. As the navy's undergraduate institu-tion, the academy trains students to become officers in the U.S. Navy and Marine Corps.

MARYLAND'S STATE HOUSE, completed in 1788, is the oldest capitol to see continuous legislative use, but the building's dome (RIGHT) is famous in its own right. The structure—held together by wooden pegs strengthened with iron straps—is topped with a lightning rod designed by Benjamin Franklin. In 1967, Baltimore native Thurgood Marshall became the first African-American to be appointed to the U.S. Supreme Court. The Thurgood Marshall Memorial (OPPOSITE), designed by Maryland artist Antonio Tobias Mendez, was dedicated in 1996 and stands on Annapolis' State House Square—formerly known as Lawyers' Mall.

THE
MARYLAND
INN
HISTORIC INNS

F ROM ANNAPOLIS' DINING establishments and upscale shopping to its row houses and Revolutionary War-era inns, the colorful history of Maryland's capital remains visible in its buildings and businesses.

Aᴸᴸ ᴀʟᴏɴɢ ᴛʜᴇ ᴡᴀᴛᴄʜᴛᴏᴡᴇʀ: The 1879 Hooper Strait Lighthouse (ᴀʙᴏᴠᴇ) has been a permanent exhibit at the Chesapeake Bay Maritime Museum in St. Michaels since 1967. Built in 1856 to mark the mouth of the Patapsco River, the Seven Foot Knoll Lighthouse (ᴏᴘᴘᴏsɪᴛᴇ) now greets visitors to the Baltimore Maritime Museum. Both structures are screw pile lighthouses, equipped with cast-iron pilings that allowed them to be literally screwed into the floor of the Chesapeake Bay.

FROM PLEASURE CRAFT IN the Chesapeake Bay to cargo freighters at the Inner Harbor, the Baltimore area's waterways remain a vibrant and critical source of revenue. The Port of Baltimore, the fifth busiest in the country, was initially established in 1706 to facilitate crop transportation along the eastern seaboard. Today, some 30 million tons of diverse cargoes pass through the port—one of the nation's top container terminals—each year (PAGES 264-267), providing some 127,000 jobs and reaping nearly $2 billion annually.

R ISING PROUDLY FROM NEIGH-
borhoods of row houses,
skyscrapers stand as a testament to Baltimore's status as the
15th-largest city in America and a
strong presence in commerce.

BALTIMORE

THE *Pride of Baltimore*, WHICH undertook its task as Goodwill Ambassador for the State of Maryland and the Port of Baltimore in 1977, was lost in a storm in 1986. Her successor, the *Pride of Baltimore II*, was commissioned in 1988, and today continues her mission of forging strong cultural and commercial links between Maryland and the state's international trading partners.

ARMISTEAD

Baltimore takes pride in the part it played during the country's fight for independence. Federal Hill Park (LEFT), atop an 80-foot rise, still bears vestiges of its military past in the form of cannons and other tributes. A statue of Major George Armistead (OPPOSITE), who led the defense of Fort McHenry during the 1814 bombardment, stands outside the fort's Visitor Center.

I⎺ T WAS KURT L. SCHMOKE, BALTI-
more's mayor from 1987 until
1999, who first called Baltimore
the City That Reads. Today, ambitious
students and teachers still work to
ensure that the phrase is more than

just a slogan. Through the Healthy
Start Men's Services program, Joe
Jones (OPPOSITE, ON LEFT) reads to
fathers and children like Floyd Young
and his daughter Destiny as part of
ongoing community outreach.

278   B A L T I M O R E

Having a ball: Regardless of which sport is closest to their hearts, Baltimoreans have no shortage of potential athletic heroes. The city's impressive stadiums draw legions of fans to the area each year.

WINE

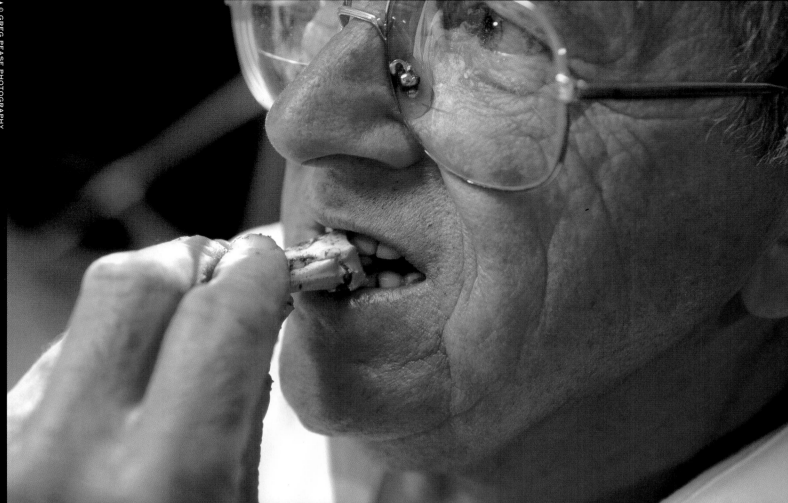

B ALTIMORE'S NUMEROUS seafood establishments, with atmospheres that range from casual to fine dining, are guaranteed to leave any patron happy as a clam. Faidley's Seafood (OPPOSITE) at the Lexington Market, was founded in 1886, and today serves up more than 1 million oysters each year.

CAPT JOES

CRAB HOUSE

IT'S EASY TO FALL IN LOVE WITH Baltimore. From the hubbub of the Inner Harbor to the stately streets of outlying neighborhoods, life in the city teems with excitement and opportunity (PAGES 282-285).

TO
GEORGE WASHINGTON
BY THE
STATE OF MARYLAND

Profiles in Excellence

A look at the corporations, businesses, professional groups, and community service organizations that have made this book possible. Their stories— offering an informal chronicle of the local business community—are arranged according to the date they were established in the Baltimore area.

Absolute Quality Inc. ◆ Action Business Systems ◆ Aether Systems Inc. ◆ Ajilon ◆ Alter Communications Inc. ◆ American Urological Association, Inc. ◆ Anne Arundel County ◆ Baltimore Business Journal ◆ Baltimore City Community College ◆ The Baltimore Development Corporation ◆ Baltimore Magazine ◆ The Baltimore Sun ◆ Baltimore Symphony Orchestra ◆ The Baltimore Zoo ◆ Branch Banking and Trust Baltimore Metro Region ◆ Bob Ward Companies ◆ Booz•Allen & Hamilton Inc. ◆ Center Stage ◆ Chesapeake Telephone Systems ◆ CIENA Corporation ◆ CitiFinancial ◆ Comcast Cable Communications, Inc. ◆ Corvis ◆ The Country Fare Group ◆ Daft-McCune-Walker, Inc. ◆ Dahne & Weinstein ◆ The Daily Record ◆ DAP Inc. ◆ Deutsche Banc Alex. Brown ◆ DMJM+HARRIS ◆ Edenwald/General German Aged People's Home, Inc. ◆ Eller Media Company ◆ Emerging Technology Center ◆ EMS Limousine, Inc. ◆ Erickson Retirement Communities ◆ EULER American Credit Indemnity Company ◆ Fidelity & Guaranty Life Insurance Company ◆ FMC Corporation Agricultural Products Group ◆ G1440 ◆ General Physics Corporation ◆ getintegrated ◆ Gilden Integrated ◆ GKV ◆ Gr8 ◆ Great Blacks In Wax Museum Inc. ◆ Greater Baltimore Alliance ◆ Greater Baltimore Technology Council ◆ Gross, Mendelsohn & Associates, P.A. ◆ Guilford Pharmaceuticals Inc. ◆ Harkins Builders, Inc. ◆ Headhunter.net ◆ HMS Insurance Associates, Inc. ◆ Hyde Incorporated Interior Design ◆ I. C. Isaacs & Company, Inc. ◆ IWIF ◆ The John D. Lucas Printing Company ◆ Kaiser Permanente Mid-Atlantic ◆ Kelly & Associates Insurance Group, Inc. ◆ kforce ◆ Legg Mason, Inc. ◆ Leonard Paper Company ◆ Long & Foster Real Estate ◆ Louis J. Grasmick Lumber Company ◆ Magco Inc. ◆ Marks, Thomas and Associates, Inc. ◆ Maryland Environmental Service ◆ Maryland Historical Society ◆ Maryland Science Center ◆ Maryland Sound International/ Maryland Sound and Image, Inc. ◆ Mentor Technologies Group, Inc. ◆ Meridian Medical Technologies, Inc. ◆ Merritt Properties, LLC ◆ The Mid-Atlantic Coca-Cola Bottling Company ◆ Middle River Aircraft Systems ◆ Monumental Life Insurance Company ◆ Morningstar Systems, Inc. ◆ MRI Worldwide Baltimore/Timonium ◆ Municipal Employees Credit Union ◆ National Aquarium in Baltimore ◆ Network Security Wizards ◆ Network Technologies Group, Inc. ◆ Nevamar Decorative Surfaces ◆ O'Conor, Piper & Flynn ERA ◆ P. Flanigan & Sons, Inc. ◆ Patuxent Publishing Company ◆ Port of Baltimore ◆ PricewaterhouseCoopers LLP ◆ PrimeNet, Inc. ◆ Radisson Plaza Hotel Baltimore Inner Harbor ◆ RDA ◆ Rifkin, Livingston, Levitan & Silver, LLC ◆ Rock Spring Village ◆ The Rouse Company ◆ Schaefer & Strohminger Management Services, Inc. ◆ Sierra Military Health Services, Inc. ◆ Sinclair Broadcast Group Inc. ◆ Skil-aire, Division of Tithe Corporation ◆ Spectera, Inc. ◆ State Employees Credit Union of Maryland, Inc. ◆ Stingray Internet Communications ◆ SunTrust Banks, Inc. ◆ SYSCOM, Inc./THINQ Learning Solutions, Inc. ◆ System Source ◆ T. Rowe Price Associates, Inc. ◆ Tate Access Floors, Inc. ◆ TESSCO ◆ Towson University ◆ Tremont Suite Hotels ◆ Unilever Home & Personal Care—USA ◆ URS Corporation ◆ Verizon ◆ W. R. Grace & Co. ◆ Wells Fargo Home Mortgage ◆ Whitman, Requardt and Associates, LLP ◆ Wills & Associates, Inc. ◆ WMAR-TV ◆ Wyndham Baltimore Inner Harbor Hotel ◆ Zurich North America ◆

Profiles in Excellence 1650–1899

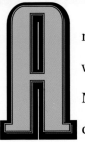

Anne Arundel County is located in the Baltimore metropolitan region, within the fourth-largest marketplace in the country. As home of Maryland's historic state capitol and many of the region's high-tech companies, Anne Arundel County is a unique blend of old and new,

a place where technology and history meet. Anne Arundel County, with the assistance of the Anne Arundel Economic Development Corporation (AAEDC), has experienced strong economic growth. The county's population now exceeds 486,000, and offers one of the most highly skilled workforces in the nation. Businesses and families are drawn to the county for its proximity to Baltimore, strong transportation infrastructure, affordability, and superior quality of life.

The Land of Pleasant Living

Anne Arundel County's quality of life makes it an easy sell for companies looking to recruit or relocate valued employees. The county has been called "the land of pleasant living," and residents agree. In Anne Arundel County, residents enjoy more than 500 miles of Chesapeake Bay shoreline and almost 40,000 acres of protected greenspace. Nature lovers appreciate the more than 70 parks in the county, which include wetlands sanctuaries, biking and hiking trails, fishing spots, boat rentals, and historic sites. The Annapolis Sailing School is the first and largest sailing school in the nation. It is not surprising, then, that boating is a popular pastime in Anne Arundel County and that Annapolis has become known as America's Sailing Capital. Many boating enthusiasts, sail or power, choose the county for their home because of its water access.

Although surrounded by nature at its best, county residents can also enjoy the culture and amenities of city life, both in Anne Arundel and beyond. The museums, restaurants, theaters, and sports arenas of Baltimore and Washington, D.C., are just a short drive away. The historic state capital city of Annapolis is located in Anne Arundel County, overlooking the Chesapeake Bay. It is home to some of the state's most charming sights and is still reminiscent of the booming, 18th-century seaport it once was. The cozy, cobblestoned streets in the downtown Annapolis district lead past buildings with architecture that has stood for more than 200 years. The Maryland State House, for example, is one of the oldest state capitol buildings still in legislative use in the United States.

The U.S. Naval Academy is a popular tourist destination, and Annapolis' picturesque architecture, shops, and restaurants attract tourists and locals alike. Anne Arundel County is also home to many local cultural organizations, including the Annapolis Opera, Annapolis Symphony Orchestra,

THE MARYLAND STATE HOUSE, LOCATED IN ANNAPOLIS, IS ONE OF THE OLDEST STATE CAPITOL BUILDINGS STILL IN LEGISLATIVE USE IN THE UNITED STATES.

Ballet Theater of Annapolis, Maryland Hall for the Performing Arts, and Chesapeake Center for the Performing Arts.

The county offers a variety of quality housing, both old and new, affordable to all income levels, and excellent access to public and private education and health care. Anne Arundel Medical Center (AAMC), a subsidiary of Anne Arundel Health Systems Inc., has been rated the top overall hospital in the Baltimore area. AAMC has also been rated first in cardiology, second in oncology, and fourth in orthopedics.

Attracting Businesses and Residents

Anne Arundel County offers a variety of attractive features for businesses and residents alike. As a business hub, few areas can match the county's transportation infrastructure. Three international airports are located in the region, including Baltimore/Washington International in Anne Arundel County. The county also has an extensive rail (commercial and commuter) system, one of the country's largest deepwater ports, and access to major interstate highways, making it possible for distribution operations in the county to reach one-third of the U.S. market overnight.

The county, located in the heart of the Baltimore/Washington corridor, boasts a labor pool with one of the highest concentrations of scientists and engineers in the country. With more than 30 top-flight colleges and universities in the region, businesses in Anne Arundel County are in an ideal position to capture a young, educated workforce. A superior quality of life helps attract and retain a highly skilled workforce. Once families locate in the area, they are reluctant to leave the excellent school systems, health care access, and recreational opportunities on the Chesapeake Bay that Anne Arundel County affords.

Anne Arundel County also helps local businesses provide ongoing training assistance for the workforce through a partnership with Anne Arundel Community College. A dynamic set of programs and courses allows Anne Arundel Community College to annually serve more than 50,000 county residents, meeting their employment and/or personal needs. Customized, employer-specific programs are aimed at upgrading workforce skills, from basics to highly specialized needs. This partnership has helped a variety of companies retain and retrain employees, and it has opened up new opportunities for county residents, training citizens for high-paying jobs.

New and existing businesses benefit from the county's supportive business climate, demonstrating the region's commitment to sustainable growth. The county's businesses enjoy a low tax structure, as well as a variety of financing options to bolster start-ups and expanding businesses. Small businesses can take advantage of the Arundel Business Loan (ABL) fund, an AAEDC program that provides business loans for up to $300,000. This program provides funding to facilitate growth and employment opportunities for small businesses seeking to start, relocate, or expand in Anne Arundel County. Since its inception in 1987, the ABL fund, also a certified U.S. Small Business Administration (SBA) lender, has provided more than $8 million in loans for Anne Arundel County small businesses, resulting in the creation and retention of many quality employment opportunities.

AAEDC's mission, on behalf of Anne Arundel County, is to recruit new employers, support existing employers, and help businesses grow. In addition, AAEDC helps

build a strong alliance with surrounding counties in Maryland to improve the state's competitive advantage. AAEDC helps to encourage quality development in Anne Arundel County, while preserving the historic charm that makes the county unique.

Representing Diverse Industries

Anne Arundel County has a diverse business community, with a strong presence in both the private and the public sectors. Northrop Grumman Corporation is the leading employer in the private sector, with some 6,500 employees throughout the county. The traditional industries of transportation, health care, and utilities are also large employers. In the public sec-

tor, the county benefits from the location of the National Security Agency in Fort Meade, which employs approximately 25,000 people. Government employers at the federal, state, and local levels provide a stable, solid foundation to Anne Arundel County's economy.

Building on this foundation are traditional industries, and Anne Arundel County has targeted leading growth industries of the future to diversify employment opportunities. An initiative to attract high-tech companies to the county has paid off, with particular strength in the e-commerce, photonics, and telecommunications markets. Anne Arundel County recently welcomed major corporations including General Dynamics and Computer Sciences Corporation. As part of the burgeoning

Baltimore/Washington high-tech corridor, Anne Arundel County boasts some 19,000 miles of fiber-optic cable, with more capacity on the way.

Anne Arundel County is also an attractive option for corporate headquarters, with its central location, convenient transportation access, and highly skilled workforce. The hospitality industry has been a growth area, with many new hotels built to meet the increasing business and tourism travel demand. The international business presence is also growing, with major organizations such as BP/Solar Corporation and RAG American Coal Holdings establishing their U.S. headquarters in Anne Arundel County.

Whether a new business is just getting started, or an established

THE DAVID TAYLOR RESEARCH CENTER, A FORMER NAVAL BASE, IS PROPOSED TO BECOME A HIGH-TECHNOLOGY BUSINESS PARK.

business is looking to expand or relocate, Anne Arundel County offers a variety of office space and the resources to help business find the perfect fit. With more than 50 business parks in the county, businesses can choose from retail, research and development, industrial, warehouse, flex, or traditional office space.

Commitment to Growth

Success stories in Anne Arundel County's business community are numerous. They include companies like CIENA Corporation, a world-class pioneer in the development cutting-edge fiber-optic equipment, and USinternetworking, an Internet-based application software provider, that have helped solidify the county as a technology leader. New technology companies have provided a pleasant balance to longtime, established tech firms in the county like ARINC, which provides communications and information-processing systems to the aviation, travel, and government industries, and Gould Fiber Optics, a leading worldwide manufacturer of fiber-optic components.

Arundel Mills Mall—a new, exciting retail project in Anne Arundel County—is a 1.3 million-square-foot, superregional shopping and entertainment complex that is expected to be one of the largest tourism attractions in the state of Maryland, attracting some 15 million to 17 million visitors each year.

A new redevelopment opportunity is under way at the David Taylor Research Center. The one-time U.S. Navy military research and development center is proposed to become a glittering, high-tech business park overlooking the Chesapeake Bay and the Severn River.

Baltimore/Washington International Airport, the fastest growing major airport in the country, is beginning a $1.8 billion expansion program of passenger and cargo facilities that will ensure its reputation well into the future as a consumer- and business-friendly airport.

Anne Arundel County is the location of choice for quality development with an exceptional quality of life. As more and more businesses decide to make it their home, Anne Arundel County truly is "where technology and history meet."

GENERAL DYNAMICS, A LEADING SUPPLIER OF SOPHISTICATED DEFENSE SYSTEMS TO THE UNITED STATES AND ITS ALLIES, IS PART OF THE GROWING LIST OF HIGH-TECHNOLOGY FIRMS LOCATED IN ANNE ARUNDEL COUNTY.

Port of Baltimore

Founded in 1706 on the banks of the Patapsco River, the Port of Baltimore has grown to become one of the busiest ports on the East Coast. Originally established to transport farmers' crops to market, today the port thrives on diversity. From automobiles to zinc, from Akron to Zhenjiang, this maritime center handles about 40 million tons of all types of cargo from around the world each year.

Nestled on the northwest branch of the Patapsco River, a tributary of the Chesapeake Bay, the Port of Baltimore consists of 45 miles of waterfront dotted with publicly and privately owned facilities. Six public terminals, owned by the Maryland Port Administration (MPA), handle containers and other general cargo such as roll-on/roll-off cargoes, automobiles, forest products, and machinery. Private terminals handle bulk cargoes such as coal, grain, and raw sugar. In addition, both public and private terminals handle automobiles, steel, aluminum, and chemicals.

Thriving Location

It has long been said that one of the Port of Baltimore's greatest advantages is its strategic mid-Atlantic location. The port's inland setting makes it the closest Atlantic port to major midwestern population and manufacturing centers, while putting it in the heart of the fourth-largest, and second-wealthiest, consumer market in the country. One-third of the U.S. population and manufacturing base is within an overnight truck ride from Baltimore's piers.

The Port of Baltimore has maximized its enviable locale by combining on-site, state-of-the-art facilities with efficient connections to points north, south, and west. Close proximity to major highway systems puts all of Baltimore's terminals within a traffic light from an interstate highway ramp. Two Class A railroads provide north-south and east-west connections to major markets in the Northeast and Midwest.

Along with being a major container port, Baltimore is the number one port for roll-on/roll-off cargoes in the United States. The port is among the top three automobile ports in the country, and is number one in automobile exports and imports of wood pulp, raw sugar, and aluminum.

Developing Heritage

Over its nearly 300-year history, the Port of Baltimore has kept pace with changing times. Its modern evolution took root following World War II, when the railroads decided to give up operating marine terminals. In 1950, a group of local business leaders, recognizing the economic potential of Baltimore's neglected piers, commissioned a study that recommended a $129 million, state-sponsored improvement plan. This plan, initiated six years later, resulted in the creation of the Maryland Port Authority and an explosion in pier renovations and new terminal developments.

The port authority developed the Dundalk Marine Terminal on a former harbor airfield; launched a $30 million reconstruction program on the Locust Point piers that created 15 modern berths to accommodate both rail and truck traffic; and purchased the Pennsylvania Railroad Pier I

THE PORT OF BALTIMORE OFFERS CUTTING-EDGE CONTAINER HANDLING AT SEAGIRT MARINE TERMINAL, ONE OF ITS FOUR CONTAINER TERMINALS. SITUATED IN A VAST TRANSPORTATION HUB, PUBLIC AND PRIVATE FACILITIES OFFER WELL OVER 32 MILLION SQUARE FEET OF STORAGE SPACE IN THE BALTIMORE AREA.

▼ DAN BREITENBACH PHOTOGRAPHY

▼ DAN BREITENBACH PHOTOGRAPHY

terminal in Canton. At the same time, many private terminals began to expand and improve their facilities. The MPA also had the foresight to see the coming containerization revolution and, earlier than most ports, built facilities to accommodate this innovation in shipping. Included in the plan was the deepening of Baltimore's channels to meet the needs of larger ships. Baltimore is now one of the few East Coast ports with a 50-foot channel.

In 1971, the Maryland Port Authority was merged into the Maryland Department of Transportation, and its name changed to the Maryland Port Administration (MPA). In 1977, the MPA finished construction on one of Baltimore's signature landmarks, the I.M. Pei-designed World Trade Center. In 1988, the Fairfield Auto Terminal opened as a turnkey project for Toyota Motor Sales, USA, cementing the port's position as a major center for East Coast auto distribution. The Seagirt Marine Terminal, completed in 1990, is regarded as one of America's top container terminals, sparking technological advances that have transformed port operations from clipboard to keyboard. Opened in 2000, the Masonville Auto Terminal sets the global standard for automobile processing.

Working with Labor

The focus on the development of new facilities and introduction of state-of-the-art technology is only one side of the Port of Baltimore's success story. While Baltimore is justifiably proud of its computerized cranes and automated gate complexes, the men and women who operate the high-tech equipment make the operation successful.

Integral to the port's standard of excellence are Baltimore's longshoremen. The International Longshoremen's Association (ILA) and the Steamship Trade Association (STA) have formed a progressive partnership that enhances both the state's competitive position and the skills of the port's workers. The workers' ability to handle any shipment—at any time and in any weather—keeps cargo moving and customers coming back.

Baltimore is ahead of the pack with its award-winning, portwide total quality initiative. Working groups addressing various portwide issues have earned two national efficiency awards. The port's Quality Cargo Handling Team (QCHAT) focuses on auto handling, bringing together labor, carriers, processors, and stevedores with one goal in mind: to set the standard for global quality and excellence in cargo handling.

As it nears its third century of service, the Port of Baltimore is still on the move, keeping pace with the times. With a tradition of service and excellence, the Port of Baltimore is now meeting the modern challenges of the industry, and is prepared to evolve with any changes that the future may bring.

BALTIMORE STANDS AT THE TOP OF THE LIST NATIONWIDE WHEN IT COMES TO ITS "WHITE-GLOVE" AUTOMOBILE HANDLING. BOTH IMPORTS AND EXPORTS ARE MOVED QUICKLY AND EFFICIENTLY BY A LABOR FORCE THAT MAKES CONTINUOUS QUALITY IMPROVEMENT ITS MISSION.

Deutsche Banc Alex. Brown

Deutsche Banc Alex. Brown combines two powerhouses in the financial industry: Deutsche Bank, the world's largest financial institution, with more than 93,000 employees worldwide, and Alex. Brown, America's oldest investment bank. These two respected names joined forces in 1999, and today represent Deutsche Bank's North American investment banking and brokerage businesses.

With a 200-year legacy of turning change into opportunity, Deutsche Banc Alex. Brown provides its corporate and private clients with customized solutions to their investment needs. The firm provides a complete range of advisory, financing, research, risk management, and investment services through its 18 offices across the United States and in London.

A Proud History in Baltimore

While Deutsche Bank is new to Baltimore, the name Alex. Brown is almost as old as the city itself. In 1800, Alexander Brown, an Irish merchant, chose the port of Baltimore to launch a small linen-import business. With Brown's business savvy and the support of his four sons, Alex. Brown & Sons grew into a large family business engaged in merchant trading and shipping, as well as—in later years—deposit and investment banking. Not only did the firm prosper, but it also played a key role in the development of the young nation. The company's speedy clipper ships—flying the firm's traditional red-and-white flag—helped revolutionize commerce by reducing shipping times between markets on both sides of the Atlantic. The company financed America's first railroad, the Baltimore and Ohio, which opened markets to the emerging West.

The firm helped rebuild the South after the Civil War; was instrumental in creating the Federal Land Bank, which was the first reliable credit resource for farmers; and pioneered the financing of major public works projects like roads and bridges. It weathered the Great Depression by taking advantage of unique investment opportunities, and actually expanded during the 1930s, while many other businesses were failing.

More recently, the firm has played a major role in the initial public offerings of such leading companies as Microsoft, Oracle, Sun Microsystems, Starbucks, and America Online. Alex. Brown went public itself in 1986, taking on the new name of Alex. Brown, Inc. Alex. Brown merged with Bankers Trust Corp. in 1997 prior to that bank's merger with Deutsche Bank in 1999.

Serving Corporate and Private Clients

The firm's Global Investment Banking unit focuses on 11 key industry groups, including media and communications, technology, chemicals, energy and utilities, and health care. The Investment Banking unit also

THE BALTIMORE CLIPPER
CIRCA 1800
ALEX. BROWN & SONS

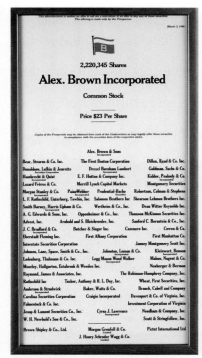

provides customized services to the venture capital community.

In the firm's Investment Services Group, brokers strive to understand private clients' objectives and tailor investment plans to meet those goals. The firm's investment representatives consult on a wide range of financial management strategies, from bond investments to private placement to estate planning.

One of the firm's strengths is providing its investment banking clients with a wide range of additional services, ranging from corporate cash management and retirement programs to employee

stock purchase plans and wealth management for company executives. The company also provides clearing services to other brokerages through its Correspondent Services department.

◆◆◆◆◆◆◆◆◆◆◆◆◆◆◆◆◆◆◆◆◆◆◆
Supporting Baltimore's Nonprofit Organizations

Alex. Brown can boast a long-established tradition of giving back to the community. The Alex. Brown Charitable Foundation is a significant funding source for nonprofits in Baltimore.

To celebrate its 200th anniversary, the firm contributed $5.5 million to a variety of nonprofit organizations. These contributions made it possible for the Walters Art Gallery to offer a hands-on art curriculum for children. At the University of Maryland, Baltimore County, officials used funds from the foundation to establish the Deutsche Banc Alex. Brown Center for Technology and Science Entrepreneurship. Another of the firm's donations put the Maryland Institute, College of Art closer to its first new academic building since 1904. Grants have also gone to the New Song Community Learning Center for a library in one of the city's poorest neighborhoods and to the Living Classrooms Foundation to renovate the oldest industrial building in Baltimore's Harbor into an educational center.

Many other organizations benefit from the firm's contributions, and Deutsche Banc Alex. Brown's employees also donate hundreds of thousands of dollars and countless hours of their time to improving the communities in which they live and work.

Today, Deutsche Banc Alex. Brown is among the world's leading financial firms in terms of assets and global presence. Led by its Baltimore-based cochairman, Mayo A. Shattuck, the firm's legacy of commitment to its clients and its city is as strong as it was 200 years ago.

The John D. Lucas Printing Company

Founded in 1830, The John D. Lucas Printing Company is the oldest continuously operated printer in Maryland, and one of the oldest elite printers in the nation. Now as part of the Mail-Well family, the company enjoys an even more prominent place in the commercial printing industry. Today,

John D. Lucas is consistently ahead of the curve, outpacing changes in this competitive industry.

John D. Lucas employs nearly 170 people at its four-acre manufacturing site in Baltimore. The 170,000-square-foot facility is in operation 24 hours a day, seven days a week, churning out books, magazines, pamphlets, annual reports, college and university publications, maps, and other commercial products. John D. Lucas specializes in medium- to long-run web press work for full-size eight-color web, one-color web, and 40-inch sheetfed jobs. The company's work has included everything from best-selling books like the Harry Potter series to materials for the National Park Service and the State of Maryland.

The Lucas name has always been associated with quality and

JOHN D. LUCAS PRINTING COMPANY'S FOUR-ACRE MANUFACTURING SITE ENCOMPASSES THIS 170,000 SQUARE-FOOT FACILITY (TOP).

BARRY M. HEYMAN (LEFT) SERVES AS PRESIDENT OF JOHN D. LUCAS AND REGIONAL VICE PRESIDENT OF MAIL-WELL MID-ATLANTIC PRINT GROUP. BOB JANES SERVES AS GENERAL MANAGER AND VICE PRESIDENT OF SALES FOR JOHN D. LUCAS AND MAIL-WELL GRAPHICS (BOTTOM).

is now becoming associated with technological innovation. Using the latest in equipment and technology, John D. Lucas is able to provide the highest-quality work by the most efficient and cost-effective means. Recent equipment upgrades include inside/outside ink-jet imaging capabilities for saddle stitching and perfect binding production lines to better meet the needs of designers and catalogers in the direct mail print market. A new, high-speed publication web press has been installed as well, offering a six- by nine-inch book format that can save customers significant postage costs. The company installed new mechanical binding equipment to increase the range of binding options, a significant purchase prompted by a customer request.

This approach is nothing new; John D. Lucas has always led the way in new technology. In fact, the company was the first commercial printer in the Baltimore/Washington corridor to offer a complete digital computer-to-plate prepress system.

Reaching Customers in New Ways

John D. Lucas is using new technology in a different way, becoming one of the first North American printers to offer a fully integrated e-commerce solution to its customers. In a unique part-

nership with printCafé, John D. Lucas allows customers to design, order, estimate, and check job status through the PRINTMAIL WELL service. Lucas staff members review each on-line request, and respond with estimates via e-mail. This high-tech service is just one more example of the comprehensive integrated communications solutions John D. Lucas offers its loyal customers.

As a longtime member of the Baltimore business community, John D. Lucas has a commitment to its hometown city and its residents. The company regularly supports a number of organizations and causes, with donations of time and resources. In 2000, John D. Lucas and its sister companies in Mail-Well Mid Atlantic Print Group raised $9,000 for Santa Claus Anonymous, a nonprofit organization that provides holiday gifts for underprivileged children.

A Proud Member of the Mail-Well Family

In 1998, John D. Lucas became part of Mail-Well Inc., a leading consolidator in commercial printing. Mail-Well, based in Englewood, Colorado, has more than 15,000 employees and some 140 printing plants in North America. Joining the Mail-Well family has provided John D. Lucas with unprecedented opportunities

to expand its capabilities and partner with sister Mail-Well companies to provide even greater service.

After the Lucas acquisition, Mail-Well added other regional printers to the family. These companies have come together to form Mail-Well Mid Atlantic Print Group, headquartered at John D. Lucas' Baltimore site. Each addition brought new printing capabilities to the fold, and today the Mail-Well Mid-Atlantic Print Group offers some of the most comprehensive services available. One unified sales force represents all of the companies in the group, presenting unique cross selling opportunities that benefit the sister companies and their customers.

French Bray, based in Glen Burnie, Maryland, is an important part of Mail-Well's Mid-Atlantic team. The commercial printer specializes in annual report printing, with its arsenal of 40-inch sheetfed and narrow web presses, as well as its extensive computer-to-plate (CTP) capabilities. French Bray targets designers, agencies, corporations, and associations for eight-color through four-color sheetfed work, and is the printer of choice for the NFL's Baltimore Ravens. Along with John D. Lucas, French Bray also offers on-line convenience to its customers through PRINTMAIL WELL.

Another Maryland company, Cambridge's Mail-Well Graphics, specializes in printing perfect-bound books and government work. The firm also offers vast experience in a unique niche, printing on very thin paper, such as that used in Bibles. In addition, Mail-Well Graphics does contractual work for almanac publishers, along with such big names as *Sports Illustrated,* ESPN, the IRS, and a Big Three car manufacturer.

Braceland Brothers, of Philadelphia, rounds out the Mail-Well Mid-Atlantic Print Group. This book printer specializes in one-color and two-color, heat-set, perfect-bound directories, catalogs, and manuals. Braceland handles a significant amount of government work, as well as private sector

work from the Philadelphia/New York corridor. Braceland Brothers also has satellite offices in Ohio and Atlanta, lending some geographic diversity to the group.

John D. Lucas and the Mail-Well Mid-Atlantic Print Group demonstrate the best-case scenario for successful industry consolidation. While maintaining individual company identities, Mail-Well Mid-Atlantic Print Group is also able to capitalize on efficiencies and maximize competitive advantages. As a member of the Mail-Well family, The John D. Lucas Printing Company preserves its proud heritage as one of the country's oldest printers, while expanding its tradition of quality, service, and innovations in ways never before possible.

W. R. Grace & Co.

With more than 6,000 employees in more than 40 countries around the world, W. R. Grace & Co. is truly an international company. Its world headquarters is located in Maryland, where the company's history traces back to the 19th century. ◆ A $1.5 billion, leading global supplier of specialty chemicals, construction, and container products, Grace has two main divisions to serve diverse industries. Grace Davison Chemicals, based in Maryland, makes refining and chemical catalysts that improve the yield and performance of petroleum petrochemical and chemical products. Grace Davison also makes silica products and adsorbents that enhance manufacturing processes and end products in a wide range of industrial and consumer applications. Grace's Performance Chemicals division, headquartered in Cambridge, Massachusetts, produces construction chemicals and building materials for the commercial, institutional, and residential construction industries, and container products for the food and consumer products industries. Together, these entities make Grace a world leader in specialty chemicals.

THE W. R. GRACE & CO. HEADQUARTERS IS LOCATED IN COLUMBIA, MARYLAND (TOP).

GRACE MAINTAINS A MANUFACTURING COMPLEX IN CURTIS BAY, MARYLAND (BOTTOM).

Rooted in Maryland

In the state of Maryland, the company's roots go back to 1832, when Davison, Kettlewell & Co. was founded in Baltimore. Davison, Kettlewell originally produced fertilizers made from old bones and oyster shells, using the first sulfuric acid chamber in the United States. By the 1920s, the company's product line had evolved to include silica gel, which formed the basis of the modern Grace Davison Chemicals and is still in production today. The growing company continued to be a leader, developing and manufacturing the world's first synthetic fluid cracking catalyst in 1942. These catalysts played a strategic role in World War II and later, by dramatically increasing the yield of gasoline from crude oil.

Meanwhile, W. R. Grace & Co. had been expanding since its U.S. founding in 1854. William Russell Grace, the company's namesake, was an influential man who held diverse business interests. In addition to the chemical company, Grace established a merchant steamship business; Grace National Bank, a forerunner to Marine Midland Bank; and Panagra airline, jointly formed with Pan American Airways. In addition, he served two terms as mayor of New York City, beginning in 1880. His descendants were involved in the management of the company until recent years, when J. Peter Grace, the former chairman, died in 1995 at age 82.

In 1954, J. Peter Grace purchased Davison, as well as the Dewey & Almy Chemical Company of Massachusetts. The three chemical companies united under the Grace name, and the historic Davison Chemicals name was retained.

A Major Employer

Today, Grace Davison has nine manufacturing sites around the world, with a total of some 2,800 employees. Nearly 400 are employed at Davison's 150-acre, world-class research facility in Columbia, Maryland, where scientists develop catalysts and silicas. Another some 700 Marylanders work at Grace Davison's 88-acre Curtis Bay Manufacturing Works, where the catalysts and silicas are produced for distribution. Grace Davison's customers use these chemicals in paints, plastics, food, personal products, and paper, as well as in oil refining and petrochemicals. In fact, nearly one-half of all the petroleum products in the world

are made using Grace Davison's refining catalysts.

In 1999, W. R. Grace & Co. relocated its headquarters to Columbia in order to establish more convenient access to its two primary business units. With both W. R. Grace & Co. and Grace Davison based in Maryland, the company takes its role as a corporate citizen in the state very seriously, employing more than 1,100 residents.

♦♦♦♦♦♦♦♦♦♦♦♦♦♦♦♦♦♦♦♦♦♦♦♦
Commitments to Community and the Environment

As a chemical manufacturer, Grace upholds its commitment to ensuring the safety of its workers and consumers. Through the company's Commitment to Care program, Grace's manufacturing sites follow a stringent environmental, health, and safety program that is one of the strictest in the industry. In 1999, every Grace facility met all program codes established by the American Chemistry Council's Responsible Care program. In addition, comprehensive training and careful management practices have helped minimize accidents and reduce emissions.

W. R. Grace gives back to the residents of Maryland in many ways. Through the company's charitable organization—the Grace Foundation—it supports

the Columbia Festival for the Arts, Columbia Foundation, and Alliance for the Chesapeake Bay. The foundation also provides funding for the Boy Scouts of Central Maryland, Goodwill Industries, and United Way. At the Curtis Bay site, several employees regularly provide information and tours for community groups and schools. Staff members at Curtis Bay have also served as judges in local sci-

ence fairs, helping to encourage the next generation of engineers and scientists.

Every day, millions of people around the world use products made with Grace chemicals—from fuels used to propel cars and airplanes, to materials used to build homes and offices. As science and society continue to evolve, W. R. Grace & Co. intends to be one step ahead, ready to fill needs and create solutions with new applications of the company's expertise in specialty chemicals.

CLOCKWISE FROM TOP LEFT: GRACE PRODUCES CATALYSTS AND SILICAS AT ITS CURTIS BAY PLANT.

STRICT QUALITY AND PROCESS CONTROLS ARE CRITICAL TO THE PRODUCTION OF GRACE'S CATALYSTS.

STATE-OF-THE-ART-RESEARCH FACILITIES ARE HOUSED AT THE COMPANY'S HEADQUARTERS IN COLUMBIA, MARYLAND.

The Baltimore Sun

For more than 160 years, citizens of Baltimore have depended on *The Baltimore Sun* for information about their community, their country, and their world. From its roots as a penny paper to its status as Maryland's largest daily metropolitan newspaper, *The Sun* has maintained its high standards of journalism and its commitment to the communities it serves.

The Sun consistently dominates its market, comprised of Baltimore and the five-county metro area. The newspaper's roots are in the city of Baltimore, where it maintains its downtown headquarters, and in South Baltimore, where it operates a state-of-the-art, computerized printing facility. Additionally, *The Sun* maintains suburban bureaus; a Washington, D.C., bureau; a state house bureau; and foreign bureaus.

Nearly 1,800 Marylanders work for *The Sun*, making it one of the largest employers in the state. But the paper is valuable to the state in many other ways as well; its tradition of hard-hitting news and its commitment to the communities it serves makes *The Sun* an integral part of the Baltimore region.

From Penny Paper to Pulitzer Winner

The first issue of *The Sun* was published on May 17, 1837. Founder Arunah S. Abell came to Baltimore from Rhode Island to introduce a penny paper in a market filled with six-cent literary editions. Abell began the tradition of in-depth, independent news coverage that attracted middle-class readers, as well as the traditional wealthy audience. From the beginning, *The Sun* was a trailblazer; under Abell's leadership, it furthered the cooperative news-gathering process that was the forerunner of the Associated Press. Although unconventional for the times, Abell's new approach to news succeeded, and *The Sun* grew and prospered.

The Abell family maintained control of the paper until 1910, when a group of Baltimore businessmen led by H. Crawford Black assumed the helm. The Black family remained involved with the paper until 1986, when *The Sun* was purchased by the Times Mirror Company. In 2000, Times Mirror merged with Tribune Company, making *The Sun* a subsidiary of Tribune—a major-market, multimedia leader with operations in television and radio broadcasting, publishing, and interactive media. Today, *The Sun* is a vital part of Tribune Publishing, along with other leading newspapers such as *The Los Angeles Times* and *The Chicago Tribune*.

Baltimore-area residents have long recognized the excellence of their hometown paper. But national and international organizations have taken note of *The Sun*'s quality as well, lauding the paper with numerous awards for journalism and design. In 1998, *The Sun* received its 14th Pulitzer Prize. In 1999, *The Sun* was named one of the top 10 newspapers in America by the *Columbia Journalism Review*. The same year, it was named one of the world's best-designed newspapers by the Society for News Design.

Through its hard-hitting investigative journalism, *The Sun* has had a significant impact on the residents of the Baltimore region. Its in-depth coverage of the city's lead-based paint problems led city, state, and federal authorities to earmark more than $50 million for cleanup programs. A

CLOCKWISE FROM TOP: ARUNAH S. ABELL FOUNDED *The Baltimore Sun* IN 1837 AND BEGAN THE TRADITION OF IN-DEPTH, INDEPENDENT NEWS COVERAGE THAT HAS CHARACTERIZED THE NEWSPAPER THROUGHOUT ITS HISTORY.

The Sun's HEADQUARTERS IS LOCATED IN DOWNTOWN BALTIMORE.

The Sun's 1999 SERIES ON MARYLAND'S JUVENILE JUSTICE "BOOT CAMPS" IS AN EXAMPLE OF THE PAPER'S AWARD-WINNING INVESTIGATIVE JOURNALISM.

1999 series on Maryland's juvenile justice "boot camps" brought this issue to the forefront of statewide debate, and led to investigations and the closings of several facilities. *The Sun*'s commitment to investigative reporting has been noted by the journalism community; the paper's prestigious awards include the George Polk Award and the Robert F. Kennedy Award for the "boot camps" series.

While *The Sun* remains committed to balanced and accurate reporting, it also keeps pace with readers' changing needs and with the latest trends in media. In 1996, *The Sun* established its Internet presence at www.SunSpot.net. SunSpot has established itself as the dominant local news, information, and classified site for Maryland's on-line community.

◆◆◆◆◆◆◆◆◆◆◆◆◆◆◆◆◆◆◆◆◆◆◆◆◆
Encouraging Future Readers

As a longtime corporate citizen, *The Sun* is committed to contributing to the Baltimore community. The paper supports a wide range of organizations that impact the region, from education and the arts to health and human services programs.

In recent years, *The Sun*'s focus has been on education—in particular through its Reading By 9 program. The company launched this initiative in 1997 after reporting that only one-third of Maryland's third graders were reading at satisfactory levels. This innovative program raises public awareness of the childhood literacy issue, provides reading incentives for children, and recognizes the successes of students and teachers in the Baltimore area as they strive to improve reading scores.

As part of the paper's Reading By 9 program, about 100 *Sun* employees volunteer as reading tutors in area elementary schools. The paper regularly reports on schools' progress in improving reading performance and publishes a special children's section each week. Other organizations have partnered with *The Sun* to provide programs that help make reading fun for kids, such as book fairs, book giveaways, and summer reading clubs. Newspapers are regularly provided to area schools for use in the classroom, and an annual awards program recognizes the literacy efforts of parents, teachers, students, and librarians.

Baltimore is a much different place from when Abell first arrived in 1837. Each decade brought with it exciting changes, yet one thing remained the same—*The Sun* was there to cover it. Many newspapers have come and gone in Baltimore, but *The Sun* remains as Maryland's largest, and among the country's most respected, newspapers.

Maryland Historical Society

The state of Maryland and its residents feature prominently in many important events in American history—from colonial times through the Civil War and Reconstruction and into the modern era. Fortunately, much of that history is preserved and documented through the efforts of the Maryland Historical Society (MHS). Thanks to a group of diligent Baltimoreans who founded the society in 1844, the state benefits from one of the most comprehensive historical societies in the nation, with an extensive collection of books, manuscripts, art, and historical artifacts.

"Maryland's history is not just the story of white, Anglo-Saxon Protestants," says Dennis Fiori, director. "People of all heritages have built Maryland and we want to tell their stories." With that in mind, MHS features a variety of permanent and changing exhibitions, highlighting the state's diverse history. The museum and library are home to more than 7.5 million objects, manuscripts, and rare books.

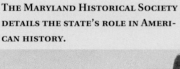

THE MARYLAND HISTORICAL SOCIETY DETAILS THE STATE'S ROLE IN AMERICAN HISTORY.

Permanent exhibitions include the Gallery of Early Maryland Life, 1634-1800; A House Divided: Maryland During the Civil War; the Pratt House period room in a historic Baltimore mansion; and the Symington Sporting Arts Gallery and Library. A variety of temporary exhibitions are displayed each year, with such titles as *Filming Maryland; Steamboat Vacations: Excursions on the Chesapeake*; and *Celebrating the Baltimore City Life Collections*. Fine artwork on display includes Charles Willson Peale's painting *Washington and His Generals at Yorktown*, and the works of African-American artist Joshua Johnson. Popular culture throughout history is reflected as well, from the memorabilia of jazz icon and Maryland native Eubie Blake to an extensive collection of American decorative and folk art.

Sharing and Preserving History

MHS strives to spread its message beyond its walls and into the community. Some 5,000 members strong, MHS is committed to sharing the wonders and insights of Maryland history in innovative ways by hosting more than 15,000 students each year and reaching more than 40,000 people through its educational outreach programs.

MHS' annual fund-raising events have become fixtures on the state's social calendar. The Maryland Historical Society Antique Show and the Maryland Hunt Club Luncheon are popular events that increase public awareness of MHS and its goals, while raising much-needed capital.

In keeping with efforts to preserve history, MHS is also committed to preserving Baltimore's historic neighborhoods. Located in the heart of the historic Mount Vernon/Howard Street neighborhood, MHS now occupies more than an entire city block and has been instrumental in the area's revitalization efforts. A unique opportunity presented itself when the City of Baltimore donated the historically significant art-deco-style Greyhound Bus garage to the society. After careful renovation and restoration, the property was reopened as MHS' Heritage Gallery. This undertaking not only provided much-needed space for MHS, but also helped the community by preserving architecture that otherwise may have been abandoned or demolished.

The Maryland Historical Society understands that history is all around us, and all of us have a responsibility to preserve it. As Fiori says, "It's our mission to connect the past to the present to the future."

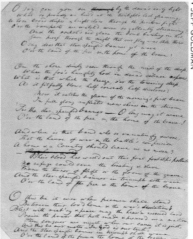

JEFF GOLDMAN

DAVID PRENCIPE

JEFF GOLDMAN

The name on the door may be new, but the commitment to the region and its customers is anything but. Branch Banking and Trust (BB&T) Baltimore Metro Region officially entered the area in 1999 through its acquisition of Mason-Dixon Bancshares, Inc. Regional roots for Mason-Dixon are traced as far back as 1850, when one of its predecessor banks first opened doors in Westminster. Like much of Baltimore, BB&T is both old and new, immersed in heritage, yet looking expectantly toward the future.

Although the name has changed, customers find the same responsiveness and service they have always enjoyed at this community bank. BB&T remains committed to the concept of community banking at the highest levels and manages its entire portfolio through this approach. All of BB&T's subsidiaries are organized into regional groups, each with its own president. "The regional concept allows us to draw on the corporation's strong infrastructure, but still allows decisions to be made close to the customer," says Michael L. Oster, president for BB&T's Baltimore Metro Region.

MICHAEL L. OSTER SERVES AS PRESIDENT OF THE BRANCH BANKING AND TRUST BALTIMORE METRO REGION.

A Strong Foundation

BB&T Baltimore Metro Region is built on a strong foundation of many long-time community banks in the Baltimore area. Three institutions were founded in the mid-1800s that were precursors to the BB&T network today: Farmers and Mechanics National Bank, First National Bank of Westminster, and Westminster Savings Bank all served the region's residents and businesses for just under 100 years before joining together as Carroll County National Bank of Westminster in 1948. A merger in 1962 created Carroll County Bank and Trust Company, and Mason-Dixon Bancshares, Inc. was formed in 1992 to provide for future expansion. In 1999, BB&T agreed to acquire Mason-Dixon and, in March 2000, the change was official.

BB&T, headquartered in Winston-Salem, is one of the South's largest bank holding companies. Originally founded by Alpheous Branch in North Carolina in 1872, the company grew and evolved, eventually establishing itself in 1931 as BB&T. Since then, the company has grown through sound management and acquisition, and operates more than 800 branch offices throughout the South. Under its new name, BB&T Baltimore Metro has continued its long tradition of giving back to the communities it serves.

Good for the Community and Its Customers

The bank supports a wide variety of organizations in the community, most notably educational institutions from area elementary schools to local colleges. BB&T conducts a banking basics program in conjunction with 18 elementary schools within the region, helping children learn about the banking system and money management. The bank also provides support for Carroll Community College and Western Maryland College.

BB&T's solid financial standing is a major factor in the success of the corporation and its subsidiaries. The holding company has total assets of approximately $61.7 billion and, in the fourth quarter of 2000, reported record earnings-per-share figures. By all measures of performance, BB&T is a leader in the banking industry, growing in size and strength.

With a wide range of services, Branch Banking and Trust Baltimore Metro Region is prepared to meet the financial needs of nearly any client. Aside from consumer accounts and lending, the bank also provides a full array of financial services, including trust, insurance, securities brokerage, and international services for business and governmental clients. The bank's commitment to small business has been recognized by the U.S. Small Business Administration, which named BB&T the number one small-business-friendly bank in the eastern United States two years in a row, and number two in the entire country in 1999.

Monumental Life Insurance Company

Monumental Life Insurance Company is one of the oldest and largest life insurance companies in the country. Chartered as the Maryland Mutual Life and Fire Insurance Company in 1858, its first field agent was licensed in 1860, the same year Abraham Lincoln was elected

president. Caught between the North and the South during the Civil War, the company suspended operations in 1862. Business resumed again in 1870 under the name Mutual Life Insurance Company of Baltimore.

The company grew steadily after the war, offering insurance protection to the area's merchants, bankers, steelworkers, farmers, watermen, and growing population of European immigrants. By 1900, Mutual Life's insurance in force had grown to $2.5 million.

In 1926, home office operations were moved to an impressive new building at the corner of Charles and Chase streets. In 1928, the company converted from a mutual insurance company to a closely held stock company. In 1935, its name was again changed to Monumental Life to reflect its strength and prominence in Baltimore, the Monumental City.

By 1957, Monumental Life had 59 field offices in 12 states and

$1 billion of insurance in force. Throughout the 1960s and 1970s, the company continued to prosper and grow. It entered the 1980s with a clearly focused marketing strategy: to sell life and health insurance products to meet the final expense and income replacement needs of America's middle-income households.

Industry leaders began to take notice of Monumental Life's consistent success and solid operating performance. In 1986, the company was acquired by AEGON Insurance Group, an international family of insurance and financial service companies headquartered in the Netherlands. Monumental's association with AEGON, one of the world's largest and most successful insurance organizations, ushered in a new era of expansion and growth.

Impressive Growth

During the 1990s, Monumental Life acquired large blocks of business from several other life insurance companies, including Washington National of Evanston; Commonwealth Life and Accident of Galveston; Reliable Life of St. Louis; and Providian Corporation's Capital Security, Commonwealth, and Peoples Security life insurance companies of Louisville. Company assets multiplied rapidly during the decade, along with policy count and the number of agents and field offices.

Today, Monumental Life is responsible for more than 6 million life and health insurance policies originally underwritten by close to 200 insurance companies. The company's field force of some 3,500 career agents, field managers, and clerical personnel operates out of approximately 200 office locations in 22 states. Teams of home office associates—totaling

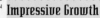

more than 470 in Baltimore and 125 in Durham—provide service and support to both policyholders and field agents.

Meeting Needs

Monumental Life is committed to helping American families improve the quality of their lives. The company fulfills this mission by educating people about the purpose of life insurance and by providing insurance coverage and benefits for families who need it most.

Monumental Life provides traditional life and health insurance products through three distinct distribution channels: career agents, retired military officers, and funeral home directors. The firm's customers are lower- and middle-income individuals and families living in inner-city or suburban neighborhoods, on farms, and in small rural or mountain communities.

Respect for Diversity

Like the United States, Monumental Life is a melting pot of diversity. Both its agents and its policyholders represent dozens of nationalities, cultures, and ethnic backgrounds. Career agents who understand their customers' language, customs, needs, and priorities are able to provide better service. That's why many agents are recruited from within the communities Monumental Life serves.

Respect for diversity and individual differences makes Monumental Life a dynamic and forward-looking organization. This is also reflected in AEGON's worldwide motto: Respect People.

Make Money. Have Fun. Professional development is a company-wide priority, and Monumental Life holds its management team responsible for developing leadership potential, for helping employees achieve their individual goals, and for providing financial reward and recognition for those who succeed.

Building Relationships

In a technical age, when much insurance is sold over the telephone and the Internet, face-to-face contact with customers sets Monumental Life apart from its competitors. The company's career agents, all full-time employees, are assigned to a specific geographic area. They visit policyholders regularly in their homes to identify needs, review coverage, and update information. They earn the right to repeat sales and referrals by providing value-added services and by building relationships based on respect and trust.

Monumental Life's field and home office employees are encouraged to support civic and charitable organizations such as the United

Way, March of Dimes, Red Cross, Girl Scouts of America, Kiwanis, PTA, and Little League. Volunteering time, talent, and resources is another way employees help families and communities improve their quality of life.

Civic Leader

Monumental Life and AEGON USA generously support education, the arts, and medical research through scholarships and donations to organizations such as the Johns Hopkins Hospital Health Systems, Kennedy Krieger Institute, Walters Art Museum, Baltimore Symphony Orchestra, Maryland Institute College of Art, Maryland Public Television, and Boy Scouts of America. Company officers are also actively involved in civic improvement organizations such as the Charles Street Renaissance and Baltimore's Downtown Partnership.

Monumental Life calls itself the Quality Life Company, and with good reason. The company earns consistent high marks from insurance rating services such as A.M. Best Company and Standard & Poor's for its financial strength. For more than 140 years, its employees have served policyholders and the broader community with an unwavering commitment to excellence.

Monumental Life aims to be the best in its chosen markets by continuing to benefit from its quality traditions and state-of-the-art technology, from its personal service and productivity-enhancing systems, and from the visibility of its local offices coupled with AEGON's status as an international insurance leader.

COMMITTED TO HELPING AMERICAN FAMILIES IMPROVE THE QUALITY OF THEIR LIVES, MONUMENTAL LIFE AGENTS OFFER BASIC LIFE AND SUPPLEMENTAL HEALTH INSURANCE AND PERSONAL, FACE-TO-FACE SERVICE TO MIDDLE-INCOME CONSUMERS IN U.S. CITIES, SUBURBS, AND RURAL COMMUNITIES (TOP LEFT AND RIGHT).

HENRY G. HAGAN, PRESIDENT AND CEO, IS PROUD OF THE COMPANY'S HISTORY AND PRESENCE IN THE BALTIMORE AREA. MONUMENTAL LIFE'S HOME OFFICE HAS BEEN LOCATED ON THE CORNER OF CHARLES AND CHASE STREETS SINCE 1926 (BOTTOM).

Towson University

In 1866, 11 students gathered in downtown Baltimore as the first class of the State Normal School. Today, more than 130 years later, the school's successor, Towson University, attracts nearly 17,000 full- and part-time students for its 60 undergraduate majors, 32 master's degree programs, and three doctoral programs. Towson University has evolved from its origins as a state teacher's college into the second-largest public university in Maryland, with nationally ranked academic programs and impressive ties to the region's business community.

TOWSON UNIVERSITY IS COMMITTED TO DEVELOPING AND MAINTAINING AN ENVIRONMENT THAT PROVIDES EQUAL EDUCATION AND SOCIAL OPPORTUNITIES FOR ITS DIVERSE STUDENT BODY. APPROXIMATELY 16 PERCENT OF TOWSON STUDENTS ARE CLASSIFIED AS MINORITIES, AND INTERNATIONAL ENROLLMENT HAS TRIPLED IN THE LAST NINE YEARS.

Solid Academic Programs

Towson's reputation for strong academic programs was recognized in 2000 when the university was ranked 10th among regional public institutions in the North in *U.S. News & World Report*'s America's Best Colleges issue. Towson was also named among the top 100 values in public education in the October 2000 issue of *Kiplinger's Personal Finance Magazine*. The university's strong programs in the arts and sciences, communications, business, health professions, education, fine arts, and computer information systems provide the foundation for its reputation, along with newly offered programs such as the Doctor of Science in Occupational Science and the Bachelor of Science in Deaf Studies.

Students often find one-of-a-kind experiences at Towson, which offers several programs and accreditations not found at any other institution in the state. Towson is the only public institution in Maryland with an accounting program accredited by the prestigious International Association for Management Education (AACSB). In addition, the university is the only institution in the state with both bachelor's and master's programs in occupational therapy. Towson is the only school in Maryland that offers a bachelor of fine arts degree in dance. The computer science major was the first—and, thus far, the only—program at a Maryland public institution accredited by the Computing Sciences Accreditation Board (CSAB). These types of distinctions demonstrate Towson's continued commitment to excellence.

Towson's highly qualified faculty and staff make all of this happen. A full 87 percent of the university's tenured or tenure-track faculty members have earned the highest degree of academic preparation available in their fields of specialization. In addition, Towson's faculty is responsible for writing and publishing hundreds of articles each year, bringing the university national and international recognition. Faculty members also hold offices in more than 200 professional organizations, helping them keep abreast of new developments in their fields.

A highly ambitious and diverse student body is continually raising the bar at Towson, making university history in academics, community service, and extracurricular activities. Overall enrollment is steadily increasing and becoming more competitive, with 283 freshmen qualifying for the Honors College in the fall of 2000. Graduate enrollment has increased 42 percent since the spring of 1995. The applicant pool includes students from all 50 states and 94 foreign countries, and international students comprise nearly 5 percent of Towson's total enrollment. In recent years, five Towson graduates have received prestigious Fulbright scholarships for postgraduate study abroad. Towson students display the same drive in their extracurricular activities, garnering awards and recognition for the university for everything from dance to debate to football.

Supporting Businesses in Baltimore and around the Nation

Towson University is a valuable resource not only for its student body, but for the entire Baltimore area as well.

The institution has established itself as a supportive member of the business community, providing a variety of programs to aid businesses, while offering unique opportunities for its students and faculty.

Since 1996, Towson has been home to RESI (formerly known as the Regional Economic Studies Institute), one of the largest business and economic research centers in the United States. A client-oriented organization, RESI provides solutions and services to government, business, and industry. Areas of expertise include organization and management consulting, training, and human services and policy analysis. RESI is a recognized authority on national and regional economics, and produces several respected publications detailing economic activity in the mid-Atlantic area. RESI also hosts Web sites and develops Web-based applications for Maryland's state agencies.

Another valued Towson program is the Central Region Small Business Development Center (SBDC), which helped Maryland's small businesses to obtain nearly $55 million in capital in its first four years. SBDC's mission is "to contribute to the economic growth of our region by preparing small businesses to become viable employers," benefiting businesses as well as future Towson graduates. Through satellite centers in Baltimore City and five surrounding counties, the SBDC network helps small businesses overcome challenges and prepares entrepreneurs to surpass start-up and expansion hurdles. SBDC's clients can take advantage of no-cost counseling services, comprehensive management and technical assistance, and affordable training programs covering all stages of business development.

While Towson University has a strong reputation as one of the region's most dynamic college communities, with a long tradition of offering quality academic programs, it is best known for its commitment to educational excellence and lifelong learning.

Profiles in Excellence

1900-1919

Eller Media Company

As far back as the days of ancient Egypt, people chiseled messages on stone tablets and placed them alongside busy public thoroughfares. That may be the earliest example of outdoor advertising, one of the most powerful, effective, and widely used media in the world. In today's world, Eller Media Company is a leader in this industry, with offices across the country and around the world.

The Eller name first entered the market in 1996, though the company's roots date back more than 100 years. Founded as Foster & Kleiser in 1901, the outdoor advertising company went through a series of acquisitions and name changes during the 20th century. In the 1950s, the company was purchased by W.R. Grace, and was subsequently sold to Metropolitan Broadcasting Company, which later became Metromedia. During these changes, the company maintained the Foster & Kleiser name and held its dominance in the industry. In 1986, Foster & Kleiser was acquired by Patrick Media Group, Inc., which became a subsidiary of General Electric (GE). Karl Eller purchased the company from GE in 1996, and changed the name to reflect his ownership. Today, Eller Media Company, now a wholly owned subsidiary of Clear Channel Communications, is one of the world's largest outdoor advertis-

ing companies, operating in 32 major American markets and 34 countries in South America, Europe, Asia, and Australia.

Better Research, Stronger Targeting

After the acquisition, Eller Media invested heavily in new marketing resources, allowing the company to provide clients with expanded research data. PROfiles, Eller Media's exclusive, state-of-the-art mapping system, helps companies determine their target audiences and pinpoint specific locations to reach them, based on demographics and lifestyle clusters. Other advanced research and analysis techniques can provide clients with accurate information to evaluate trading areas and generate comparisons in market potential, profitability, and competition. Information regarding audience measurements, ethnic and social diversity, and competitive spending are provided free of charge to Eller Media customers—just one example of the company's quality-service philosophy.

Eller Media has always recognized outstanding customer service as the most important component in achieving continued success, and Eller's people are the foundation of that success. Looking to the future, Eller Media is pioneering technological advances for the out-of-home industry that will revolutionize engineering, construction, site selection, bill posting, pictorial presentation, and research. By staying ahead of the competition in research and innovation, Eller Media is always finding new ways to market mobility.

Baltimore/Washington Metroplex: A Leading National Market

Baltimore is part of Eller Media's Baltimore/ Washington Metroplex region, composed of 21 counties in Maryland, the District of Columbia, and Virginia. With a population exceeding 5.3 million, the Baltimore/Washington Metroplex is the fourth-largest metropolitan

ELLER MEDIA COMPANY, NOW OWNED BY CLEAR CHANNEL COMMUNICATIONS, CONTINUES TO BE A LEADER IN THE OUTDOOR ADVERTISING INDUSTRY.

area in the country, making it very attractive to advertisers. Baltimore's 13 million annual visitors and central location along major north-south and east-west highways make it an ideal location. Eller Media enjoys a market share of more than 88 percent in Baltimore, making the company the largest source for outdoor media in the region.

Outdoor advertising is more than just billboards; it also covers advertising posters found in commuter rail stations, transit shelters, mall kiosks, and airports, and on buses, trains, and urban wallscapes. And even billboards are not just billboards—they come in a variety of shapes and sizes at Eller, from traditional, 12- by 25-foot, 30-sheet posters and 14- by 48-foot bulletin displays to new formats like Premier Panels and Tri-Visions. All these products converge in the out-of-home media category, designed to target certain markets and present customized strategies for advertisers.

◆◆◆◆◆◆◆◆◆◆◆◆◆◆◆◆◆◆◆◆

The Economical, Effective Advertising Choice

Outdoor advertising remains an economical, instant-impact media for many advertisers, with the least expensive cost-per-thousand levels among the major media. Marketers can target specific audiences or blanket the market with their message by utilizing a successful media mix or by standing alone. The ultimate visual medium, outdoor advertising provides unsurpassed opportunities for creative expression. Outdoor presents a unique opportunity to provide a continuous message that consumers will notice repeatedly, increasing the likelihood of action on their part. In addition, outdoor cannot be turned off, thrown away, or clicked past; instead, potential consumers can be reached all day, every day.

With such a powerful communications tool at its disposal, Eller Media Company has made it a corporate priority to provide access for worthy causes and organizations across the country. Each year, Eller Media donates more than $20 million worth of advertising space for public service campaigns nationwide. In the Baltimore region, such campaigns have increased the awareness of lead poisoning in children and the potential dangers of handguns. Nationally, Eller Media's efforts have helped non-profit organizations like the American Cancer Society get the word out on prevention, early detection, and fund-raising events.

Eller Media Company is one of the oldest, largest, and most established outdoor advertising companies in the nation. And as the population continues to grow and society becomes more and more mobile, out-of-home advertising will become an even more effective and economic means of communicating with consumers. Eller Media Company is on the move and in 2001 will be rebranded as subsidiary of Clear Channel Communications. As Clear Channel Outdoor, Eller Media will look ahead to the next challenge and set its sights on new goals for the future.

ELLER MEDIA ENJOYS A MARKET SHARE OF MORE THAN 88 PERCENT IN BALTIMORE, MAKING THE COMPANY THE LARGEST SOURCE FOR OUTDOOR MEDIA IN THE REGION.

The Mid-Atlantic Coca-Cola Bottling Company

The Coca-Cola name is most often associated with Atlanta, the founding city of the international soft drink company and its longtime corporate headquarters. But Coca-Cola has enjoyed a significant presence in the Baltimore region for nearly as long. Coca-Cola was founded in Atlanta in 1896, and first bottled in Baltimore just nine years later. That milestone paved the way for a long and prosperous association between Coca-Cola and Baltimore, which since 1908 has been home to one of the soft drink manufacturer's largest bottling and distribution sites.

A Refreshing Century

In 1905, Baltimore's first Coke bottling operation got underway, selling 1,222 gallons in its first year. The operation grew steadily, and in 1919 was incorporated as the Maryland Coca-Cola Bottling Company. Four years later, the Coca-Cola Company acquired the business, and established it as a subsidiary called the Coca-Cola Bottling Company of Baltimore. Soon, a newer, larger bottling plant was constructed on Plowman and Front streets.

In just a few years, the new plant was producing more than 400,000 cases each year. Coca-Cola's presence in Baltimore continued to grow, as new plants were constructed and existing ones enlarged. By the late 1970s, a company publication acknowledged that the Baltimore plant had achieved the highest per capita share of market and the highest share of market growth among Coca-Cola's domestic bottling subsidiaries, although the plant served the smallest territory.

In 1980, the Baltimore plant was sold to a group of investors, but the operation continued to bottle Coke products. Over time, the plant returned to the Coca-Cola family, this time as part of Coca-Cola Enterprises (CCE). CCE became a separate, publicly traded company in 1986, when Coca-Cola USA sold 51 percent of stock in the company in a public offering.

Coca-Cola Enterprises is the world's largest marketer, producer, and distributor of products of the Coca-Cola Company. The brands of the Coca-Cola Company represent some of the most popular beverage brands in the world.

Coca-Cola Enterprises also distributes Dr. Pepper and several other beverage brands. The company operates in parts of 46 U.S. states, throughout Canada, and in parts of Europe. The company's 69,000 employees worldwide work in some 437 facilities, generating net operating revenues in excess of $14 billion annually.

Today, the commitment of the Coca-Cola Enterprises Bottling Company to Maryland totals 13 facilities and more than 1,700 employees—making the state an integral part of the Coca-Cola system. Such prominence would not be possible without the invaluable contribution of the Baltimore metropolitan region and its three Coca-Cola facilities.

A seven-acre Coca-Cola bottling facility in Baltimore is home to more than 80 employees and produces more than 30 million cases per year. The bottling facility supplies Coca-Cola products throughout a region that stretches from northern Virginia to south-central Pennsylvania. Coca-Cola Enterprises also maintains a separate, nine-acre sales center in Baltimore that is home to more than 300 employees. The Baltimore Sales Center sells an average of 11 million to 12 million cases per year. Finally, a central administrative office is located in nearby Columbia, Maryland, and employs a workforce of more than 150 personnel.

With three facilities out of a total of 13 Coca-Cola facilities in Maryland, the Baltimore region truly plays a crucial role in the success of the Coca-Cola system. Mid-Atlantic Coca-Cola Bottling Company is an operation that makes Coca-Cola Enterprises one of the largest employers in the state of Maryland and a valuable corporate citizen for Howard County and the Greater Baltimore region.

COCA-COLA HAS BEEN BOTTLED IN BALTIMORE SINCE 1905.

When Baltimore's residents and visitors want to find out where to eat, what to see, and who to meet around town, they turn to the pages of *Baltimore*, the award-winning monthly lifestyle magazine that has been celebrating Charm City since 1907. ◆ For generations,

Baltimoreans have relied on the magazine to deliver the hottest news and the coolest trends, just as advertisers have relied on it to deliver a highly desirable, sharply targeted audience for their marketing messages. *Baltimore* delivers both, while presenting the kind of compelling writing and arresting design that does its namesake city proud.

Although *Baltimore* is the nation's oldest city magazine, it is also among the freshest, reinventing itself issue by issue to remain the definitive source for cultural, social, and business information in the region.

Baltimore's regular coverage runs the gamut—from the arts and travel to health and education, from dining reviews and shopping tips to politics and penetrating profiles of the people who make the region work. Each issue also features a comprehensive *Where to Eat* listing of restaurants and *Datebook*, the monthly calendar of key events throughout the region. Every issue—from its newsy, sometimes irreverent opening *B-Side* pages to its closing *Baltimore Grill* profile of local personalities—underscores the validity of the magazine's tag line: "From cover to cover, we cover it all."

Many of Baltimore's special issues have become true fixtures for readers in the city and surrounding counties. The "Best of Baltimore" issue each summer recognizes superior performance that year in dozens of categories, ranging from best crab cake and best tree surgeon to best dress shop and best neighborhood holiday displays. Just as the "Best of Baltimore" issue has been an institution since 1975, the party accompanying its publication, benefiting local charities, is one of the genuinely hot tickets in town. Other issues that attract

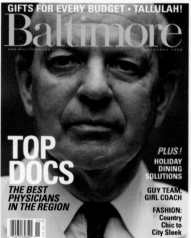

special reader interest include "Best Restaurants," "Top Doctors," "Bargain Dining," and "Top Singles."

In addition to its 12 regular issues, each year the magazine also publishes separate, stand-alone issues. *Baltimore Bride* is the only publication of its kind providing helpful, in-depth information for those getting married in and around Baltimore. *Metroguide*, an informative and interesting introduction to the area for new residents and new readers alike, has earned an established place in the marketplace. *Baltimore*'s special millennium issue, *B2K*, won widespread reader acceptance and remains a popular collector's item.

Baltimore's varied content

appeals to an active, upscale audience throughout the region, making the magazine a favorite with advertisers. With education levels and household incomes well above national averages, readers regularly demonstrate their loyalty to the magazine: Eight out of 10 readers read every issue and spend nearly an hour on each issue. That attention is not lost on advertisers, who recognize that nine out of 10 readers use the magazine to make buying decisions.

Baltimore is published by Rosebud Entertainment LLC, a local company owned by Stephen Geppi, and is a member of the City and Regional Magazine Association.

WHEN BALTIMORE'S RESIDENTS AND VISITORS WANT TO FIND OUT WHERE TO EAT, WHAT TO SEE, AND WHO TO MEET AROUND TOWN, THEY TURN TO THE PAGES OF *Baltimore*, THE AWARD-WINNING MONTHLY LIFESTYLE MAGAZINE THAT HAS BEEN CELEBRATING CHARM CITY SINCE 1907.

URS Corporation

While URS Corporation is currently the second-largest design firm in the engineering design/contracting industry, with an international reach and impressive list of clients and projects, the firm's Baltimore roots reach back to the turn of the century. With its international engineering, architecture, and contracting credentials and Maryland pedigree, URS is built on a strong foundation of pioneering excellence and designed to withstand the test of time. URS is a major force in its industry, both in the Baltimore region and around the globe.

URS' Baltimore roots reach back to the early 1900s, when civil engineering legend John E. Greiner started his own one-man business. For two decades, Greiner had been an impressive force in the engineering community. His groundbreaking work with the B&O Railroad served as the basis for many new national standards, and his presentations before the American Society of Civil Engineers were legendary. When the Engineer's Club of Baltimore was founded in 1904, Greiner was one of its 32 charter members, and he went on to serve two terms as president, a distinction yet to be repeated. But Greiner's engineering legacy really took off in 1908, when he started the Baltimore engineering firm that bore his name.

Legendary Engineering on Landmark Projects

Greiner's reputation provided a strong foundation for the company, which soon flourished with assignments. Throughout the 20th century, Greiner engineers worked on some of the most significant projects in the United States, from railways to bridges to highway systems. Greiner constructed the B&O Railroad Piers 8 and 9 in 1917, Baltimore structures that are still in use today. The firm designed and built many noteworthy bridges, including the Potomac River Bridge in Charles County, Maryland; the historic Bridge of Lions in St. Augustine, Florida; and both spans of the Chesapeake Bay Bridge.

Greiner was also instrumental in the development of state turnpikes, working on systems in Indiana, Michigan, New Jersey, Ohio, Pennsylvania, Washington, and Wisconsin. In later years, Greiner developed specialties in mass transit systems, constructing portions of Boston's Massachusetts Bay Transportation Authority (MBTA) system and the Metro system in Washington, D.C. The firm also constructed several award-winning airports, such as Florida's Tampa International and Orlando International. More recently, Greiner was chosen by NASA to develop its Orbiter Landing Facility at the Kennedy Space Center, an efficient and environmentally friendly design that won many awards.

The Greiner firm enjoyed more than 75 years of excellence in engineering, and continued Greiner's legacy long after his death in 1942. In 1995, the company merged with worldwide engineering powerhouse URS to become URS Greiner. The next year, the company acquired another engineering firm, Woodward Clyde, and became known as URS Greiner Woodward Clyde. URS followed this pattern of acquisition across the country, assembling a collection of regional engineering firms and maintaining separate names in different geographic areas. In 1999, the acquisition of the Dames & Moore Group—an environmental, chemical, and process engineering firm—took place. Then, in 2000, all URS companies consolidated under the URS name, forming a global

architectural, engineering, and environmental presence that is one of the most formidable in the world.

Today's Global Presence and Local Involvement

Today, URS has nearly 16,000 employees in more than 300 offices in 30 countries. The San Francisco-based company's team of planners, engineers, architects, scientists, and program and construction managers serve a wide range of public and private sector clients in a variety of specialty areas. According to *The Engineering News-Record*, a leading industry publication, URS is the leading firm for hazardous waste engineering, ranks second for transportation and general building, and is in the top 10 for manufacturing, sewer/waste, water, power, and industrial processing. URS has enjoyed steady, solid growth in recent years, and was noted by *Fortune* magazine as one of the fastest-growing companies in 1999. In fact, revenues grew by 76 percent in fiscal 1999, bumping URS up four slots in the industry rankings to become the second-largest engineering/architecture/contracting firm in the world.

In Maryland, URS maintains a strong presence, with six offices throughout the state. Close to 800 employees work in URS' offices in Baltimore, Hunt Valley, Bethesda, Gaithersburg, Germantown, and Linthicum. The Maryland offices continue in the Greiner tradition, focusing on surface and air transportation, environmental, and building projects, and maintaining active involvement in the community.

Commitment to Education

Much of URS' community involvement in the Baltimore area revolves around education, both primary and secondary. Senior executives serve on the Maryland Business Roundtable for Education, and the company's employees and managers support educational efforts with their time and resources. Through the Day with an Engineer Program, students from Baltimore City and surrounding counties spend a day in URS' offices, learning firsthand from professional staff. The firm has also participated in many local high schools' career days, allowing employees time to speak to students about careers in engineering and related fields. URS has also participated in the Upward Bound Program, a national initiative to encourage first-generation and low-income children to attend

college. Maryland employees of URS have even organized the collection of supermarket receipts for a city elementary school to raise funds for the purchase of computers.

Throughout its long history, URS and its predecessors designed and built some of the most significant structures of our time. As a new, united company, URS Corporation will continue to make history, providing outstanding engineering, architecture, and contracting services to clients around the world.

SOME OF URS CORPORATION'S MOST NOTABLE PROJECTS INCLUDE (CLOCKWISE FROM TOP LEFT) THE OBSERVATION GALLERY AT BWI AIRPORT, CHESAPEAKE BAY BRIDGE, JONES FALLS EXPRESSWAY, AND (OPPOSITE TOP) FRANCIS SCOTT KEY BRIDGE.

CitiFinancial

Baltimore-based CitiFinancial holds a claim to fame as being one of the first companies to put Americans behind the wheel and on the road to financial stability. Founded in Charm City in 1912 as Commercial Credit, CitiFinancial pioneered consumer lending and paved the way for others.

From its initial offices in the Garrett Building, which still stands on East Redwood Street, founder Alexander Duncan had grand ideas for the company he started with just two associates and $300,000 in borrowed capital.

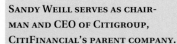

A History of Innovation

With the introduction of the Model T Ford in 1916, Duncan helped hundreds of thousands of families finance the purchase of new cars. For the first time in history, Americans could drive home a brand-new car without having to hold the cash in hand to pay for it. Instead, they could borrow money from the company and pay it back monthly. And so the term installment lending was born.

This installment plan was soon adopted by other financial institutions and continues to be the foundation for CitiFinancial's success. The company later introduced similar buying plans for home appliances and consumer goods, becoming a leader in the field of sales finance. By 1940, CitiFinancial began direct lending to consumers. The company now offers a full range of personal and home equity loans, plus related products and services, including financing through national retailers.

Established early on as "the people's lender," CitiFinancial today reaches more than 4 million customers, who live mostly in small towns or suburban areas within a few miles of one of the company's 2,100 branches in the United States and Canada.

CitiFinancial was the first company in what became Travelers Group. In 1998, Travelers Group merged with Citicorp to form Citigroup, the world's largest financial services company, providing products and services to both consumers and corporate customers all around the globe. The Citigroup family also includes Citibank, Travelers Property Casualty, Travelers Life and Annuity, Salomon Smith Barney, and Primerica.

Main Street Roots

While CitiFinancial has grown to become one of the most profitable lending institutions in the world, President Mike Knapp says the company continues its tradition of doing business locally and personally. In fact, the company's corporate headquarters is still maintained within Baltimore's downtown business district, only a few blocks from its birthplace.

"Even though we're a large company with more than 15,000 employees, our team members establish personal relationships with all of their customers in the communities where they live," Knapp says. "We truly understand the needs of our customers and work with them to develop affordable solutions so they can live their dreams."

Not only does CitiFinancial help consumers with their financial needs, but the company also lends a hand in the local community. Through grants from the Citigroup Foundation, the company helps finance education programs for minority and low-income students and residents. Citigroup was a major donor in the development of the children's museum Port Discovery. More recently, CitiFinancial funded the museum's first traveling exhibit. Employees also have helped the community by volunteering for Baltimore-area projects including Our Daily Bread, Maryland Special Olympics, and Habitat for Humanity.

Well on its way to achieving even higher levels of success, CitiFinancial is sure to pave another path for companies to follow in the future.

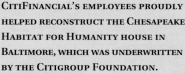

Thanks to I. C. Isaacs & Company, Inc., Baltimore can claim a place among the acclaimed international fashion capitals of New York, Paris, and Milan. Since 1913, I. C. Isaacs has contributed to the international fashion scene, first with original designs and today with some of the world's most popular

licensed brands. Millions of men, women, and children around the globe wear I. C. Isaacs brands, reflecting the cutting-edge styles and diverse reach of this hidden treasure of Baltimore.

When Harry Z. Isaacs opened his Baltimore plant in 1913, the business focus was on riding habits, produced and merchandised under the slogan The House of Good Habits. In 1932, Isaacs was granted a U.S. Patent for "a new and useful improvement" in the breeches category. The business quickly grew, expanding into other styles of breeches, riding habits, western wear, and, finally, military garments under the brand name Over the Top. In the 1950s and 1960s, the company introduced several new lines, including a collection of slacks, fine shirts, dungarees, slim pants, and the stylish Zacari label by Paris designer Antonio del Castillo. The Zacari line featured European-haute-couture-inspired, high-fashion sportswear.

Adapting to the times, I. C. Isaacs produced bell-bottoms and disco fashions in the 1970s, and designer jeans and the *Miami Vice* look in the 1980s.

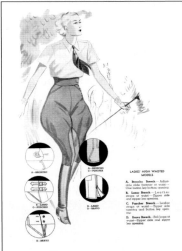

Manufacturing and Marketing High Fashion

In the late 1980s, fashions changed again. But more important, there was a change in the business of fashion. I. C. Isaacs became a limited partnership, and strategically repositioned itself from a manufacturing-oriented company to a marketing and brand-driven marketing company. In keeping with that objective, the company acquired licensed brand labels like Marithé & François Girbaud, BOSS, and Beverly Hills Polo Club throughout the 1990s, and became publicly traded on Nasdaq.

I. C. Isaacs now holds the licenses to manufacture and market these popular sportswear lines in the United States and Puerto Rico, and, for Beverly Hills Polo Club, also in Europe. With these licensed brands, I. C. Isaacs enjoys a presence in more than 2,500 specialty and major department stores in the United States, Puerto Rico, and Europe, including Bloomingdale's, Macy's, and JC Penney. In addition, the company continues to make pants and jeans styles for women under its own I. C. Isaacs brand name.

Although the Baltimore plant no longer produces apparel, I. C. Isaacs maintains its corporate offices, including a pattern design and sample room, at the original site on Bank Street. Today, the company includes offices in New York City, which house executive management, sales, and merchandising staff, as well as manufacturing facilities and sales offices throughout the United States, Mexico, and Europe.

Supporting Baltimore

As a longtime corporate citizen of Baltimore, I. C. Isaacs is committed to giving back to its hometown. The company annually supports the Ed Block Courage Awards, a Baltimore-based program named for a longtime Baltimore Colts trainer. This award, which recognizes one player from each NFL team who exemplifies sportsmanship and courage, has become one of the most prestigious awards in the NFL. The company has also been a generous supporter of the Maryland School for the Blind, as well as many other organizations and events in the Greater Baltimore area.

With a reputation for high quality, high fashion, and a genuine sense of corporate citizenship, I. C. Isaacs & Company, Inc. has made a name for itself in the Baltimore area and well beyond.

SINCE 1913, I. C. ISAACS & COMPANY, INC. HAS CONTRIBUTED TO THE INTERNATIONAL FASHION SCENE, FIRST WITH ORIGINAL DESIGNS AND TODAY WITH SOME OF THE WORLD'S MOST POPULAR LICENSED BRANDS.

From the town of Accident in Garrett County to the town of Gratitude on the eastern shore, employers all over the state of Maryland count on the Injured Workers' Insurance Fund (IWIF) to provide fairly priced insurance coverage and just compensation for on-the-job injuries.

A Special Role in Maryland

Maryland's legislature created IWIF in 1914 to provide a stable source of workers' compensation insurance coverage. Through its nearly nine decades of service to Maryland, IWIF has been the only insurance organization in the state that ensures workers' compensation insurance is available at a fair market price to all Maryland employers. This unique role has become especially important during the past decade, as private insurers have repeatedly declined to provide work-related coverage in some industry segments.

Through its service to Maryland employers, IWIF has evolved far beyond its origins as a state agency to become a fully self-supporting insurance trust fund, operating with a social purpose and funded entirely by premiums and investment income. With financial stability, exceptional customer service, innovative product offerings, and in-depth knowledge about local business, IWIF has become the insurer of choice for one out of every five Maryland businesses.

Building on Strength

With $1 billion in assets accumulated through decades of sound management, IWIF has the capacity to underwrite Maryland's entire workers' compensation market. The organization's unique status as a nonprofit insurer allows it to return profits to policyholders through its rates, incentive plans, and dividend programs. In addition, by returning profits from its investments in the form of lower premiums, IWIF is in the position to establish the competitive pricing benchmark for Maryland's workers' compensation industry, assuring that the state's workers' compensation insurance costs remain among the most competitive in the nation.

IWIF has emerged as a carrier of choice among Maryland employers, especially small to medium-sized companies. Small businesses paying as little as $800 over three years, for example, are able to enjoy discounts for good loss experience, a benefit usually reserved by private insurance companies for only their larger policyholders.

A Service Orientation

IWIF is a specialist in the field of workers' compensation, with all efforts concentrated on elevating the services and operations of this one line of insurance.

By focusing on workers' compensation insurance alone, IWIF is continuously expanding and improving the services it provides. For example, IWIF has as many loss control consultants working to help its policyholders prevent accidents as some insurance firms have for the entire East Coast.

IWIF also excels in managing claims and the medical component of workers' compensation care. Through IWIF's state-of-the-

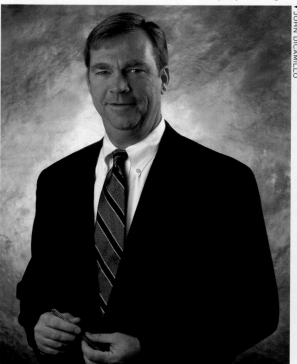

INJURED WORKERS' INSURANCE FUND (IWIF) IS LED BY DANIEL MCKEW, CHAIRMAN (LEFT), AND PRESTON D. WILLIAMS, PRESIDENT AND CEO.

art managed medical program, IWIF COMPrehensive Care, and its local network of health care providers, IWIF claimants have access to local case managers who have firsthand knowledge of Maryland's medical providers.

IWIF's strong and growing market share in Maryland is reflective of the quality and value IWIF provides its policyholders.

Striving for Workplace Safety

Educational programs are a key component in IWIF's successful approach to reducing risks in the workplace. In addition to policyholder visits, IWIF conducts and participates in many safety workshops, policyholder seminars, and conferences. These policyholder seminars are unique to the industry and are

free of charge for the company's policyholders.

For those Marylanders who do become injured on the job, IWIF embraces the social and humanitarian principles of fair and equitable benefits for the compensable injuries of Maryland's workers. IWIF created *Guide for the Injured Worker*, which is distributed to all claimants. This industry-first pamphlet educates injured employees about their benefits and responsibilities.

No private workers' compensation carrier does more for Maryland's injured workers than IWIF. In fact, a major focus of the IWIF COMPCare program is to ensure that an injured worker receives the highest-quality medical care in a timely manner. IWIF's commitment is to provide services, information, and benefits that are

consistent with the way workers' compensation was intended to function.

As committed as IWIF is to the fair treatment of injured workers, the company is equally committed to investigating and prosecuting workers' compensation fraud. IWIF pioneered the creation of an in-house fraud unit, and is leading the fight in Maryland to reduce unnecessary costs resulting from fraud.

A Promise Kept

When IWIF was established, the goal was to ensure that all Maryland employers, regardless of their size or risk profile, could offer insurance to their workers for on-the-job injury. Today, IWIF is still the only guarantor of that promise. Accessible, affordable, and accountable have been the hallmarks of IWIF's service to Maryland—a dependable resource that will continue to serve generations of Maryland's workers to come.

CLOCKWISE FROM TOP:
IWIF IS LOCATED ON LOCH RAVEN BOULEVARD IN TOWSON, MARYLAND.

IWIF'S MANAGEMENT TEAM VICE PRESIDENTS INCLUDE (FROM LEFT) LISA KRUSKA, POLICYHOLDER SERVICES; ROBERT MARSHALL, INFORMATION SYSTEMS; GEORGE MATTHEWS, MARKETING AND BUSINESS DEVELOPMENT; DEBRA ZEZESKI, CLAIMS; ROBERT MERRITT, CHIEF INVESTMENT OFFICER; DONNA WILSON, COMMUNICATIONS AND CUSTOMER SERVICE; AND THOMAS PHELAN, CHIEF FINANCIAL OFFICER.

IWIF'S BOARD OF DIRECTORS INCLUDES (SEATED, FROM LEFT) STEPHANIE L. FINK, GREGORY D. CHASNEY, GAIL C. MCDONALD, (STANDING, FROM LEFT) MICHAEL J. WAGNER, THEO C. RODGERS, AND JOSEPH M. COALE III.

Wells Fargo Home Mortgage

The name Wells Fargo is synonymous with the American West, as the company helped scores of the country's early citizens blaze a trail toward California. In those days, Wells Fargo was committed to serving its clients' transportation, delivery, and banking needs as they established themselves in the new frontier. More than a century later, Wells Fargo Home Mortgage is still helping people establish themselves in new homes across the country, through its innovative home financing programs.

Wells Fargo was formed in 1852, when Henry Wells and William Fargo united to provide transport and delivery services in the new American West. The pair had experienced success with the establishment of American Express on the East Coast, and they were convinced that people going out west could benefit from the same services. The advent of the gold rush made Wells Fargo's long-distance delivery and transportation services very valuable, and almost overnight there was a Wells Fargo in every major trading town in the West.

THROUGH INNOVATIVE FINANCING, WELLS FARGO HOME MORTGAGE HELPS FAMILIES AROUND THE COUNTRY ESTABLISH THEMSELVES IN NEW HOMES.

Going West with Wells Fargo

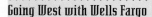

As mining towns and camps sprang up all over the western territories, Wells Fargo expanded its business to provide banking services to the new communities. Wells Fargo immediately became the most trusted name in personal banking, and its banknotes and checks became the new currency of the West. The company's name became synonymous with security, as the Wells Fargo stagecoaches sped across the open plain, delivering goods and valuables to prospectors and store owners, and always returning with the signature chests full of gold.

The subsequent decades brought new changes and challenges for the evolving company. The invention of the telegraph soon made it possible to wire money from one city to another, and Wells Fargo was the first to pioneer its use in this manner. During World War I, the government used the company's communication and transportation lines to support the war effort. Left with little but its name after the war, Wells Fargo set out to rebuild itself into one of the most successful banking franchises in American history.

Wells Fargo then focused on personal banking and mortgages. In the 20th century, more than 1,000 organizations merged with Wells Fargo, giving it one of the strongest and most consistent patterns of growth of any financial institution in America. As the company's home financing arm, Wells Fargo Home Mortgage carries on the tradition of strength. The company finances one out of every 15 new homes in America, and helps service loans for more than 2.5 million Americans. More than half of the Fortune 100 companies turn to Wells Fargo to handle their employee relocations, as well.

A Leader in Baltimore

In Maryland, Wells Fargo holds a large share of the state's market for resale and new construction financing. Its 25 home mortgage offices in the Baltimore/Washington, D.C., metro area transact some $1 billion in business each year and employ more than 1,100 people. The company's strong partnerships with leading builders promise continued growth for Wells Fargo in this region.

Wells Fargo Home Mortgage prides itself in extending the buyer's edge to customers, whether they are buying their first home, relocating, or searching for an investment property. With a massive network of representatives armed with extensive knowledge of local real estate markets, the company is prepared to help home buyers through every step of the process.

Home ownership is a vital part of the American dream, and Wells Fargo is committed to making that dream a reality for everyone. Through its Subprime Lending programs, Wells Fargo offers loans to home buyers with less than perfect credit. The company's Emerging Markets department is dedicated to increasing home ownership among low- and moderate-income, ethnic minority,

and immigrant populations. Due to those efforts, Wells Fargo is the number one lender for first-time and ethnic minority buyers, and is ranked second in lending to low- to moderate-income home buyers and FHA/VA loans. In fact, nearly one in every four Wells Fargo loans is made to a home buyer whose income is less than 80 percent of the area's median income.

While mortgages are the bulk of its business, Well Fargo also provides for the home owner's other financial needs. The company provides home equity loans for renovations and home improvements to improve a home's value. In addition, Wells Fargo offers home owners' insurance as a convenience to mortgage customers.

An Enduring Philosophy

In 1882, Wells Fargo outlined its value-based customer service philosophy: "The most polite and courteous treatment of all customers is insisted upon. Proper respect must be shown to all, let them be men, women, or children, rich or poor, black or white." In almost 120 years, this philosophy has not changed.

Wells Fargo is committed to the communities it serves, and demonstrates that through service and support of various organizations. In the Baltimore area, Wells Fargo is proud of the money, time, and materials it donates to Habitat for Humanity. Through this organization, Wells Fargo is again furthering the American dream and helping to create homes.

In its endeavors—both business and community—Wells Fargo Home Mortgage's attention to service and satisfaction demonstrate the reasons for the company's enduring leadership, which will continue for generations to come.

FMC Corporation Agricultural Products Group

A t a 90-acre site on the edge of Baltimore's Curtis Bay, hundreds of workers travel the streets of a minicity on bicycles and golf carts. This metropolis in miniature is actually the FMC Corporation Agricultural Products Group chemical plant, one of the largest of its kind in Maryland. FMC Baltimore makes many of the active ingredients used for crop protection and specialty pesticide products, supplying agricultural product manufacturers across the country. At the same time, FMC Baltimore takes an active role in preserving the environment, through meticulous internal procedures and extensive outreach efforts.

Years of Service to Baltimore and Beyond

FMC's Baltimore plant has been in operation since 1915, when Curtis Bay Chemical Company was established as a joint venture between Hercules Powder Company and U.S. Industrial Alcohol Company. At that time, the facility made chemicals used in the production of smokeless gunpowder, as part of the World War I effort.

After the war, U.S. Industrial Alcohol Company took sole ownership of the plant, and used the facility to manufacture sterno and automobile antifreeze. FMC Corporation acquired the site in 1954, using it to produce a variety of specialty chemicals. The plant became part of FMC's Agricultural Chemical Group in the late 1970s, and since then has concentrated solely on the manufacture of agricultural chemicals.

An Industry Leader

FMC Corporation is a Fortune 400 company with headquarters in Chicago. The corporation is composed of five operating groups, which manufacture such products as agricultural, specialty, and industrial chemicals; energy systems; and specialized machinery. The company's some 16,000 employees work in 90 manufacturing and mining facilities located in 25 states and 16 foreign countries, with annual sales of $3.7 billion.

Upon acquiring the Baltimore facility, FMC Corporation modernized the plant and enhanced plant capabilities to better serve its customers. Today, some 370 employees work at the Baltimore location. Operations run nonstop—24 hours a day, seven days a week, 365 days a year.

Large agricultural clients and formulators from all over the world purchase the firm's products, such as 7-Hydroxy, used to make Furadan, a pesticide that rids 50 different crops worldwide of more than 300 different pests. FMC Baltimore also manufactures Clomazone, the herbicide that controls weeds and grasses that damage soybean crops, and Pyrethroids, a synthetic version of pesticide found naturally in chrysanthemums. The firm makes the basic compound, while other sites create finished products.

Commitment to Safety and Environmental Protection

FMC Baltimore takes an active, leading role in safeguarding Baltimore's public health and educating others about proper safety precautions. In 1982, the company helped organize the South Baltimore Industrial Mutual Aid Plan (SBIMAP), an association of more than 55 companies, government agencies and community groups that deal with hazardous substances. In response, the Chemical Manufacturers Association (CMA) presented FMC with one of its first Community Awareness and Emergency Response Awards. SBIMAP works with local fire departments and city government, pooling resources to develop a comprehensive emergency response plan. Since 1985, the organization has conducted annual drills with increasingly complex scenarios of hazmat (hazardous materials) incidents in the region; FMC Baltimore has hosted two of these drills in that time.

FMC Baltimore uses sophisticated and effective environmental controls and waste minimization methods throughout its operation. The company accepts cradle-

CONSTRUCTED IN 1915 TO PRODUCE COMPONENTS USED IN SMOKELESS POWDER, FMC'S CURTIS BAY PLANT HAS EVOLVED INTO A MODERN AGRICULTURAL PRODUCTS FACILITY.

DAVID WALLACE

STONEHOUSE COVE, LOCATED TO THE WEST OF THE PLANT, IS A NATURAL WILDLIFE REFUGE.

to-grave responsibility for its materials—from the shipping process to end use and waste disposal. Through FMC's comprehensive efforts, annual organic emissions at the Baltimore plant are lower than those of the average gas station. Employees of all levels of the firm are intensively trained, and safety is consistently monitored through hazards reviews, systems safety analysis, periodic facilities design reviews, and field safety audits. This commitment to safety has resulted in the firm's outstanding safety record of 2.5 million man-hours without a lost-time accident.

Training and Experience: A Valuable Resource

With its stellar safety record and unique experience in hazardous materials handling, FMC is a valuable resource for local, state, and federal public safety organizations. FMC has provided training assistance for local police and fire departments, and for other groups across the country. The Environmental Protection Agency has featured the plant's waste minimization technology and emergency response practices through training videos and tours. Recently, agents from the CIA, the Defense Department, and the National Security Agency used the plant as part of their training on chemical weaponry and terrorist response. Many government and regulatory agencies have honored FMC with awards in recognition of the company's commitment to public safety and health.

FMC's agricultural products help farmers battle against weeds, plant diseases, and pests—playing a major role in sustaining our world's food supply. At the same time, FMC is a valuable asset to local and federal officials, as the company takes an active role in environmental protection and education. FMC's record demonstrates that science and nature can coexist for the benefit of all.

FMC'S CHEMICAL PRODUCTION OPERATORS ARE HIGHLY TRAINED, RECEIVING SOME 10 MONTHS OF EDUCATION BEFORE WORKING ON THEIR OWN (LEFT).

THE MOST RECENT ADDITION TO FMC'S BALTIMORE PLANT IS THE SULFENTRAZONE MANUFACTURING FACILITY, WHICH REQUIRED A LOCAL INVESTMENT EXCEEDING $100 MILLION TO CONSTRUCT (RIGHT).

Whitman, Requardt and Associates, LLP

Whitman, Requardt and Associates, LLP (WR&A) has built Baltimore from the ground up—literally. For more than 85 years, this comprehensive engineering and architectural firm has been serving the needs of the Baltimore community by putting a solid infrastructure into place. Today, WR&A continues to build on that strong foundation, offering a wide variety of services to its clients in government, business, and industry.

A Solid Foundation

WR&A traces its roots back to 1915, the year that Ezra B. Whitman, William J. Norton, and Paul B. Bird forged a partnership to form Norton, Bird and Whitman. Whitman, a local World War I hero, came into the business with a solid engineering reputation. After Baltimore's Great Fire of 1904, Whitman was instrumental in the city's rebuilding effort. He also served a successful term as Baltimore's water engineer, implementing the world's first rapid sand filtration plant for a major city. Whitman contributed to the design of the city's Back River Wastewater Treatment Plant, the first such central plant for a large city in the United States. The small firm quickly became known throughout the Baltimore region for its expertise in water and wastewater projects.

After several additions to the partnership, the firm took on its current name in 1943. WR&A continued to focus on the water and wastewater aspects of civil engineering until the 1960s, when the company began to diversify and expanded its services to include highway transportation, building design, and marine engineering. Today, the WR&A provides a variety of engineering services, including architecture and building design, industrial facilities, land development and site planning, geotechnical, solid waste and environmental engineering, construction management, surveying, and other services. The firm now has more than 350 employees in eight offices in Maryland, Virginia, Delaware, and Pennsylvania.

The Growth of Baltimore

Baltimore's current water delivery and wastewater conveyance and treatment systems still utilize the engineering put in place by WR&A years ago. The firm's foresight and careful planning helped prepare the city for decades of growth without costly and time-consuming overhauls. The Prettyboy and Loch Raven reservoirs were both planned and designed by WR&A, and the firm engineered the 108-inch main water line that still brings water to the city from the Susquehanna River. The firm designed the system that recycles water from the Back River Wastewater Treatment Plant for Bethlehem Steel's Sparrows Point

railways and roadways. The firm worked on the renovation of Penn Station and the construction of its new parking garage, and helped to establish Baltimore's light-rail system. WR&A also designed the west approach to Baltimore's Fort McHenry Tunnel, one of the most heavily traveled routes in the region.

Contributions to Communities

A corporate citizen of Baltimore's Charles Village neighborhood for many years, WR&A plays an active role in the revitalization of that community. The firm was a founding member of the Charles Village Community Benefits District (CVCBD), a nonprofit organization formed in 1994 to represent residents and business owners in the neighborhood. CVCBD provides private security and sanitation services for the 100-block area, as well as sponsorship of regular events and promotions.

Through much change within the firm and throughout the region, the engineering done by WR&A has stood the test of time. Though needs and requirements will continue to evolve, the name Whitman, Requardt and Associates, LLP will always stand for thorough engineering with innovative solutions.

Plant. WR&A also contributed to the planning and design of the Montebello and Ashburton filtration plants, which treat a combined total of 248 million gallons of water each day.

WR&A provides a variety of services in Baltimore's maritime community, helping to design the bulkheads and infrastructure to support the Inner Harbor from the World Trade Center to Fells Point. Included in this area is the world-renowned National Aquarium's Marine Mammal Pavilion, for which the firm provided the engineering design. WR&A also designed two of the largest dry docks in the world—for Bethlehem Shipbuilding (Bal-

timore Marine Industries) and for the Newport News Shipbuilding and Dry Dock Company. This experience enabled WR&A to become one of the leaders in dry dock certification for the U.S. Navy.

WR&A's engineers are also experts in residential and commercial land development, including complete utility infrastructure, roads, and lot layout. In the Baltimore region, WR&A provided land development engineering services during the construction of the White Marsh Mall, and to the towns of Joppatowne, Columbia, and St. Charles.

In the transportation arena, WR&A has been instrumental in the development of the region's

WR&A HAS COMPLETED A VARIETY OF PROJECTS IN THE BALTIMORE AREA, INCLUDING THE MARINA MAMMAL PAVILION AT THE NATIONAL AQUARIUM (TOP) AND PENN STATION (BOTTOM).

Schaefer & Strohminger Management Services, Inc.

Louis M. Schaefer and David G. Strohminger have known about cars for as long as they can remember. They should—they represent the second generation of Schaefers and third generation of Strohmingers to sell cars in Baltimore since 1917. Schaefer & Strohminger (S&S) is the oldest car dealership in Baltimore; today, it is one of the largest as well, with eight locations in the area. The business credits its success to its commitment to complete customer satisfaction, and its reputation in and around Baltimore for professionalism and fairness. As Strohminger, S&S president, says, "We care about people. We try to make this a very easy place to do business."

Three Generations of Family Leadership

In 1917, Michael Schaefer and Henry Strohminger founded their Baltimore business as an auto repair shop. The two brothers-in-law had worked together as mechanics for Baltimore Gas and Electric before striking out on their own. As they built their clientele, the partners began selling used cars, and eventually added new vehicles as well. Over the years, Schaefer & Strohminger sold a variety of cars, including DeSotos, Kaiser-Fraziers, Nash Ramblers, and Simcas.

In 1955, the second generation took the helm. Under the leadership of Louis Schaefer, chairman and CEO, and George and Henry Strohminger, the business began expanding. S&S established a second location—the Towson dealership—in 1960, followed by a third in Dundalk, in 1969. The Dundalk dealership was one of the first in the area to sell Toyotas, as import cars entered the U.S. market.

The third generation of Schaefers and Strohmingers grabbed the wheel with the families' trademark enthusiasm and savvy. The business now includes four dealerships in Baltimore County, one in Baltimore City, two in Harford County, and one in Cambridge, Maryland, with a total of some 450 employees. Customers can purchase new and used trucks, minivans, and cars from 12 lines of vehicles: Dodge, Pontiac, Jeep, Chrysler, Honda, Mazda, Toyota, Chevrolet, Oldsmobile, GMC, Daewoo, and Mitsubishi.

Making It Easy to Buy a Car

The S&S team is proud of its approach to car sales. The company's employees are committed to educating their customers and to helping them find the best cars for their needs and budgets. The management staff has more than 100 cumulative years of intensive consumer sales training, and managers have more than 200 combined years of experience.

S&S likes to make shopping for a vehicle as easy as possible. The firm's Web site—www.sandsauto.com—allows prospective buyers to review in-stock vehicles from the comfort of their homes. In addition, every S&S dealership has access to the more than 2,000 cars, trucks, and minivans in stock, providing customers with an extensive selection.

The finance team at S&S understands that when buyers are ready for new cars, they want results fast. The company offers easy, on-site financing with more than 20 accredited lending institutions. This broad reach allows S&S to approve credit within 20 minutes, enabling most buyers to leave with their cars on the day of purchase. S&S' credit specialists can also help provide fresh-start financing for those with less-than-perfect credit. Most prospective customers can find cars to meet their needs at S&S; the dealerships offer everything from brand-new luxury vehicles to car leases with low down payments.

Used car sales are still an important part of the company's business, and S&S remains committed to providing high-quality, reliable used vehicles. The dealerships' some 100 state-certified, factory-trained, authorized technicians put all used vehicles through a complete, 70-point mechanical

IN 1917, MICHAEL SCHAEFER (LEFT) AND HENRY STROHMINGER FOUNDED WHAT HAS TODAY BECOME SCHAEFER & STROHMINGER MANAGEMENT SERVICES, INC. (S&S).

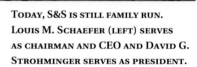

inspection before the cars reach the lot, and each car is professionally cleaned, inside and out.

At S&S, the staff is not satisfied until the customer is satisfied. Buyers can exchange vehicles—up to five days after purchase—for a car of equal or greater value, paying just the applicable taxes, title and processing fees, and difference in price, if any. A full-time staff of five customer service representatives routinely contacts each customer, after a sale or service visit, to ensure complete customer satisfaction.

S&S knows that the relationship is not over once the car leaves the lot. The dealerships make every effort to ensure stress-free repair or maintenance visits to their service centers. Customers receive free towing within a 25-mile radius of any S&S dealership, and can utilize the convenient "night owl" drop-off service. Replacement vehicles can be rented at a discount while vehicles are being serviced, or customers can use the dealerships' free shuttle service, which runs within a 10-mile radius of the service center.

In recognition of S&S' commitment to quality, Chrysler has named the company a five-star dealership for several consecutive years. To receive Chrysler's top designation, companies must pass rigorous sales, service, and follow-up tests.

Giving Back to the Communities It Serves

As longtime Baltimoreans, the S&S family is committed to supporting its hometown. The company regularly supports a variety of community organizations, from sports teams to schools. The dealerships have provided funding for books for the city's elementary schools, and they provide support for a number of area schools. S&S also sponsors

alcohol-free prom parties at four local high schools each year, reinforcing the message of responsible driving.

For more than 80 years, Schaefer & Strohminger has been serving Baltimore's automotive needs. Over the years, the types of cars have changed, but the fundamentals have remained the same: commitment to family, quality of service, and a hard-won reputation as one of Baltimore's most respected car dealerships.

TODAY, S&S IS STILL FAMILY RUN. LOUIS M. SCHAEFER (LEFT) SERVES AS CHAIRMAN AND CEO AND DAVID G. STROHMINGER SERVES AS PRESIDENT.

S&S IS COMPRISED OF SEVEN DEALERSHIPS IN THE BALTIMORE AREA, INCLUDING THIS ONE IN TOWSON.

Baltimore Symphony Orchestra

Internationally recognized as one of the world's most distinguished orchestras, the Baltimore Symphony Orchestra (BSO) is renowned for its imaginative interpretations of masterworks and its uncompromising artistic innovation. The BSO has been hailed as a prototype for the performance of classical music in the 21st century.

In October 1997, the BSO's prospects for even greater artistic achievement were enhanced when Maestro Yuri Temirkanov accepted the position as the orchestra's 11th music director. Widely recognized as among the most talented conductors of his generation, Temirkanov is also the music director and chief conductor of Russia's legendary St. Petersburg Philharmonic, conductor laureate of London's Royal Philharmonic, and principal guest conductor of the Danish National Radio Symphony Orchestra. Temirkanov's 1999-2000 inaugural Baltimore season attracted the adulation of many of the nation's leading music critics and generated statewide enthusiasm.

THE JOSEPH MEYERHOFF SYMPHONY HALL HAS BEEN HOME TO THE BALTIMORE SYMPHONY ORCHESTRA SINCE 1982.

A Long, Rich History

Organized in 1916, the BSO is the only major American orchestra originally established as a branch of the municipal government. Reorganized as a private institution in 1942, the orchestra maintains close relationships with the governments and communities of Baltimore and its surrounding counties, as well as with the state of Maryland.

The BSO's modern history dates from 1965, when Baltimore arts patron Joseph Meyerhoff became president of the symphony orchestra, a position he held for 18 years. Meyerhoff appointed Romanian-born conductor Sergiu Comissiona as music director; together, the two men ensured the creation of an artistic institution that has become an integral part of the arts community of the mid-Atlantic region.

MAESTRO YURI TEMIRKANOV SERVES AS MUSIC DIRECTOR OF THE BALTIMORE SYMPHONY ORCHESTRA.

A True Musical Ambassador

The BSO's reputation for musical excellence and artistic achievement has spread far beyond the shores of the Chesapeake Bay. Through its international tours of the Soviet Union and Asia, the orchestra has developed appreciative audiences across the globe.

The BSO's prolific recordings have also helped the orchestra reach music lovers around the world. The BSO and Conductor David Zinman won their first Grammy award in 1987 for a recording of cello concertos by Samuel Barber and Benjamin Britten with soloist Yo-Yo Ma. Since then, the BSO has collected two more Grammy awards, as well as several nominations, for its recordings. The orchestra recently released *I Will Lift Up Mine Eyes*, a CD recording of works of prominent African-American composer Adolphus Hailstork. This CD received national attention and was the subject of a special National Public Radio broadcast.

Community Outreach

The BSO gives back to the community not only through its music, but also through its community outreach efforts and educational partnerships. The innovative Arts Excel initiative involves BSO musicians in teaching core-curriculum subjects to primary and secondary students using musical concepts. Additionally, the orchestra performs more than 40 education concerts annually for some 70,000 area students from kindergarten through 12th grade.

In 1989, the BSO established its Community Outreach Committee to address the interests and needs of the African-American community. The committee aims to involve this audience in the full range of the BSO's concert, management, and volunteer activities.

Venturing onward, the BSO is establishing a second home at a new, 2,000-seat concert hall at the historic Strathmore Hall arts center in north Bethesda. The pursuit of this initiative is in keeping with the symphony's mandate to serve as a cultural resource for all Maryland residents, while achieving the finest in musical performance excellence.

"We are proud that our orchestra has triumphed on the world stage and enticed an enthusiastic international following," says John Gidwitz, BSO president. "However, the primary mission of the organization is, as it has always been, serving the artistic, civic, and educational life of the Maryland community."

Profiles in Excellence 1920–1959

Middle River Aircraft Systems

In 1929, the Martin Company broke ground in a sleepy town along the Chesapeake Bay in Baltimore County, making many of the locals skeptical. Few believed that these newfangled contraptions called airplanes would meet with much commercial success. Martin soon made believers out of Middle River's residents—as well as of skeptics around the world—with its trendsetting aircraft design and successful manufacturing practices.

Over the ensuing generations, the Martin Company's Middle River facility has undergone many adaptations, including establishing itself as an independent entity called Middle River Aircraft Systems. But its impact on the surrounding community and the field of aviation has remained constant.

A Leading Name in Aviation

Glenn L. Martin established his aircraft manufacturing company in 1919, and the world of aviation has never been the same since. Martin was an enthusiastic amateur pilot and a driven businessman, although he lacked technical engineering skills. That didn't keep him from building airplanes, and building them well; for four decades, the Glenn L. Martin Aircraft Company was a leading aircraft manufacturer in the United States, while Martin maintained direct control of the company. In those 40 years, Martin trained some of aviation's best-known names, including William Boeing, James McDonnell, and Donald Douglas.

Like those names, the Martin name is still synonymous with excellence in aviation. After Martin's death in 1955, the Martin Company merged with American-Marietta Company, creating the aerospace giant, Martin-Marietta. In the mid-1900s, Martin-Marietta merged with Lockheed, forming the world's largest defense contractor, Lockheed Martin.

Through each of these mergers, the Middle River factory remained an integral part of the company's plans. In 1997, the facility became an independent entity and changed its name to Middle River Aircraft Systems (MRAS). Today, MRAS works with the industry's major airframe makers and engine producers to design and build component parts of their products, and to provide ongoing maintenance and support.

A Place in History

In the early days under Martin, the Middle River factory was responsible for the manufacture of many historic aircraft. The plant's first project was the B-10

bomber, which was introduced in 1932, and immediately received the Collier Trophy, aviation's highest award. One year later, the Middle River facility unveiled the China Clipper, the world's first trans-oceanic luxury passenger plane. As the shadow of war spread across Europe, activity at the factory intensified. Martin manufactured scores of bombers, including the PBM Mariner, the B-26 Marauder, and the JRM Mars. By the end of World War II, the some 50,000 employees at Middle River had produced more than 10,000 aircraft.

In 1955, the Middle River facility finished production of its final aircraft, the XP6 SeaMaster. With nearly three decades of aviation experience under its belt, the factory turned its attentions to the emergent fields of missiles, rocketry, and spacecraft. The Martin-Marietta merger in 1961 positioned the company for further growth, and for three more decades the Martin-Marietta Company stayed at or near the top of the world's aerospace industry. The now-sprawling facility in Middle River served as a nucleus for hundreds of projects during the Martin-Marietta years, including missiles, launch vehicles, satellites, and sonar and radar systems. During the Great Space Race, which pitted former allies against each other in a rush to put a man on the Moon, many of America's best astronauts studied, trained, and lived in the newly remodeled Middle River facility.

Throughout the 1960s, the factory hummed with ideas and machines. While the satellites Martin-Marietta built were being launched into orbit, Middle River began work on some of the earliest single stage to orbit (SSTO) vehicles. The X-24A, grandfather of today's space shuttle and great-grandfather of the forthcoming VentureStar, was designed and built by the forward-thinking Middle River team.

◆◆◆◆◆◆◆◆◆◆◆◆◆◆◆◆◆◆◆◆◆◆
Establishing World Leadership

Today, MRAS' 1.7 million-square-foot facility, situated on 180 acres, focuses on the specialized needs of the modern aircraft industry. The company is one of the world's leading suppliers of jet engine thrust reversers, the brakes of a jet engine. MRAS is the sole source of life to the contract supplier of GE's entire line of CF6 engines, and also provides reversers for Pratt & Whitney, another leading aircraft engine manufacturer.

In addition, MRAS manufactures a variety of specialized structures for major aircraft manufacturers, including Boeing and Lockheed Martin. The company provides overhaul and repair services for a variety of aero structures, and offers high-quality, around-the-clock support and repair services to commercial airlines worldwide. MRAS also supports a variety of military programs, including the air force's TF-39 reverser, the navy's P3 Orion, and the JT3D reverser, part of the JSTARs.

For more than 70 years, Middle River Aircraft Systems has been designing, building, and servicing the world's best aircraft. Through its many incarnations, the company has made aviation history—contributing to some of the most defining events in the nation's history.

TODAY, MIDDLE RIVER AIRCRAFT SYSTEMS' 1.7 MILLION-SQUARE-FOOT FACILITY FOCUSES ON THE SPECIALIZED NEEDS OF THE MODERN AIRCRAFT INDUSTRY.

unicipal Employees Credit Union of Baltimore, Inc. (MECU) is a dynamic financial institution that offers convenience, service, and competitive financial products to its members. However, MECU also offers something a commercial bank can't—the unique benefits of a credit union,

including status as a member/owner, attractive rates on savings and credit, and low fees. More and more people are recognizing all that MECU has to offer, and making the credit union their first choice for their financial services needs.

MECU has aggressively managed to maintain its competitive position in the modern financial service industry. "We must provide service to our members or other institutions will do so," says Bert J. Hash Jr., president and CEO. Customer service, delivery options, and product lines have all been updated to bring current and prospective members the very best.

Once viewed as a credit union exclusively for city employees, MECU's services are now available to a broader group. Any current or retired employee of the City of

Baltimore is eligible, as are other qualifying select groups, including employees of the Baltimore City Convention Center, Baltimore City Development Corporation, Baltimore City Zoo, Baltimore Museum of Art, National Aquarium, Walters Art Gallery, and many more. In addition, the families of city employees and retirees—spouses, children, grandchildren, and siblings—are eligible for membership.

In today's competitive financial services industry, more and more people are taking advantage of the unique benefits of credit unions. Above-market savings dividends, below-market lending rates, and low fees, combined with all the convenience and service options of a commercial bank, make MECU an attractive option to many Baltimoreans.

A Proud Tradition of Service

When MECU was founded in 1936, the credit union's main goal was to provide city employees with a safe, inexpensive alternative to the outrageous interest rates charged during the Depression era. The organization's 15 charter members helped establish the credit union, raising an initial capital of $150. MECU's low-cost membership and affordable loans proved popular, and soon its services were expanded. The credit union continued to grow, and in 1977, MECU moved to its current office on Fayette Street, at the Old Armistead Hotel site.

Through the 1980s and 1990s, large financial institutions dominated, and technology changed the face of consumer financial service. MECU's ability to adapt with the times and deliver modern conveniences while maintaining its commitment to its members has proven to be sound business. By the end of 1999, MECU's assets totaled more than $521 million, a 5.5 percent increase over 1998. Total net income and deposits have experienced similar growth, positioning MECU for future success in the years to come.

Convenient Access Options

Through a variety of means, MECU has improved access to its services. Members can conduct transactions and receive information in branches, at an ATM, via telephone, by mail, or by home computer. Through a unique partnership with a regional financial institution, MECU members now enjoy convenient, surcharge-free access to their accounts at some 550 ATM locations. The credit union also effectively doubled its 24-hour, seven-day Telephone Teller capacity, mak-

UNDER THE LEADERSHIP OF HERMAN WILLIAMS JR. (LEFT), CHAIRMAN, AND BERT J. HASH JR., PRESIDENT AND CEO, MUNICIPAL EMPLOYEES CREDIT UNION (MECU) HAS GREATLY EXPANDED ACCESS TO ITS MEMBERS BY OPENING THREE NEW BRANCH OFFICES IN LESS THAN A YEAR.

ing the system more responsive, efficient, and better equipped to handle high caller volume. A new mail-processing department provides accurate service to members who bank by mail. MECU is even on the Internet, with a user-friendly Web site that provides membership and account information, rates, ATM locations, PC banking, and an on-line loan application.

Members can apply for a loan through the credit union's 24-hour, seven-day lending center. The telephone center handles a variety of credit products, including preferred home equity; auto, boat, and recreational vehicle loans; mortgages; and personal loans. Through its participation in the Credit Union Auto Loan Network, MECU offers members the convenience of applying for vehicle loans at more than 100 automobile dealers.

If members want to visit a MECU office, it is easier than ever to find one in a convenient location. In addition to the credit union's flagship branch in downtown Baltimore, MECU has in recent years opened three new branch offices: on Reisterstown Road, Northern Parkway, and Martin Luther King Boulevard. These additions bring its services closer to the homes and offices of members.

MECU offers a variety of account options, such as checking, savings, certificates of deposit, individual retirement accounts, and club accounts. Members can take advantage of convenient account services like VISA Check cards, ATM cards, direct deposit, and ACH direct payments. The credit union also offers VISA Classic and Gold credit cards to qualifying members.

Rooted in Community

In keeping with its mission, MECU is committed to giving back to the communities in which its member-owners live and work. The company actively supports the Sandtown Habitat for Humanity, a variety of Baltimore literacy initiatives, and has adopted a school in the city school system. Community service is not just a corporate ideal; it is an initiative for MECU's employees as well. More than 98 percent of MECU employees volunteered for the Combined Charities Campaign in 1999, a figure that far exceeded any other participating agency's total.

Municipal Employees Credit Union enjoys a rich history, steeped in the credit union tradition. At the same time, MECU is a leading financial institution that offers a competitive array of products and services. Both elements meld successfully at MECU, due to sound leadership and a clear vision, which will be the hallmarks of the organization for years to come.

T. Rowe Price Associates, Inc.

Thomas Rowe Price Jr. may be an investment legend today, but more than 60 years ago his peers were skeptical about some of his investment ideas. Price believed that corporations, like people, have life cycles of growth, maturity, and decline. If investors were able to identify leading growth companies and hold onto them for many years, he believed, they would be rewarded with growth in their market value and dividend income. Price also believed that investors would be better served by an investment firm that charged a fee on assets under management rather than by the prevailing transaction-based revenue structure. A fee-based system meant that the firm would prosper only if the clients also prospered. Thus, investment choices would require thorough research, which Price's firm would provide.

In 1937, as the Great Depression persisted, investors were not feeling particularly adventurous. Though Price's investment philosophy was generally unknown and untested, he remained steadfastly committed to implementing his ideas for investing and investment counseling.

An Established Industry Leader

T. Rowe Price Associates, Inc., the company that bears Price's name and was founded on his theories, is one of the financial industry's largest managers of no-load mutual funds, as well as one of its largest providers of full-service 401(k) retirement plans. Thousands of clients rely on T. Rowe Price to put the company's founding principles to work for them every day.

T. Rowe Price provides a broad range of investment services for pension, profit sharing, and other employee benefit plans; endowments; foundations; and individuals. The firm and its affiliates serve as investment adviser for more than 75 stock, bond, and money market funds. Solid investment results over time, sensitivity to investment risk, low costs, and high-quality services to shareholders have made T. Rowe Price a leader in the financial services industry.

Around the Country, around the World

As of December 31, 2000, T. Rowe Price managed $167 billion in total assets for more than 8 million individual and institutional investor accounts, including $106 billion in mutual fund assets under management. With more than 4,000 employees in its offices in Baltimore; Boston; Colorado Springs; Los Angeles; Owings Mills, Maryland; San Francisco; Tampa; and Washington, D.C., T. Rowe Price is truly a national leader. The firm has also established an international presence. T. Rowe Price International, Inc. is one of the largest

T. ROWE PRICE ASSOCIATES, INC.'S HEADQUARTERS OVERLOOKS BALTIMORE'S SPARKLING INNER HARBOR.

managers of international assets for U.S. investors, with about $33 billion under management, as of December 2000. This wholly owned subsidiary has offices in London, Paris, Hong Kong, Singapore, Tokyo, Buenos Aires, and Baltimore.

More than 1,900 corporate and public retirement plans across the country benefit from T. Rowe Price's investment and administrative services. The firm provides investment management, state-of-the-art record keeping, and participant communications, all adapted to the unique needs of each client. Customized services such as special reporting and flexible processing help to assure that clients are getting the information and services they need to meet their goals.

The experience and commitment of its employees makes T. Rowe Price stand out among its peers. A team of some 50 portfolio managers and more than 46 equity and credit analysts work to uncover new investment opportunities, evaluating the balance between risk and reward. Customers can access information on their investment holdings seven days a week through the firm's toll-free customer service center. More than 400 knowledgeable service representatives are ready to answer investors' questions, utilizing

the latest technology to provide real-time information. Customers can also obtain account information, make fund transactions, and access various financial planning calculators on the firm's Web site, www.troweprice.com.

"I may be a darn fool for taking this unnecessary risk, but I am going to have the satisfaction of

knowing that I tried to build my own business," wrote Price in 1937. "If I later fail, I will have no regrets." More than six decades later, there is certainly no cause for regret. One man's vision has expanded beyond his wildest dreams, providing an array of valuable services for millions of people around the world.

JACK LAPORTE, A DIRECTOR OF THE FIRM AND MANAGER OF ITS NEW HORIZONS FUND, REVIEWS A PORTFOLIO HOLDING WITH A COLLEAGUE (TOP).

MARY MILLER, DIRECTOR OF THE FIRM'S MUNICIPAL BONDS DIVISION, DISCUSSES CURRENT MARKET DEVELOPMENTS (BOTTOM).

Unilever Home & Personal Care-USA

After marketing America's first brand of soap, the Lever Brothers Company has maintained a tradition of providing consumers with quality products at a sensible price for more than 100 years. Over the years, Lever Brothers became Unilever, a global leader in consumer products with brands in foods, household care, personal care, and fragrances. In 1997, the name in front of the Baltimore plant changed from Lever Brothers to Unilever Home & Personal Care-USA to reflect the combining of the Lever Brothers, Chesebrough-Pond's, and Helene Curtis businesses. That strong heritage remains.

Brothers William and James Lever, sons of a wholesale grocer, originally established the Lever Brothers Company in England. Their first product, Sunlight, was a pure laundry soap and an immediate success in Britain. Lifebuoy bar soap was introduced in 1894. The company's business in the United States began in 1895, when William Lever opened a sales office in New York. In 1919, the company expanded its sales structure with offices in Chicago, Kansas City, New York, Philadelphia, and San Francisco, and introduced Rinso, the first granulated laundry soap. This product eliminated the chore of cutting bar soap into chips for the newly introduced home washing machine. Lever Brothers further strengthened its business in 1926 with the precedent-setting introduction of Lux soap, the first white, milled, perfumed soap to be made and sold in America at a reasonable price. In a few years, it was the largest-selling beauty soap in the country.

Today, Unilever is a worldwide leader in the consumer products industry, and manufactures such well-known brands as Wisk®, all®, and Surf® laundry detergents; Snuggle® and Final Touch® fabric softeners; Dove®, Caress®, and Lever 2000® bars and shower gels; and a whole host of others.

THE UNILEVER HOME & PERSONAL CARE-USA MANUFACTURING PLANT IS LOCATED ON HOLABIRD AVENUE IN BALTIMORE.

BOB STOCKFIELD

A Baltimore Beginning

The 1938 opening of the Lever Brothers plant in Baltimore marked a new era in the company's history. After acquiring the plant—located on a onetime dairy farm—from the Hecker Products Corporation, the company modernized the original five-story building and expanded it into a large manufacturing complex, including a 460,000-square-foot distribution center.

Lux soap and Lifebuoy were the first Lever brands produced at the Baltimore plant. The manufacturing center scored a number of firsts in new product development, including the 1950 production of Dove, a non-soap, moisturizing beauty bar, and Wisk, an all-purpose, heavy-duty laundry detergent. Currently, the Baltimore facility, which employs some 500 people, manufactures the popular household brands of Wisk, all, and Surf laundry detergent; Snuggle and Final Touch fabric softeners; and Dove and Caress beauty bars.

PRODUCTS MANUFACTURED AT UNILEVER'S BALTIMORE PLANT INCLUDE WISK®, ALL®, AND SURF® LAUNDRY DETERGENT; SNUGGLE® AND FINAL TOUCH® FABRIC SOFTENERS; AND DOVE® AND CARESS® BEAUTY BARS.

BOB STOCKFIELD

From the beginning, the company's Baltimore plant has been a trendsetter in work practices and employee recognition. Even in the early days, Baltimore employees enjoyed progressive benefits, such as investment and pension plans, company-paid life insurance, profit sharing, and tuition reimbursement. Today, employees at Unilever's Baltimore plant enjoy these benefits and many more, and are proud to be part of the Unilever family. Employee loyalty is strong; the plant's Quarter Century Club, for employees with 25-plus years of service, has a membership of 737, of which 45 are active employees and 692 are retirees. Even after retirement, Unilever employees gather for social events and work projects through the Lever Brothers Retirees' Association, which was established in 1986.

◆◆◆◆◆◆◆◆◆◆◆◆◆◆◆◆◆◆◆◆

Commitment to Community

Unilever's commitment to its Baltimore manufacturing facility also extends to the local community—so much so that the company was honored in 1996 with the Mayor's Business Recognition Award for outstanding service.

Recognizing the importance of environmental initiatives, Unilever was the first corporate sponsor of Tree-Mendous Maryland, a statewide conservation program. It also has underwritten programs like Project C-Wrap, a wetlands conservation and environmental education project benefiting Baltimore-area schools. Unilever employees also have joined community volunteers for worthwhile projects with the National Park Foundation at Fort McHenry to promote recycling, as well as with the mayor's office for a cleanup project at Gwynn's Falls Park. In 2000, the plant was awarded the Business for the Bay Excellence Award for Outstanding Achievement. This award recognized the Baltimore plant among businesses from Maryland, Virginia, and Pennsylvania for the many achievements and initiatives made to protect the environment.

The Baltimore plant makes a concerted effort to be a good neighbor to Baltimore and an asset to the Dundalk community. Through charitable donations, Unilever supports such organizations as the Johns Hopkins Children's Center, United Way of Central Maryland, Our Daily Bread, My Sister's Place, and Family Crisis Center of Baltimore County. Unilever has donated to and partnered with local educational institutions, such as Southeast Middle School, Sollers Point/Southeastern Technical High School, and Dundalk Community College. The Baltimore plant began a new annual program with the Baltimore County Schools in 1999 as a corporate sponsor of the Science Screen Report for Kids, a videotape series that focuses on recent developments in science, technology, and engineering. In addition, the Unilever employees participate in food and clothing drives with their Adopt-A-Family programs.

From the historic beginnings of Lever Brothers Company to Unilever's many innovative products, its progressive systems development, and its environmental and community initiatives, Unilever Home & Personal Care-USA in Baltimore is poised to meet the 21st century with an eye on the future, while honoring the company's rich heritage.

EMPLOYEE LOYALTY IS STRONG AT UNILEVER'S BALTIMORE PLANT.

Dahne & Weinstein

It is apparent from the moment the doors open that Dahne & Weinstein is not just another jewelry store or just another jeweler. The store is clearly a step above the rest, and Dahne & Weinstein treasures its reputation as much as its customers treasure the exquisite pieces the store offers. From rare, historical collections to contemporary, one-of-a-kind designs, Dahne & Weinstein is a unique place where customers and staff share their passion for fine jewelry.

Dahne & Weinstein has been serving the Baltimore community since 1939, when Irvin and Rose Weinstein first opened their store in downtown Baltimore. Although the business has since moved to a spacious, modern building in Lutherville's Greenspring Station, the Weinstein family remains at the helm. Rose Weinstein acts as president emeritus, son Stephen is president, and Stephen's wife, Elinor, serves as vice president. With more than 60 years of experience in Baltimore, the Weinstein family has served several generations of the city's prominent families, as well as many newcomers who appreciate the finer things in life.

Jewelry as Art

Dahne & Weinstein employs only trained gemologists, who recognize quality and understand the intricacies of gemstones and jewelry design. The store's inventory focuses on the finest works of jewelry as art, rather than on the formula designer pieces seen at most retail jewelry outlets. Extremely fine precious and semiprecious gemstones are a specialty, as well as exquisitely cut diamonds of exceptional quality. Dahne & Weinstein also offers many unusual pieces that reflect its customers' unique tastes without being trendy. The store's jewelry and gifts are priced to fit anyone's budget, ranging from less than $200 to more than $200,000.

Estate jewelry is another passion at Dahne & Weinstein, and the store's staff plays at the very highest levels of the estate market, competing with internationally renowned names like Sotheby's. Dahne & Weinstein purchases estate pieces from all over the world, developing a national and international clientele for major pieces. Other jewelers across the country also rely on Dahne & Weinstein as a supplier for estate jewelry.

"We have a close relationship with our customers, and we really care about what we sell," says Stephen Weinstein. "That relationship is apparent as customers come into the store and are greeted

DAHNE & WEINSTEIN HAS BEEN SERVING THE BALTIMORE COMMUNITY SINCE 1939, WHEN IRVIN AND ROSE WEINSTEIN FIRST OPENED THEIR STORE IN DOWNTOWN BALTIMORE. TODAY, THE STORE IS LOCATED IN LUTHERVILLE'S GREEN SPRING STATION.

by name." Dahne & Weinstein's passion for jewelry is unquestionable. Weinstein, a leading figure in the international jewelry scene, has been invited to participate in prestigious events all over the world, such as the Fabergé Young Jewelry Designers Competition in St. Petersburg, Russia, where he served as judge.

Stavenhagen Collection

Dahne & Weinstein has also received international recognition as the owner of the Stavenhagen Collection, the third-largest privately held collection of ancient rings in the world. The collection includes 525 historic finger rings from all over the world, including Egyptian, Etruscan, and Roman pieces, as well as rings from medieval German guilds, the Renaissance, and the Victorian era. Kurt Stavenhagen, a second-generation German jeweler who immigrated to Mexico to escape the Nazi regime, originally amassed the collection. The collection survived Stavenhagen's journey to Mexico, and was added to during his time there. However, no documentation of the collection survived, and Weinstein and his staff

have painstakingly worked to analyze and catalog the collection since acquiring it in 1996. The Stavenhagen Collection has been made available to museums and jewelry shows, and in 1999, it was the main cultural exhibit at the Vicenza Fair in Vicenza, Italy.

Though Dahne & Weinstein appreciates history, the store also recognizes the power of new technology. It was one of the first jewelry stores to establish a presence on the Internet through its cutting-edge virtual store.

On Dahne & Weinstein's Web site, located at www.dahneandweinstein.com, visitors can see a layout of the store with individual display cases, zoom in on a case, and then zoom in on one particular piece displayed in that case. In this way, Internet users can view any item on display in the store at any time with amazing clarity. Specific pieces are marked with item numbers and prices, and visitors can e-mail any sales associate for more information directly from the Web site or contact a sales associate via the store's toll-free number.

Dahne & Weinstein also operates an upscale gift store, which is open to the public and houses the

company's corporate gift division. Dahne & Weinstein has provided corporate gifts for many of Baltimore's most prominent corporations, and the gift store has been consistently included in *Baltimore Magazine*'s Best of Baltimore issue.

As a longtime resident of the Baltimore area, Dahne & Weinstein is an active corporate citizen. The company regularly supports a wide variety of local churches, synagogues, and schools, and it contributes to organizations such as Meals on Wheels. Dahne & Weinstein's customers are active civic leaders and volunteers, and the company is always eager to support their events and causes.

For more than 60 years, Dahne & Weinstein has been building its reputation as "the local jeweler with the international reputation," and the company has lived up to its tag line. Dahne & Weinstein's commitment to quality and service is apparent in everything it does. From its dealings with jewelry experts to helping local Baltimoreans select the perfect gift, Dahne & Weinstein knows its business well and works diligently to help others in their quest for quality jewelry, "one customer at a time since 1939."

ROSE WEINSTEIN, PRESIDENT EMERITUS AND COFOUNDER OF DAHNE & WEINSTEIN, DISPLAYS THE STAVENHAGEN COLLECTION OF ANCIENT RINGS.

Nevamar Decorative Surfaces

ost consumers may not be familiar with the name Nevamar Decorative Surfaces, but chances are they encounter one or more of the company's products every day. For more than 60 years, Nevamar has been making decorative laminates and other surfacing materials for a wide variety of applications. The company's products are used everywhere from airport rest rooms to bowling alleys, retail store displays to luxury yachts, office to home. With products that combine extreme durability and cost-effectiveness with the latest in sophisticated style, Nevamar is firmly positioned as one of the top manufacturers of high-pressure laminates in North America.

Blazing a Trail over Half a Century

Nevamar's roots stretch back to 1939, when the Winer family founded a company called National Plastics in Baltimore. Within a few years, the family business moved to Odenton in Anne Arundel County—a location that remains the hub of Nevamar's operations today. Over the years, the company changed ownership and its name several times. The name Nevamar came into use in 1970, a clever play on the product's durability. Today, the name is well recognized and respected in the construction and design industries, and the company enjoys a legacy as a design and technology innovator.

That trailblazing attitude has been a part of the Nevamar culture since its earliest days. In the early 1940s, when the company first moved to Odenton, it was one of the first to move into the manufacture of high-pressure laminates, a product that was virtually just off the drawing board. During wartime, the company adapted quickly, producing products for the navy's rocket program and the army's Signal Corps. In fact, Nevamar received the Army/Navy E Award for "converting its operations to the manufacture of war material and excellence in production and development." After the war, the company returned its focus to high-pressure laminates and began improving the product's design and performance.

NEVAMAR DECORATIVE SURFACES MAINTAINS HIGH EMPLOYEE LOYALTY FROM RESEARCH AND DEVELOPMENT TO MANUFACTURING TO QUALITY CONTROL.

Nevamar is responsible for many breakthroughs in high-pressure laminate manufacturing, including the development of dimensional laminates, cane-textured laminates, and many original designs. The ARmored Protection (ARP) Plus Surface, standard on all Nevamar textured finish laminates, provides longer wear and improved design clarity and fidelity. Innovations like the exclusive ARP Plus Surface, ChemArmor, Impressions premium surfacing, and LamMates matching thermofused melamine panels make Nevamar products even more durable and beautiful than ever before, and offer clients even greater value for their money.

Blending Form and Function— Beautifully

Few products offer all that Nevamar does: durability, high style, and affordable pricing. Plus, the products are extremely flexible, lending themselves to a wide range of applications. With a seemingly endless array of colors, textures, and finishes, Nevamar products can simulate much more costly surfaces like marble, metal, and wood. The Nevamar team even collaborates with customers to create custom designs to fit a specific purpose. Using sophisticated color-matching technology, Nevamar designers can meet exacting specifications, matching a particular wood grain or shade of color.

A recent custom design resulted in yet another technological breakthrough for the company: in a style the design team calls Fetch, sheets of high-pressure laminate are decorated in a black-and-white-spotted, dalmatian pattern. This type of design had not been thought possible before, as the high pressure used in manufacturing caused the color of the spots to run and streak. With a characteristic can-do attitude, Nevamar's team found a way, and the result has been warmly received by both the customer and the industry. Now, through the company's Custom Print program, any image, photography, text, or logo can be integrated directly into Nevamar laminates.

Not a group to rest on its laurels, the Nevamar design team is constantly introducing new styles, designs, finishes, and colors to the product line. The company's designers stay on top of color and style trends, and strive to be at the front of the curve. Each year, a new line is introduced, providing customers with the very latest styles to create a modern, sophisticated look.

From Camden Yards to Grand Central Station

Leading companies in a wide variety of industries rely on Nevamar's products. The company's decorative laminates are found in Grand Central Station, Borders bookstores, and Harley-

Davidson retail stores. Nevamar products are in the new Denver Broncos stadium, as well as the new Cincinnati Reds stadium. In the Baltimore area, Nevamar laminates can be found in Oriole Park at Camden Yards and at the Marberry Pavilion at Johns Hopkins Bayview campus. They're even found in some places you'd never expect: Nevamar products are used on the Royal Jordan yachts, in O'Brien water skis, and in Martin guitars. Nearly everywhere you turn, you may encounter a Nevamar product—and, chances are, it will

CLOCKWISE FROM TOP LEFT: A LAMINATE BACKDROP IS PERFECT TO ACCENTUATE MERCHANDISE.

PAINTED WOODLANDS IS ONE OF MANY DISTINCTIVE NEVAMAR DESIGNS.

SAND 'N' SHELLS IS A VISUAL DELIGHT THAT INVITES THE HAND TO TOUCH.

CLOCKWISE FROM TOP LEFT: LAMINATE IS A PRACTICAL CHOICE FOR DESKTOPS, AT WORK OR AT HOME.

CUSTOMIZED WOOD EDGE INTEGRATES THE TOTAL ROOM DESIGN.

NEVAMAR COUNTERTOPS ANSWER NEEDS FOR STYLE, DURABILITY, AND EASE OF MAINTENANCE.

look great every time, year after year after year.

The company also produces an array of specialty products, which lend the benefits of laminate to very specific sets of needs. Nevamar's laminated access flooring panels are a highly durable, easy-to-maintain choice for high-traffic areas, and offer low static generation, making them a natural fit for computer rooms and clean rooms. The company's line of Static Dissipative Laminates takes that feature one step further, with specially designed products that meet the exacting requirements of electronically sensitive applications. Elevators, store fixtures, and other public building construction projects take ad-

vantage of Nevamar's fire-rated laminates, which provide UL-listed, fire retardant products in a variety of styles and finishes. A distinct line of products, colors, and designs meets the needs of the bus, railcar, and motor home manufacturers, providing high-style fixtures like dining tables, wainscoting, bulk-heads, and ceiling panels. The company even offers ready-to-use ThickLam panels for use in public rest rooms, office cubicles, lockers, and wall systems. For nearly any need, there is a Nevamar product to fit it—and fit it with high style.

Nevamar's successful combination of practicality and style has not gone unnoticed. The company's products have been repeatedly recognized by design industry publications for their versatility and innovation. Most recently, Nevamar's ARP Plus Surface received top honors at *Home Magazine*'s third annual Kitchen & Bath Awards in the countertop surfaces category. The editorial review board noted the product's high style and low maintenance as key factors in its decision.

The company has also received kudos for its imaginative product advertising. Over the years, Nevamar has made a mark for itself through highly stylized, colorful, creative advertising. The images used in the ads stand on their own as art; framed prints of many of these campaigns decorate the halls of the Nevamar offices. The company's ads are just one more way that Nevamar demonstrates its commitment to design creativity

and its culture of breaking the industry mold.

Commitment to Community

While the company is constantly pursuing new innovations, one thing remains constant: its commitment to the Odenton community. Nevamar is a fixture in this corner of Anne Arundel County, and has been for more than half a century. Back then, the company's arrival was a major boon to the local economy, which had been decimated by the railroad's decline. The firm remains a major economic force in the county, and now boasts many multigenerational families of Nevamar employees. But whether related by blood or not, all Nevamar employees enjoy the family atmosphere at the company.

The company's family atmosphere is demonstrated through the Odenton plant's outstanding safety record. A comprehensive safety program, managed by the employees themselves, has resulted in more than 4 million hours without a lost-time incident. This is just one example of the company's focus on its employees' health and wellness both on and off the job.

Nevamar's focus on safety benefits the environment as well. In 2000, the company recycled more than 780,000 pounds of paper, and worked with Anne Arundel Community College to create a wetlands nursery with the noncontact cooling water from its laminate presses. Nevamar has even installed innova-

tive multifuel boilers that can burn waste sander dust as fuel. In 1999, more than 3.8 million pounds of sander dust were used to generate steam for the plant—material that previously would have been sent to a landfill. For its efforts to reduce its environmental impact, Nevamar has been repeatedly recognized by Anne Arundel County's Green Efforts program.

The company's caring attitude carries over to the community at large as well. Both employees and management at Nevamar are heavily involved in the Odenton community, supporting a variety of organizations and causes. Nevamar employees have organized food and clothing drives, walk-a-thon teams, and blood drives. Many local organizations benefit from this volunteerism, such as Sarah's House, a home for battered women and children; the local chapter of the American Cancer Society; and the Babe Ruth Museum after school program (which educates inner city youth through a collaborative effort with the Enoch Pratt Library). Nevamar continues to address the needs of non-profit organizations such as the Chesapeake Bay Foundation and Anne Arundel Medical Center targeting assistance in communications where its employees live. The grant program primarily focuses on environmental, economic, extraordinary education, and community needs, and assists organizations where its employees actively volunteer. On a corporate level, Nevamar helped the Anne

Arundel County YWCA establish the national Tribute to Women in Industry (T.W.I.N.) awards program. Since the program's inception, several women from Nevamar have been recognized for their leadership both in their careers and in the community.

◆◆◆◆◆◆◆◆◆◆◆◆◆◆◆◆◆◆◆◆◆◆

Forging a Better Nevamar for the Next Century

In 1995, Nevamar merged with Micarta, another leader in the high-pressure laminate industry. Founded in 1905 by George Westinghouse, Micarta was a force in the industry for decades. By uniting under the Nevamar name, the two industry leaders expanded their design selections, product availability, and technical support, and formed an even stronger company.

Today, Nevamar Decorative Surfaces employs more than 650 people at its Odenton, Maryland, facility and satellite centers, and another 600 work at its sister manufacturing plant in Hampton, South Carolina. The company also operates a network of customer service and distribution centers throughout the United States, and a national sales force that reaches from coast to coast. The sum has proved to be greater than the parts, melding together to form a bigger and better Nevamar that is well positioned for the new century.

The Rouse Company

Since its founding in Baltimore in 1939, The Rouse Company has grown to become one of the country's largest real estate development and management companies. In Baltimore, Rouse is also known as a hometown success story, having been responsible for some of the most significant development projects in the city's history.

Initially, the firm capitalized on the housing boom created by returning World War II veterans. In the decades that followed the war, the company shifted its focus to commercial real estate development; large, mixed-use projects; and full-scale community development. Today, The Rouse Company manages approximately 250 properties, encompassing retail, office, research and development, and industrial space.

The company has completed significant projects across the country, but several of its most well-known projects are right in its hometown of Baltimore. The creation of the city of Columbia and the development of Harborplace at Baltimore's Inner Harbor has changed the face of the region, and helped propel The Rouse Company to even greater success.

THE ROUSE COMPANY'S HARBORPLACE PROJECT WAS THE SPRINGBOARD FOR THE DEVELOPMENT OF BALTIMORE'S INNER HARBOR, AND SPURRED THE CITY'S RENAISSANCE IN THE EARLY 1980S.

HARBORPLACE CELEBRATED ITS 20TH ANNIVERSARY DURING THE 2000 INDEPENDENCE DAY WEEKEND.

Prestigious Projects

In the early 1960s, when The Rouse Company embarked on the Columbia project, community development was just emerging as a new trend. In partnership with Connecticut General Life Insurance Company, the firm founded the Howard Research and Development Corporation (HRD) and set out to develop 14,100 acres in Howard County. Columbia was conceived as an ideal for American suburban life, incorporating all elements of the community into self-contained villages. The initial development was completed in 1963, and Columbia continues to thrive and grow as one of the most popular communities in the Baltimore/Washington corridor.

The Inner Harbor is one of Baltimore's most popular locations for tourists and locals alike. Central to the Inner Harbor is Harborplace and the Gallery, a Rouse development project that recently celebrated its 20th anniversary. Retail shops and restaurants make Harborplace a natural gathering place, with water views and easy access to the National Aquarium and downtown businesses. The development of Harborplace was the springboard for development of the entire Inner Harbor area, and spurred Baltimore's renaissance in the early 1980s.

Rouse also has a considerable retail presence in Baltimore beyond Harborplace. Popular retail centers such as Owings Mills, Towson Town Center, White Marsh, and Village of Cross Keys were all developed by Rouse. The company remains committed to the needs of urban residents, as well, as evidenced by its continuing commitment to Baltimore's Mondawin Mall.

Investing in Communities

In its role as a developer, The Rouse Company recognizes the importance of strong community involvement. For the better part of the 20th century, The Rouse Company has demonstrated true corporate citizenship in the Baltimore area and beyond by generously donating its resources to the arts, education, and various community organizations. In the city of Baltimore, the company continually supports all major cultural institutions, and the firm provides annual contributions to community outreach programs for educational enrichment and affordable housing.

By remaining focused on quality real estate development and contributing to the communities in which it operates, the company is poised to be an integral part of the continued renaissance of Baltimore in the decades to come.

As North America's oldest and largest trade credit insurer, EULER American Credit Indemnity Company (EULER ACI) offers its clients more than a century of experience in minimizing the risk of nonpayment. EULER ACI brings value to its customers by offering cash flow security and predictability that lead to profitable growth opportunities.

EULER ACI provides insurance to businesses that extend credit for their products to domestic and international clients. If an insured business' customer is unable to pay, the policy would cover the loss, allowing the business the security and flexibility needed to remain competitive. With EULER ACI coverage, businesses can avoid catastrophic bad-debt losses, safely expand sales to new and existing customers, secure better financing terms, accurately predict cash flow, and reduce bad-debt reserves.

A History of Service

The same was true even in the late 1800s, when American Credit Indemnity (ACI) was founded in New Orleans. In the era after the elimination of the Bank of the United States, the commercial credit industry was struggling to establish itself. ACI survived through turbulent financial times, and began the modern era of growth and expansion in 1936, when Commercial Credit Company of Baltimore purchased the majority of its stock. ACI's headquarters was moved to Baltimore in 1940, and its product line and reach were expanded. The company continued to grow and prosper, becoming the largest trade credit insurer in the country. In 1992, Paris-based EULER, the world's premier credit insurer, purchased a 5 percent share of the company, and steadily increased its share until assuming 100 percent ownership in 1998. The company changed its name to EULER American Credit Indemnity in 1999 and embarked on a new chapter in the firm's history.

As customers of EULER ACI, businesses benefit from years of experience and the sound backing of the world's largest insurer.

But beyond its status as the oldest and largest, EULER ACI also provides some of the best service and benefits in the industry. Clients can utilize EOLIS, EULER ACI's on-line policy management system, to get fast decisions on new coverage, submit claims, review policy information, or contact their EULER ACI agent and service team. Customers also benefit from access to the company's direct agency force—the largest in the world, with more than 35 offices in the United States and Canada—as well as to EULER's database of excellence, with information on more than 40 million companies. The company has regional offices in Atlanta, Charlotte, Chicago, Los Angeles, Seattle, Montreal, Toronto, and New York, with risk management offices in Miami, San Francisco, and Mexico City.

With some 300 employees in the United States and Canada, EULER ACI provides coverage on shipments to more than 160 countries. ACI's partnership with EULER has fortified its position as the top trade credit insurance provider in the United States and as the largest private credit insurer in Canada. EULER ACI has consistently received excellent ratings from industry sources, including an AA+ rating from Standard & Poor's and an A (excellent) rating from the A.M. Best Company. In 1999, the company reported gross premiums in excess of $113 million.

Giving Back to the Community

Although EULER ACI deals with clients all around the world, the company remains proud of its status as a longtime corporate citizen of Baltimore. The firm and its employees support a variety of local organizations and causes with their time and resources. For several consecutive years, EULER ACI employees have participated in a voluntary payroll deduction program benefiting Johns Hopkins Children's Center. Employees also donate their time manning phones for the center's annual telethon.

Around the world or at home in Baltimore, EULER ACI is a valuable partner.

EULER AMERICAN CREDIT INDEMNITY COMPANY'S (EULER ACI) NORTH AMERICAN HEADQUARTERS IS LOCATED IN THE HEART OF BALTIMORE'S INNER HARBOR (TOP).

EULER ACI'S AFFILIATION WITH PARIS-BASED EULER HAS ENHANCED THE COMPANY'S GLOBAL MARKETING STRATEGY (BOTTOM).

Leonard Paper Company

Leonard Paper Company (LPC) doesn't just sell paper products. In fact, the leading wholesale distributor of janitorial maintenance supplies and food service disposables sells a wide range of items, from air fresheners to vacuum cleaners. It all started more than 60 years ago when Charles Burke Leonard founded the company. Today, Leonard family members are still at the helm, serving the needs of a variety of companies and businesses throughout the Baltimore and Washington, D.C., region.

IN 1940, LEONARD PAPER COMPANY FIRST BEGAN SELLING BUTCHER PAPER AND TWINE TO BALTIMORE MEAT MARKETS AND GROCERY STORES FROM ITS ALICEANNA STREET LOCATION.

LEONARD'S NEW TRAINING FACILITY HAS MANY DIFFERENT TYPES OF FLOORING—IN ADDITION TO A COMPLETE SAMPLE REST ROOM—TO TRAIN JANITORIAL CUSTOMERS FOR EVERY POSSIBLE APPLICATION.

Leonard Paper Company, Past and Present

In 1940, Leonard first began selling butcher paper and twine to Baltimore meat markets and grocery stores. A one-man operation, he served as the salesman and deliveryman, handling all deliveries from his Aliceanna Street location in downtown Baltimore with only one truck. When the pulp market diverted all its resources to the World War II effort, Leonard quickly diversified, learning and serving the needs of the food service industry. From there, the business took off, quickly outgrowing its space on Aliceanna Street. Over the years, the company has occupied a variety of buildings in Baltimore, including sites on

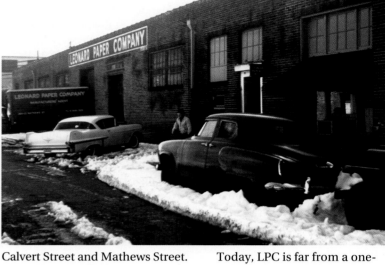

Calvert Street and Mathews Street. LPC also grew through several mergers and acquisitions in the 1950s and 1960s, and was briefly known as New York Paper Company. The Leonard name was soon reestablished and growth continued. The company moved to its current location on North Haven Street in 1979, not far from the original Aliceanna Street location it occupied six decades ago.

Today, LPC is far from a one-man operation, boasting more than 90 employees. Over the years, LPC has continued to expand its current East Baltimore location and now manages more than 140,000 square feet of warehouse space, with new acquisitions pending. The warehouse services more than 21 trucks, which handle deliveries to customers throughout the region. LPC's central location provides easy access to major interstate highways and the Conrail rail system, making it an ideal site to serve the company's broad territory. Leonard serves customers in Maryland from Havre De Grace and Frederick to the north and Annapolis to the east. In Virginia, customers extend as far south as Manassas and Quantico, and as far west as Dulles, making LPC the premier wholesale supplier in the greater Baltimore and Washington, D.C., area.

▲ DANA LEONARD

Serving Well-Known Institutions

Throughout the region, LPC serves some of the most well-known institutions and facilities in the Mid-Atlantic states. Johns Hopkins Hospital, Morgan State University, and the National Institute of Health are all satisfied customers, along with many of the area's major hotels and restaurants. Clients appreciate the efficient, friendly service they receive from the LPC staff. The company's extensive sales team has recently adopted a system so that account representatives can instantly complete and submit customer orders via laptop computer. LPC employees are encouraged to assist their customers, not just by meeting their supply needs, but by working one-on-one with individual clients in order to maximize each supply budget. The company offers competitive prices and prompt delivery of quality products from highly reputable vendors, including 3M, EcoLab, Kimberly-Clark, Reynolds, Rubbermaid, and Sweetheart.

In addition to its comprehensive selection of products, LPC also offers productivity-improvement training for client's janitorial employees. At the company's new, state-of-the-art training facility, LPC staff train up to 35 people at a time on more efficient and effective use of their equipment and supplies. This training is just another example of the company's dedication to its customers.

All in The Family

Not every employee is named Leonard, but every one is part of the LPC family. The company recognizes the value of its employees and invests in them as part of its future. This sense of family contributes to the company's success, and has helped maintain the loyal, dedicated workforce that LPC has enjoyed for generations. In fact, many LPC employees have more than 25 years of service with the company.

Receiving Praise from the Community it Supports

The company has cultivated an excellent reputation with clients and suppliers for dependability and quality. Many of LPC's vendor partners have recognized the company over the years for its outstanding sales and service achievements. LPC has earned awards for high-volume sales from companies such as Dart Container and Sweetheart Cup.

As a lifelong corporate citizen of Baltimore, LPC is committed to giving back to the city it calls home. The company is known for its frequent financial contributions, as well as its generous gifts of time and supplies to local non-profit institutions. The Baltimore Zoo, the United Way, Food and Friends, the Baltimore Association of Retarded Citizens, and the St. Agnes Foundation are just some of those that benefit from Leonard's philanthropy.

Leonard Paper Company has been one of Baltimore's stellar successes for more than 60 years, a continuing example that dedication, hard work, and commitment form the foundation for a thriving business. Maintaining its founder's philosophy of always providing the best products and service to its customers, four generations of Leonards and dedicated employees continue to serve the people of this extensive region.

TODAY, LEONARD PAPER IS FAR FROM A ONE-MAN SHOW. THE FIRM'S 140,000-SQUARE-FOOT BUILDING IN EAST BALTIMORE HOUSES MORE THAN 90 EMPLOYEES AND A FLEET OF 21 TRUCKS TO HANDLE DELIVERIES TO CUSTOMERS THROUGHOUT THE REGION (TOP AND BOTTOM).

HMS Insurance Associates, Inc.

HMS Insurance Associates, Inc. is much more than an insurance agency. The firm proudly combines the best of risk management, loss control, and financial planning for its commercial clients, helping them realize the full potential of their businesses. For nearly 60 years, HMS has been insuring and assisting some of the region's most well-known companies, and growing along with its hometown city.

In many ways, HMS' growth parallels Baltimore's growth. HMS was founded in Charm City in 1943 as Hartman, McClean Inc., and quickly became a valuable member of the business community. In 1964, the company became Hartman, McLean & Schmidt, Inc. As specialists in construction and commercial real estate insurance, HMS proved a valuable asset in Baltimore's development. That remains true today: HMS enjoys long-standing partnerships with many of the mid-Atlantic region's largest contractors, and the construction industry is still prominently featured in HMS' client base.

HMS' construction industry clients benefit from the firm's depth of knowledge and understanding of this complex field. From construction insurance to surety bonding, HMS' experienced team can assess risks, help develop a strong financial plan, and prepare clients for the bonding credit process. In addition, HMS partners with clients to find ways of reducing their insurance costs through effective loss control.

HMS also serves the commercial insurance needs of a variety of other industries, including wholesale and retail business, commercial real estate and property management, manufacturing and technology, and transportation. Residential, commercial, manufacturing, and

▼ THOMAS GRAVES

mercantile properties can require a wide variety of specialized coverage, from building ordinance to rental income. Manufacturers and retail and wholesale businesses need to protect inventory from damage and theft, while providing for potential business interruptions. The transportation industry has unique needs for cost containment programs. HMS can serve the special needs of each industry, with specialized teams that truly understand the field. And all HMS clients benefit from a consultative, efficient approach that helps minimize costs while providing the most comprehensive coverage available.

THOMAS GRAVES

Living a Culture of Client Service

Client service isn't just lip service at HMS; management and employees say, "We live it here." The firm's team of more than 70 insurance professionals and support staff develop long-term relationships with their clients, and become intimately familiar with their clients' needs. Low turnover at HMS makes this possible, bolstered by a service culture that is nurtured at the very highest levels.

That commitment to service is backed up by the best tools and training available today. HMS takes pride in its systematic approach to communications, research, and client data. Performance and response are continually assessed, and improvements are frequently implemented. All HMS staff members are continually learning as well; continuing education is a high priority at the firm, with employees attending an average of three training seminars each year. All of this proves that HMS is living its commitment to client service every day.

HMS' service culture has served the company well, as HMS enjoys its current status as one of the largest independent insurance brokers in the mid-Atlantic region. The firm represents many of the leading insurance carriers in the country, and is represented in some of the industry's most prestigious organizations. HMS is an active member of the National Association of Surety Bond Producers, and sits on the Council for Insurance Agents and Brokers, a national group that represents the leading brokers in the

country. HMS also participates in organizations that serve the company's client industries, such as the Building Congress and Exchange, Association of Builders and Contractors, and American Subcontractors Association.

In 1997, HMS decided to apply its winning formula to the world of financial planning by establishing HMS Financial Services. The affiliated company offers personal health and life insurance, as well as hospitalization coverage and estate planning. This addition made HMS a full-service provider of financial protection services, and made HMS' legendary service available to a whole new group of clients.

HMS also has an outstanding group of personal insurance professionals to meet the need for personal auto, homeowners, farm, and marine coverage. This growing HMS unit has helped round out service to all segments of the Baltimore community.

Giving Back to the Community

As a longtime member of the Baltimore community, HMS also enjoys strong ties to civic and charitable groups in the area. HMS is represented on the board of Baltimore's Council for Economic and Business Opportunity, which supports the development of minority businesses in enterprise zones throughout the city. Through the Building

Congress and Exchange Foundation, HMS supports continuing education programs that encourage young people to enter the construction field. In addition, HMS generously donates time and resources to a number of local charities, including the Make-A-Wish Foundation and the American Heart Association.

Many Baltimoreans know HMS for its longtime ownership and occupancy of the historic Canton House on Water Street, overlooking the Inner Harbor. In 1978, the structure was added to the National Register of Historic Places, a welcome honor for one of Baltimore's oldest office buildings. HMS eventually outgrew the Canton House offices and, in 1985, the company moved to its current location at Greenspring Station in Brooklandville. The site now serves as the headquarters for HMS Insurance Associates and HMS Financial Services.

Since 1943, HMS Insurance Associates, Inc. has been providing Baltimore's businesses with protection and peace of mind. The firm offers an unbeatable combination of experience, knowledge, commitment, and service that businesses and families need to protect their assets, minimize losses, and reduce costs. Through a partnership with HMS, businesses can mind their own business—and realize their goals.

HMS' CLIENTS CAN DRAW ON THE FIRM'S MANY YEARS OF EXPERTISE IN HANDLING INSURANCE NEEDS FOR ALL ASPECTS OF BUSINESS AND PERSONAL COVERAGE.

WMAR-TV

On October 27, 1947, televisions in homes all across Maryland tuned in to the state's first television broadcast. That broadcast—horse races from the Pimlico Race Course—was brought to Maryland's viewers by Baltimore's own WMAR-TV, and from that moment on, the station has been a leader in local programming.

Since that auspicious beginning, WMAR has continued to make history. The station is Baltimore's ABC affiliate, and is owned and operated by the Cincinnati-based E.W. Scripps Company, an industry leader in broadcast, print, and Internet media. WMAR provides the region with ABC network favorites like *Jeopardy!*, *Who Wants to Be a Millionaire*, *Monday Night Football*, and *The Practice*. But beyond its network offerings, the station is a proud member of the Baltimore community, and a consistent leader in broadcast technology, news, and programming.

An Industry Leader and Innovator

Technologically, WMAR has always been a leader and an innovator in the television field. WMAR, in conjunction with CBS, broadcast the first color television pictures in North America. The Baltimore-based news station also had the first color film processor for television news and production, and helped pioneer the use of the zoom camera lens for both film and tape cameras.

WMAR was also the first TV station in Maryland to do a remote telecast of an operation at Sinai Hospital in 1949, and it broadcast the first blue baby operation from Johns Hopkins Hospital. WMAR also aired the country's first national talk show, *The National Review*, setting a model for countless variety shows since.

A leader in local sports, WMAR was the first TV station to televise direct pickups of major sporting events, from football to regattas.

STUART ZOLOTOROW

WMAR is the leader in local sports coverage, broadcasting *The Lacrosse Game of the Week*, high school football, and college basketball. WMAR also celebrates a long history with Maryland's horse racing community by televising Preakness coverage each year.

WMAR is nominated for local Emmys every year, and has won in recent years for programming, promotion, and news. WMAR was also the 1997 and 1999 winner of the best newscast award from the Chesapeake Associated Press Broadcasters Association. The station has also been recognized by organizations like the Maryland Society of Professional Journalists, PROMAX International, and National Association of Black Journalists, to name a few.

News and Programming for All of Baltimore

The station's StormTrak system, the most powerful Doppler radar in Maryland, can pinpoint weather systems down to a specific street. *2News* provides more than 20 hours of local news per week, starting at 5:30 a.m.

STUART ZOLOTOROW

STUART ZOLOTOROW

and continuing on through the day until 11:30 at night. *2News* is known for its leading role in investigative reporting, which has earned the station national attention.

WMAR also features great local broadcasting. *Around the House*, the station's weekly home improvement show, airs every Saturday morning with hands-on advice on home renovation. The station's *Kindertime* caters to the whole family, bringing children, parents, and grandparents together with entertainment from many cultural backgrounds. *Entertaining Seafood*, *Senior Living*, and *College Tour Shows* are also WMAR-produced programs.

WMAR is proud to be one of Baltimore's most interactive studios. Talking 2Us is one of WMAR's largest community initiatives, bringing station managers and employees to local community associations every month to hear firsthand the concerns of their viewers. The Neighborhood Network initiative encourages community leaders to share news and events with one another, helping to bring Baltimore's diverse neighborhoods closer together. WMAR's telephone polls survey 1,000 people every day, and the station's number-one-rated Web site, www.insidebaltimore.com, allows Internet-savvy viewers to get newscast and community information at their convenience.

‍HARRY KAKEL

Giving Back to the Community

WMAR's slogan—Real People. Real News.—sums up the station's philosophy. The station understands its responsibility to the community, and has been actively demonstrating that commitment for more than 50 years.

WMAR uses its local programming to help build a better tomorrow for Baltimore. Special reports seen on the station's newscasts help citizens personally put a stop to unethical and illegal practices. Another regular feature showcases the efforts of Baltimore neighborhoods in changing their streets for the better. *2 the Point*, a weekly, 30-minute program, focuses on Baltimore's underserved popula-

tions, giving viewers "news you can use."

For more than 18 years, WMAR has helped raise more than $24 million for the Johns Hopkins Telethon, which benefits the Johns Hopkins Children's Center. And for more than 30 years, WMAR has also donated 21 hours of airtime to the Muscular Dystrophy Association's annual Jerry Lewis Labor Day Telethon. WMAR also helps raise funds for the Maryland Food Bank and many other organizations. In 1994, WMAR began its 2 Save a Life campaign with the Baltimore City Fire Department. Since then, more than 65,000 free smoke detectors have been placed in the city's homes. Most important, the campaign has helped to reduce fire fatalities by 50 percent in the city.

WMAR is a proud sponsor of the Afram Expo, a forum recognizing the efforts of Baltimore's African-American community. WMAR also works with the Arena Players, sponsoring an annual drama competition in honor of Black History Month in which hundreds of area youngsters submit plays. The winning entry is

performed by the Arena Players and produced for broadcast in prime time.

For more than 50 years, WMAR has been providing quality programming and community leadership to the Baltimore region. Moving into the new millennium under the management of Drew Berry, vice president and general manager, WMAR promises to continue that tradition of being a community leader by keeping its finger on the pulse of the people.

WMAR's Dante Wilson directs the cast of *Nana's Room*, winner of the station's 19th annual playwriting contest (top).

Hector Torres, battalion chief of the Baltimore City Fire Department, speaks at WMAR's 2 Save a Life campaign kickoff (bottom).

Louis J. Grasmick Lumber Company

For some 50 years, the Louis J. Grasmick Lumber Company has been providing shipping, packing, and building materials to Baltimore-area businesses. But today, the company's reach extends far beyond Maryland; Grasmick is now the leading supplier of industrial lumber on the East Coast. ◆ Over the years, the business has evolved from a shipping supplier for Baltimore's maritime community to one of the nation's largest building materials suppliers. Although the company now ships from Maine to Florida, Grasmick has maintained its hometown roots, as well as its commitment to building relationships and giving old-fashioned customer service.

LOUIS J. GRASMICK LUMBER COMPANY IS CURRENTLY LOCATED JUST OFF I-95 IN EAST BALTIMORE.

A Bright Beginning

Louis J. Grasmick started his company in 1951 to address the needs of Baltimore's maritime industry. In the middle of the 20th century, the maritime shipping industry relied heavily upon blocking and bracing materials supplied by lumber companies to secure cargo. Grasmick was in the perfect position to serve the Port of Baltimore, supplying these materials to many of the ships that came into port.

Over the next 20 years, Grasmick was able to provide its services to numerous other ports on the eastern seaboard. In the 1970s, however, the advent of containerization reduced that industry's need for lumber, and Grasmick had to diversify to ensure its long-term viability. With this in mind, the company began supplying lumber and building materials to industrial and manufacturing plants. When this new venture succeeded, Grasmick branched out further, looking for new markets that would appreciate its service-oriented philosophy.

Today, Grasmick has established business relationships with a variety of contractors in residential housing, commercial construction, and bridge and highway building. The company also produces a large array of pallets, skids, boxes, and crane mats, as well as concrete forms used in the manufacturing, distribution, and construction industries.

The Leader of the Industry

Now with the second generation firmly established, Grasmick Lumber Company is still going strong. Grant I. Grasmick, current president of the firm, has led his 55 employees to new heights, reaching $48 million in sales in 1999. This 37 percent growth in total sales from 1998 to 1999 resulted in recognition by a major national publication honoring the nation's top construction suppliers. As the company's local distribution facility is directly serviced by Norfolk Southern, Grasmick makes for an ideal situation in terms of shipping by truck or railcar. This strategic location has enabled Grasmick to ship materials quickly and easily throughout the entire eastern seaboard, and has

GRASMICK'S ROOTS WERE ESTABLISHED IN BALTIMORE'S INNER HARBOR.

helped Baltimore continue to be a hub for commercial business via truck, rail, or vessel.

Grasmick has never been afraid to buck industry trends in pursuit of progress. When the company diversified from its maritime focus, the firm also decided to change its approach to pricing. At the time, the norm for the lumber industry was pricing at time of shipment, which left contractors guessing about the great fluctuations of lumber prices. Grasmick adopted a guaranteed pricing policy, establishing set prices at the time the order was placed, which allowed contractors to budget or estimate more accurately. This novel idea took the contracting world by storm and helped propel the company into a leading position in the building supply industry.

◆◆◆◆◆◆◆◆◆◆◆◆◆◆◆◆◆◆◆◆◆◆◆◆◆
A Part of the Baltimore Landscape

Grasmick has become part of the Baltimore landscape in more ways than one. The company's materials have been used in many of the region's residential housing projects and in many of Baltimore's significant landmarks. Grasmick has supplied building materials for the National Aquarium, World Trade Center, Sylvan Learning Center, and Oriole Park at Camden Yards. The USS *Constellation*, a historic ship permanently docked in Baltimore's

Inner Harbor, was almost totally refurbished with lumber from Grasmick. The firm also has relationships with many of the city's industrial powerhouses, including Bethlehem Steel, Baltimore Gas and Electric, and Lockheed Martin Middle River Aircraft Systems.

Grasmick also believes strongly in giving back to the community and being a good corporate citizen. Louis Grasmick was the founder of the House with a Heart Foundation, a nonprofit organization that raises money for Maryland's homeless every year. Additionally, the company is a contributor of funds and materials for Habitat for Humanity,

and many of Habitat's homes are built with Grasmick lumber. Many other civic contributions are made each year to organizations, such as the YMCA, Johns Hopkins Hospital, Catholic Charities, and Metro Maryland Youth for Christ, to help support those who make a difference in the lives of Baltimore's youth.

For more than 50 years, the Louis J. Grasmick Lumber Company has thrived on change, constantly adapting to meet the needs of its customers. Today, the company welcomes the challenges the new century brings while continuing to be a good corporate citizen giving back to the community.

⊥ SECU also gives back to the

any things have changed since the State Employees Credit Union of Maryland, Inc. (SECU) was founded in Baltimore in 1951, but one

TESSCO

The exciting world of wireless technology is changing lives. Every two seconds, someone subscribes to a wireless phone or data device. Apartment buildings and churches rent out antenna space to wireless carriers. Internet access is available on pagers. Computer networks are being

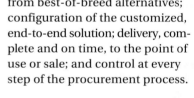

installed in hospitals, campuses, and office buildings—without wires. Consumers demand anytime, anywhere communication, and TESSCO is there for industry professionals and consumers throughout the world, 24 hours a day, seven days a week, helping to make that happen.

TESSCO, a leading provider of solutions for wireless communications, supplies the end-to-end product and service solutions necessary to build, operate, maintain, and use wireless communications systems. The company's solutions encompass the entire wireless industry: voice, data, messaging, location, tracking, and Internet systems. As wireless technology expands into new horizons, TESSCO is at the forefront.

Marketing Innovation

TESSCO's guiding vision is to be the vital link between buyers and manufacturers. The firm's mission is to virtually link knowledge and delivery of the right product, in the right configuration, at the right time, to the point of use. Since its inception, TESSCO's marketing innovation and operational excellence has kept the company at the leading edge, linking the latest developments in wireless commu-

nications to those providing anytime, anywhere communication.

For its manufacturers, TESSCO provides a cost-effective channel to a broad and diverse customer base. The company presents, markets, and sells its products as part of a total customer solution. TESSCO's manufacturers produce everything from the antenna systems that can be observed next to highways to the batteries used in cellular telephones.

Solutions That Make Wireless Work

TESSCO's product and service solutions allow its customers to deploy its financial and people capital to the projects that will generate revenue and profits fast—not to the man-

agement and storage of inventories. TESSCO's solutions are based on providing the knowledge to choose from best-of-breed alternatives; configuration of the customized, end-to-end solution; delivery, complete and on time, to the point of use or sale; and control at every step of the procurement process.

Operational Excellence

TESSCO's closed-loop, integrated capabilities are managed by a sophisticated Internet and information technology platform. This highly effective enterprise management platform incorporates operations, as well as integrating all customer, manufacturer, product, configuration, sales, and delivery activities.

TESSCO originally developed its enterprise management system before such systems were common, and has continued to refine it, staying ahead of the curve. As a result, the company's scalable system allows it to increase order throughput while enhancing customer satisfaction and improving productivity.

TESSCO's e-commerce system assures real-time, interactive customer connectivity with its facilities in Hunt Valley, Maryland, and Reno. These centers configure orders for complete, on-time delivery throughout the world. TESSCO's support operations are centralized in its Global Logistics Center, the company's ISO 9002-registered headquarters in Hunt Valley. All of the firm's showcase facilities represent its commitment to world-class performance.

◆◆◆◆◆◆◆◆◆◆◆◆◆◆◆◆◆◆◆◆◆◆◆

The People Promise

World-class performance is just one of the principles outlined in the TESSCO Way, the foundation of the firm's planning and daily business activities. The company's mission, basic strategy, promises, and expectations are spelled out for all stakeholders—customers, manufacturers, investors, and team members. The People Promise addresses inspirational vision, empowerment, opportunity to grow and emerge, and personal well-being. TESSCO Magic calls for creating a fun, enthusiastic environment that inspires individual involvement and development. TESSCO Magic defines the spirit of ingenuity, creativity, and innovation that not only attracts

the company's talented team members, but also fosters the firm's entrepreneurial and performance-oriented culture.

TESSCO's culture is its foundation—a legacy from its early years that has flourished despite growth. Today, the company is an international leader in the wireless industry and one of the largest publicly traded companies in Maryland. The firm was founded in 1952 by Robert B. Barnhill Sr. as a manufacturers' representative, Towson Engineering Sales & Service Company (TESSCO), serving the electronic component and equipment industry. TESSCO's current chairman and chief executive officer, Robert B. Barnhill Jr., refounded the company in 1982 as a Your Total Source® distributor to serve the mobile and then-fledgling cellular telephone industry.

TESSCO's history and its guiding principles have shaped its community involvement philosophy. The company strives to foster long-term relationships in the community, helping to improve the environment where its team members live, learn, and enjoy their families. Illustrating a deep-seated commitment to its team members, many of the company's service programs have been initiated and organized by team members. Programs have included fund-raisers, food and clothing collections, and blood drives. TESSCO and its team members have also lent support to a variety of local and national organizations, including the Alzheimer's Association, American Cancer Society, Baltimore Museum of Art, Neighbors in Need, and the YWCA of Greater Baltimore.

TESSCO provides structured and supportive employment opportunities for citizens with limited abilities. The company provides outsource and on-site employment opportunities through win-win relationships with the nonprofit organizations PennMar, Chimes, and the Baltimore Association of Retarded Citizens. TESSCO has been recognized for contributions that have resulted in improved quality of life for these citizens.

Education, the key to a strong and bright tomorrow, is a primary focus for TESSCO. The company has been a loyal supporter of national scholarships awarded by the Personal Communications Industry Association (PCIA) Foundation. Through the Wireless Partnership for Education, PCIA strives to promote the role of wireless telecommunications technology in education through college scholarships. TESSCO and other industry leaders have contributed generously to fund these scholarships, which foster the next generation of telecommunications innovators.

When wireless communication began its rapid expansion into the consumer market in 1983, TESSCO was ready with a revolutionary solution for bringing technology to consumers. Innovation continues at a rapid pace, expanding the definition of anytime, anywhere communication. As wireless communication options increase, and the worldwide consumer base grows, TESSCO will continue to improve the way business is done through its dynamic business model, its talented team members, and a continuous emphasis on striving to be the best.

CLOCKWISE FROM TOP LEFT: THE STAR CAFÉ IS JUST ONE OF THE WAYS IN WHICH TESSCO CREATES TESSCO MAGIC—A FUN, ENTHUSIASTIC, SHOWCASE ENVIRONMENT THAT INSPIRES INDIVIDUAL INVOLVEMENT AND DEVELOPMENT.

SOPHISTICATED INTERNET AND VIDEOCONFERENCING TECHNOLOGIES ALLOW TESSCO TEAM MEMBERS TO COMMUNICATE DIRECTLY WITH CUSTOMERS AROUND THE WORLD, MAINTAINING AN INTENSE CUSTOMER FOCUS, AS WELL AS PROVIDING SERVICES THAT PRODUCE THE HIGHEST LEVEL OF VALUE, RESULTS, AND SATISFACTION.

ROBERT B. BARNHILL JR., TESSCO FOUNDER, CHAIRMAN, AND CHIEF EXECUTIVE OFFICER, FOSTERS A PROCESS OF CONTINUAL IMPROVEMENT TO DELIVER VALUE TO CUSTOMERS, SHARE OWNERS, MANUFACTURERS, AND TEAM MEMBERS. HIS VISION FOR IMPROVING THE WAY BUSINESS IS DONE COMES TO REALITY THROUGH TESSCO'S HIGH-TECH/HIGH-TOUCH APPROACH TO BUSINESS.

Center Stage

Baltimore's Center Stage was a leader in the regional theater movement that swept the country in the early 1960s. Along with the Guthrie Theater in Minneapolis; Washington, D.C.'s Arena Stage; the Milwaukee Repertory Theater; and the American Repertory Theatre in Boston, Center Stage changed the way Americans experience professional theater. For nearly 40 years, Baltimoreans have enjoyed the work of some of the world's leading playwrights, actors, and artisans without ever leaving Charm City.

Center Stage suffered a crushing blow on January 9, 1974, when the theater burned to the ground from a fire set by drunken arsonists. Peter W. Culman, managing director, and his team persevered and found a new location at the old Loyola College and High School in the heart of historic Mount Vernon. The Calvert Street facility opened in 1975, and today it welcomes more than 100,000 patrons each season.

Diverse Offerings

Through the guidance of its dedicated staff, Center Stage is committed to reaching a wider audience through diversified programming. Stan Wojewodski Jr., who served as artistic director for 14 years, led a period of expansion, combining the works of emerging writers such as Eric Overmyer and August Wilson with the likes of Ibsen and Shakespeare in a challenging and expanding repertory. Irene Lewis, who took over as artistic director in 1992, diversified the theater's repertoire by developing Off Center, a performer-generated theater series, presenting well-known performance artists such as Spalding Gray and Anna Deavere Smith. Both the Mainstage and Off Center productions are presented in either of the two state-of-the-art auditoriums: the 541-seat Pearlstone Theater and the smaller, flexible configuration Head Theater. The community's response has resulted in subscriptions totaling nearly 13,000 and a volunteer base of almost 1,000 participants.

Center Stage attracts the nation's finest actors, directors, and designers. All of the theater's productions are rehearsed and created on-site, employing more than 100 artisans and professional administrators in a year-round operation. Docents conduct tours of the bustling backstage scenic, props, and costume shops at the request of schools and other groups.

In 1993, Center Stage received a $1.4 million grant from the Lila Wallace-Reader's Digest Resident Theater Initiative, aimed at increasing its audience of 14- to 30-year-olds. This gave birth to Theater for a New Generation (TNG), Center Stage's educational outreach program. The program has been a success, with a jump from 9 percent to nearly 25 percent of the total audience under age 30—nearly double the national average of 12 percent.

Art before Commerce

Center Stage places art before commerce. Accordingly, while production quality is high, prices are low. The theater offers pay-what-you-can days of performance, when theatergoers can literally set their own ticket prices. The theater also offers student rush tickets and group and senior discounts, and it donates tickets to nonprofit organizations throughout each season. Even during periods of economic downturn, the theater has maintained a record of a break-even or better operation, a tribute to Center Stage's institutional vitality and vision.

Time magazine called Center Stage "an unsung regional of the first rank." Recently, Thomas Pechar, formerly of Seattle Children's Theatre, replaced Peter Culman as managing director of Center Stage. Under his leadership, the theater's commitment to the art, the community, and its patrons will remain strong for many seasons to come.

The Baltimore Development Corporation (BDC) is a private, nonprofit company that has managed all economic development initiatives for the City of Baltimore for more than three decades. Perhaps its best-known success is the internationally acclaimed Inner Harbor, which transformed an abandoned port area into a tourist destination that today attracts more than 13 million visitors each year.

Most recently, BDC has helped facilitate such projects as Oriole Park at Camden Yards; the Power Plant entertainment complex, featuring the first-ever sports-themed ESPN Zone; the American Visionary Art Museum; and a multimillion-dollar incubator for Internet technology companies specializing in education and training.

Citywide Economic Development

BDC's reach extends far beyond downtown, with more than 75 percent of its efforts concentrated in Baltimore's neighborhoods and business parks. Examples include the attraction and retention of businesses in the Seton Business Park; the revitalization of the Fairfield Business Park; and the conversion by Johns Hopkins University of a former high school into a technology incubator and office center. From 1997 to 2000, BDC's aggressive outreach effort has resulted in the creation or retention of more than 22,000 jobs, involving 222 companies.

Focusing on targeted industries such as financial services; health care and life sciences; manufacturing; technology; tourism; and warehousing, distribution, and the port, BDC helps assemble land and provide loans that leverage public funds for maximum private investment. For example, from 1997 to 2000, $16 million in public bond funds leveraged $406 million in private investment.

A High-Tech Breeding Ground

As the public-private partnership that redeveloped downtown and the Inner Harbor expands outward, the attraction of high-tech companies to the Canton area in the east and the former Procter & Gamble plant to the south has inspired a new name for the waterfront area—the Digital Harbor.

Since 1991, BDC has been in the forefront of assisting start-up technology companies. The Technology Development Center in South Baltimore provides low-cost space and shared office services for a dozen fledgling businesses, while the Bard Labs located in the Inner Harbor offers wet lab space for small biotechnology companies. Of particular note is the new Emerging Technology Center in Canton, which is partnering with NASA's Goddard Space Flight Center for funds and access to faculty and equipment.

BDC's latest project, announced in the summer of 2000, is a multi-million-dollar incubator subsidiary of Sylvan Learning Systems, to be located adjacent to Sylvan's headquarters in Inner Harbor East. Known as Sylvan Ventures, the project will create some 2,000 jobs and serve as a magnet for similar new companies.

Leadership of the BDC Board of Directors

A 12-member board of directors, appointed by the mayor and recruited from the city's top corporate and governmental leaders, sets policy for BDC. Roger Lipitz, chairman of the board, and M.J. Brodie, president, are credited with creating a new organizational structure that is widely respected for its efficiency and accountability.

Two future projects illustrate the range of BDC's capabilities. One is a $350 million revitalization of downtown's Westside, with significant private and foundation funding, which began in 1998. Well along in planning with federal, state, and private authorities is MAGLEV, a $950 million, high-speed, magnetic levitation train that will link Baltimore to Washington with 15-minute service. Patterned after similar trains in Europe and Japan, MAGLEV will become one of the nation's newest and best transportation modes.

For three decades, the Baltimore Development Corporation has demonstrated its effectiveness as thc city's economic development agent. Whatever challenges the future business and economic environment may provide, BDC has the experience to meet those challenges with energy and innovative action.

RICHARD LIPPENHOLZ

FROM TOP:
THE BALTIMORE DEVELOPMENT CORPORATION (BDC) IS LED BY ROGER LIPITZ, CHAIRMAN OF THE BOARD (LEFT), AND M.J. BRODIE, PRESIDENT.

MOST RECENTLY, BDC HAS HELPED FACILITATE SUCH PROJECTS AS ORIOLE PARK AT CAMDEN YARDS; THE POWER PLANT ENTERTAINMENT COMPLEX, FEATURING THE FIRST-EVER SPORTS-THEMED ESPN ZONE (PICTURED); THE AMERICAN VISIONARY ART MUSEUM; AND A MULTIMILLION-DOLLAR INCUBATOR FOR INTERNET TECHNOLOGY COMPANIES SPECIALIZING IN EDUCATION AND TRAINING.

Spectera, Inc.

In today's competitive labor market, more and more employers offer comprehensive vision care as part of their benefit programs. Many of those employers turn to Spectera, Inc. to provide the service the Baltimore-based company has offered for more than 35 years. Today, the fast-growing managed care company provides vision care to more than 5.5 million members through a network of more than 9,000 eye doctors across the country.

Dr. Oscar Camp, founder of Spectera and current chairman of the board, developed the idea for a managed vision care program. Camp devised a prepaid plan for union members through United Optical and, after its warm reception, began marketing the plan to other unions and employers. The vision plan thrived through several decades. In the fall of 1997, Camp began to withdraw from actively managing Spectera and named David Hall CEO; Larry Manchio became president. With this new management team in place, the company entered a period of explosive growth. A series of strategic acquisitions increased Spectera's network and presence, and transformed the company from a regional force into a national player.

Today, Spectera serves members of unions, employees of municipal governments, and private employers through its headquarters in Baltimore and regional offices in Atlanta; Bridgewater, New Jersey; Charlotte; Chicago; Dallas; Houston; Indianapolis; Los Angeles; New York City; and Oklahoma City.

Spectera and its wholly owned subsidiaries, including Group Vision Associates and EyeCare Service Plan, provide comprehensive vision care, including eye examinations and the dispensing of eyeglasses and contact lenses. Members can utilize Spectera's national network of participating optometrists, ophthalmologists, and retail chains, or visit one of Spectera's own United Optical Stores.

Benefits for Employees and Employers

Spectera's employees control 75 percent of the company's stock, making it truly employee owned. In this unique position, Spectera's employees recognize the needs of both the individual plan participants and the subscribing employers. The company provides services to accommodate nearly every need on both sides of the benefit equation, from employee benefit communications to direct member services. Spectera helps individuals get the most from their vision care benefits, while helping employers provide cost-effective, efficient options.

Individual members appreciate Spectera's comprehensive benefits and streamlined service. Basic coverage includes annual eye examinations; a wide variety of high-quality, fashionable frames; and a generous allowance for frames outside the Spectera selection. For members who prefer contact lenses, Spectera provides one of the most generous benefits in the industry, covering four boxes of disposable contacts. Two follow-up visits are also included in Spectera's contact lens benefit. In addition, members are also able to take advantage of access

SPECTERA, INC. IS HEADQUARTERED IN BALTIMORE.

to a discounted laser eye surgery benefit.

Spectera makes it easy to use its vision plan by utilizing a paperless system that allows members to control their access to information from the privacy of their own homes. A toll-free automated benefits service line allows them to choose from a continually updated directory of providers. Members can find providers' addresses and telephone numbers on the company's Web site, www.spectera.com, and can even learn which provider is closest to their homes or offices, including door-to-door directions.

Through Crown Optical, its eyeglass laboratory, Spectera produces up to 7,000 pairs of lenses each week at a state-of-the-art eyeglass facility in Baltimore. Encompassing some 40,000 square feet and an investment of $3.5 million, this facility features leading-edge technology and software at every turn.

Though the 1990s brought spectacular growth for the company, Spectera is not ready to rest on its laurels. The company has forged a strategic alliance with the Dickerson Group of California, one of the largest minority-owned employee benefits administrative services firms in the country. Dickerson's multidisciplined, multilingual company helps serve today's diverse workforce for thousands of leading employers. The alliance of Spectera and Dickerson provides flexible, competitive vision plans with progressive customer care, targeting Fortune 500 companies on the West Coast and across the country.

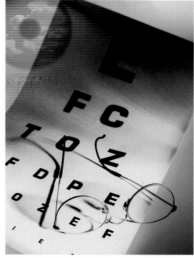

Helping Clients Maximize Health Care Dollars

Under its Certified Admission Review and Evaluation (CARE) umbrella, Spectera has provided utilization management services since 1983. CARE specialists analyze claim data, implement medical review programs, and budget administrative dollars in efforts to help clients provide high-quality benefits in the most cost-effective manner. The utilization team fields more than 1 million calls each year in pursuit of this goal, and consistently exceeds clients' performance goals. The Utilization Review Accreditation Commission, Inc. (URAC), a national organization that sets the standards for the utilization review industry, accredits Spectera's CARE program.

As a pioneer in managed care, Spectera has helped set the standards for vision care and utilization review coverage in America. Its client-driven approach, combined with sound management practices, has helped it become one of the nation's leading vision care and utilization review providers.

Spectera's more than 750 employee-owners look excitedly into the future with a clear vision: to continue to expand and develop services to meet their clients' needs.

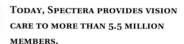

TODAY, SPECTERA PROVIDES VISION CARE TO MORE THAN 5.5 MILLION MEMBERS.

UNDER ITS CERTIFIED ADMISSION REVIEW AND EVALUATION (CARE) UMBRELLA, SPECTERA HAS PROVIDED UTILIZATION MANAGEMENT SERVICES SINCE 1983. CARE IS ACCREDITED BY THE UTILIZATION REVIEW ACCREDITATION COMMISSION (URAC).

Wyndham Baltimore Inner Harbor Hotel

Hundreds of thousands of visitors each year choose to make the Wyndham Baltimore Inner Harbor Hotel their home away from home. Whether visitors come to Baltimore for business or pleasure, they can choose the location, luxury, and professional service that Wyndham offers to make their stay a memorable one.

Owned and operated by Wyndham International, the Wyndham Baltimore is part of a network of more than 286 hotels throughout the United States, Canada, the Caribbean, Mexico, and Europe. Wyndham, the fourth-largest hospitality and lodging company in the United States, offers upscale luxury hotel and resort accommodations in major metropolitan business centers and leading vacation markets.

A Prime Location

With 707 tastefully appointed guest rooms, 30,000 square feet of meeting space, a variety of dining options, and a whole host of complementary services, guests can stay at the hotel to enjoy a profitable business meeting or a relaxing getaway. But most choose to take advantage of the Wyndham's prime location in the center of the city's business, financial, and entertainment districts. The Baltimore Arena, Convention Center, Oriole Park at Camden Yards, Inner Harbor, and historic Mount Vernon are all just a short walk away, as are many of the city's major businesses. A variety of dining and entertainment options are within walking distance, and give guests a whole host of choices for meals and nightlife.

Many of Wyndham's guests and locals choose to dine and relax at one of the hotels' two restaurants. Both restaurants are part of football legend Don Shula's restaurant network, and provide excellent food and atmosphere. Shula's Steakhouse is a fine dining experience, featuring fine cuts of Angus beef and other specialties seven nights a week in an elegant, clublike atmosphere. For a more casual option, guests can visit Shula's 2, a sports bar and restaurant offering a menu of soups, sandwiches, and inventive entrées. With banks of televisions tuned in to nearly every available sports event, Shula's 2 is a favorite for lunch or a meal before or after a game. Another popular spot at the Wyndham is the Hall of Fame Lounge, a sophisticated spot for a late-night drink, with deep leather armchairs, classic billiard tables, dark wood furnishings, and on-

THE WYNDHAM BALTIMORE INNER HARBOR HOTEL IS THE LARGEST HOTEL IN THE STATE OF MARYLAND (TOP).

WITH 30,000 SQUARE FEET OF MEETING SPACE, THE WYNDHAM ATTRACTS AN IMPRESSIVE NUMBER OF BOTH LARGE AND SMALL GROUPS FOR ALL TYPES OF MEETINGS (BOTTOM).

site humidors for serious cigar aficionados.

A hotel has been in operation at the Wyndham's site since 1964, and many Baltimoreans remember the property's long history as a Statler Hilton and, later, an Omni Hotel. But in 2000, the hotel became a Wyndham and has since been transforming itself to meet the company's high standards. Fresh off a $6 million renovation, the hotel sparkles with newly appointed guest rooms designed with the business traveler in mind. Thoughtful touches include pillow-top mattresses; two-line, cordless telephones; T-1 high-speed Internet access; and Herman Miller Aeron ergonomic workstations.

The Wyndham By Request Program

The Wyndham Baltimore also participates in Wyndham By Request, a worldwide Wyndham program. After three stays in any Wyndham hotel, guests are entered into a special database that tracks their personal preferences. With this program, frequent Wyndham guests can check into a room prepared especially for them. For example, the radio may be tuned to their favorite style of music, their hometown newspaper delivered first thing in the morning, and their favorite snack foods stocked in the minibar.

"The Wyndham By Request program is a fine example of our commitment to our guests," says Jeffery Keefe, Wyndham Baltimore general manager. "We want to be the first choice of business travelers visiting Baltimore."

Outside of the guest rooms, the commitment to guest convenience continues, with a wide range of services to meet nearly every need. Complete, all-day room service is available for those who prefer a quiet meal or for intimate catered parties. A business center offers dataports, fax and copier access, and computer rentals for travelers who need to stay connected. For dining, entertainment, and transportation advice, a concierge is available from 7 a.m. to 11 p.m. to answer questions and make arrangements. Those last-minute necessities can be picked up in the lobby gift shop. And guests can take advantage of Wyndham's comprehensive exercise facility, which features Lifecycles, treadmills, and rowing machines, or they may utilize the hotel's complementary membership at a local health club.

Giving Back to Baltimore

Wyndham is an important employer in the city of Baltimore, and has been even more instrumental in city officials' efforts to move citizens from welfare to work. Through the hotel's participation in the innovative FUTURE program, hundreds of city residents have found meaningful employment.

FUTURE is an aggressive collaboration between Goodwill Industries and the Baltimore City Department of Social Services. Designed to provide employment opportunities to former welfare recipients, FUTURE identifies and actively recruits prospective employees for the hospitality industry, who are then trained by a well-established organization and placed in jobs with growth potential. The Wyndham has been recognized by the Maryland Hotel and Motel Association for its commitment to this important program, and the program's achievements have received glowing endorsements from city officials.

Location, service, convenience, and luxury—all of these come together at the Wyndham Baltimore Inner Harbor Hotel. For an important business meeting or a family getaway weekend, the Wyndham Baltimore is the ideal location to take in the charms of Charm City.

THE WYNDHAM'S INTERNATIONAL BALLROOM EASILY ACCOMMODATES MEETINGS AND PARTIES (TOP).

THE WYNDHAM FEATURES 187 KING ROOMS, 133 QUEENS, 365 TWO-DOUBLE-BED ROOMS, 11 CLASSIC LIVING ROOMS (WHICH CONNECT ONE OR TWO BEDROOMS), AND 11 SUITES (BOTTOM).

Harkins Builders, Inc.

For more than 35 years, Harkins Builders, Inc. has been designing and constructing hundreds of buildings throughout the mid-Atlantic area. As a diversified general and design/build contractor, Harkins lends its preconstruction expertise and on-site construction ability to a variety of projects, such as life-care facilities, multifamily housing, institutional projects, and commercial enterprises.

Whether a project involves rehabilitating an existing structure or starting at the drawing board, Harkins can provide the services clients need to complete the project on time and within their budget. Much of Harkins' success is attributed to the excellent reputation the company has developed in the region. More than 73 percent of the company's business comes from repeat customers, proving that Harkins' customers are more than satisfied.

Building on Success

Harkins has grown steadily through the years. Thomas P. Harkins founded the company in 1965 in a small office in Silver Spring, Maryland. Today, the business has some 280 employees in three offices in the mid-Atlantic region.

Since 1993, J.P. Blase Cooke has been at the helm as chairman and chief executive officer of the company. Under Cooke's leadership, Harkins has continued to follow the principles of its founder, while adapting to meet the needs of clients. Through its headquarters in Howard County and satellite offices in Virginia Beach and Me-

HARKINS BUILDERS, INC. CONSTRUCTED THE HOTELS AND RESTAURANTS AT BALTIMORE'S PIER 5.

dia, Pennsylvania, Harkins has managed more than 500 projects throughout the mid-Atlantic region, totaling more than 3 million square feet and generating more than $2 billion in revenue. While the company has worked on client projects in New Jersey, South Carolina, Florida, and Delaware, the focus remains on the mid-Atlantic states.

The Harkins Method

Harkins attributes its success to its comprehensive approach to client services, a technique the company calls the Harkins Method. Clients benefit from a complete preconstruction review, with an accurate, realistic budget and project timeline. Harkins maintains a comprehensive database of current pricing information and computerized cost histories of similar projects, allowing the company to draw on past experience for the benefit of the client.

Harkins team members remain heavily involved in the design process, adjusting the budget and plans as necessary and making recommendations along the way to save the client time and money. Continual review eliminates last-minute surprises, making for a positive experience for all involved.

The Harkins team is experienced in the construction industry and loyal to the principles of the Harkins Method. The company's executives have averaged more than 20 years with the company, while most employees have been with the firm for more than 10 years.

Industry Leadership

Harkins' success has not gone unnoticed. The company is the only general contractor in the country to be consistently ranked on both multifamily housing and commercial lists by construction industry sources. Harkins has also received gold-level recognition in the Associated Builders and Contractors (ABC) National Safety and Training Evaluation Process, and has been recognized by ABC as an Accredited Quality Contractor. In 2000, the Baltimore chapter of the American Institute of Architects presented Harkins with its President's Award, naming the company Contractor of the Year.

As an active corporate citizen, Harkins Builders also supports a variety of organizations through donations of time, talent, and resources. The firm regularly supports the efforts of Catholic Charities and the Leukemia and Lymphoma Society. Recently, Harkins contributed to the restoration of the Avalon

History Visitor Center at the Patapsco Valley State Park. Company staff donated their construction skills to the project, enabling the state to preserve this historic structure, which was the first state park building in Maryland.

◆◆◆◆◆◆◆◆◆◆◆◆◆◆◆◆◆◆◆◆◆

Benefiting Baltimore

Many of Harkins' repeat customers are familiar names in the Baltimore area: A & R Development Corporation, Catholic Charities, Shelter Development Corporation, Humphrey Associates, and the Rouse Company. Harkins has produced some 120 projects for these groups alone.

The company has also left its mark on Baltimore through renovation work on many of the city's historic buildings and development of several new sites. Harkins built the hotels and restaurants at Baltimore's Pier 5, and was responsible for transforming the old Lord Baltimore Hotel into the current downtown Hilton. The company also constructed the Redwood Place parking garage and apartments near Camden Yards, one of the cornerstones of the city's Westside renaissance. Harkins has also built dormitories for several area universities, including Salisbury State, Morgan State, Coppin State, and Bowie State, as well as military housing at Fort Meade, Oceana Naval Air Station in Virginia Beach, and other military bases.

Harkins also has experience in designing and building public housing. Through the federal Hope 6 program, the company managed the demolition of an existing public housing high-rise and the development of the new Pleasant View Gardens in Baltimore. Hope 6 provided funding for similar projects in seven cities; the Harkins project was the first to be completed, on time and within budget.

No matter what the project, the Harkins Builders team applies the same level of commitment, experience, and dedication. That is the Harkins Method—and that is the reason the company has been, and will continue to be, a true success story.

HARKINS WAS RESPONSIBLE FOR THE TRANSFORMATION OF THE OLD LORD BALTIMORE HOTEL INTO THE CURRENT DOWNTOWN HILTON.

SOME OF HARKINS' OTHER NOTABLE PROJECTS INCLUDE TOWNHOMES AT PLEASANT VIEW GARDENS (TOP RIGHT) AND THE REDWOOD APARTMENTS (TOP LEFT AND BOTTOM LEFT AND RIGHT).

General Physics Corporation

For some 35 years, General Physics Corporation (GP) has been building a name for itself in Baltimore. From its original headquarters in Columbia, Maryland, the company has evolved into an international corporation—with 60 offices around the world—providing training programs, engineering, environmental, and support services to its diverse client base.

Today, GP is one of the largest technical training companies in the world, with annual sales exceeding $200 million, and with more than 1,600 employees working in offices in North and South America, Europe, and Asia.

Founded in 1966, GP is the principal operating subsidiary of GP Strategies Corporation, an NYSE-listed company. GP originally provided operation, safety, and training services to the nuclear industry. Gradually, the company branched off to serve a wider variety of market sectors, including automotive, paper and pulp, food and beverage, metals, process industries, petrochemicals, computer and software manufacturers, and telecommunications companies, as well as the Department of Defense and other government agencies.

As a performance improvement company, GP excels at the development of training and technical programs, all of which are designed to help its clients increase their employees' quality of work and productivity. The company has developed programs for service managers and executives, engineers, sales associates, plant operators, maintenance and purchasing workforces, and informa-

tion technology professionals in the public and private sectors. GP evaluates and recommends methods for improving the processes and procedures of clients' businesses, and has the capability to provide a supply of high-tech solutions to address customers' needs and desires.

In 2000, GP proudly introduced GP e-Learning Technologies, Inc. This firm focuses on training initiatives involving the Internet as a delivery method. As the Internet increasingly emerges as a tool of the future used to train today's workers more quickly and economically, GP plans to lead the way in using this resource to its full potential.

GP's client list reads like a who's who of business and industry, with many Fortune 500 companies calling upon GP for its expertise in the training field. NASA, Aberdeen Proving Ground, General Motors, Ford, Chrysler, Coca-Cola, Kraft Foods, Oracle, Microsoft, and electric power utility companies are only a few of GP's notable customers. In 1998, the National Association of Manufacturers (NAM) chose GP to be its training partner, designating the NAM Virtual University—www.namvu.com—for the organization. NAM's some 14,000 member companies rely on this training alliance to provide them with a wide range of services.

GP has received countless accolades for its impressive work. In 1999, General Motors named the company the Supplier of the Year, and the International Society for Performance Improvement (ISPI) gave GP its Outstanding Human Performance Intervention award. In 2000, Southwest Bell Corporation honored the company with the Silver Supplier Partner Award.

GP will continue to search for innovative ways to do business in the new millennium as technology advances, reaching into the company's rich archives of experience to produce outstanding training programs.

FOR SOME 35 YEARS, GENERAL PHYSICS CORPORATION (GP) HAS BEEN BUILDING A NAME FOR ITSELF IN BALTIMORE. FROM ITS ORIGINAL HEADQUARTERS IN COLUMBIA, MARYLAND, THE COMPANY HAS EVOLVED INTO AN INTERNATIONAL CORPORATION—WITH 60 OFFICES AROUND THE WORLD—PROVIDING TRAINING PROGRAMS, ENGINEERING, ENVIRONMENTAL, AND SUPPORT SERVICES TO ITS DIVERSE CLIENT BASE.

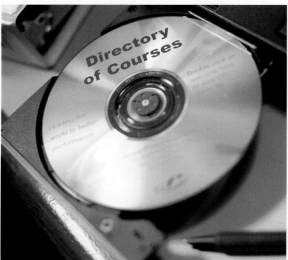

It is not a coincidence that some 250,000 Maryland residents prefer to read about their neighborhoods' happenings in one of Patuxent Publishing Company's (PPC) award-winning community newspapers. Not only does each of PPC's 13 newspapers cater to specific Maryland neighborhoods,

Patuxent Publishing Company

but each also offers its readers a connection to their community that cannot be achieved through daily metropolitan newspapers. As founder S. Zeke Orlinsky once wrote in his weekly publisher's note, "Journalism is more than just information and news. Journalism should excite and guide a community."

A History of Growth

PPC opened its doors in 1969 with a simple issue of the *Columbia Flier*. Only eight pages in length, the "shopper" was delivered to 2,000 Columbia, Maryland, households. Readers highly appreciated its town-related news and advertising. In only two years, the paper became a weekly edition that was circulated to some 9,000 households. The success of the *Columbia Flier* led to the purchase of five additional newspapers. As a result, PPC's staff, operations, and community presence grew tremendously.

PPC now publishes 13 newspapers, including the *Towson Times*, *Owings Mills Times*, *Baltimore Messenger*, and *Soundoff!* In response to readers' desires, the newspapers include innovative additions such as a section for submitted photos, a neighborhood page, and a scrapbook.

Newspapers, however, were just the beginning for PPC. In 1985, the company purchased a community telephone directory business, and now publishes eight directories for areas across Maryland. In 1988, PPC expanded into the world of magazines with the purchase of *Columbia Magazine*; since then, two other high-quality, glossy magazines have been added to the mix. More than 100 specialty publications are produced by PPC each year, with titles such as *Senior Resource Guide*, *Back to School*, and *Howard County Career Con-*

nection. PPC's quality publications have earned hundreds of writing, photography, and design awards.

Strengthening the Bond

Looking for another vehicle to support the communities it represents, PPC created the Community Relations Office. Through dedicated representatives, the Community Relations Office coordinates events, sponsors community organizations, and fosters partnerships with nonprofit groups. The office ensures that the partnerships and sponsorships formed reflect the goals of PPC's readers. The causes and missions of these nonprofit organizations are also used as content for supplements featured in PPC's newspapers.

Support from the Community Relations Office assists many nonprofit organizations in raising funds and spreading awareness of their causes in an effort to enrich the community. Representatives are also involved in the management of various fairs and festivals that bring together neighborhoods around Maryland. From event organization to providing volunteers, the office's representatives clearly display a unique interaction with PPC's readers.

Whether it is direct or indirect, Patuxent Publishing Company's involvement in the community is admired by readers across Maryland. As the voice of community for more than 30 years, PPC continues to provide quality publications that reflect the vision of Maryland residents.

PATUXENT PUBLISHING COMPANY'S NEWSPAPERS, DIRECTORIES, AND MAGAZINES ARE READ BY SOME 250,000 MARYLAND RESIDENTS.

DMJM+HARRIS

◆◆◆

Merritt Properties, LLC

Two of the biggest names in transportation engineering recently came

Merritt Properties, LLC defines its mission simply: Creating homes for businesses. Since 1967, this privately held commercial real estate firm has developed more than 11 million square feet of industrial and office properties in the Baltimore/Washington area. Merritt designs, builds, leases, and manages properties for the long term, and is committed to providing the highest-quality service to all of its clients.

Hands-on Management

From land acquisition through delivery of completed buildings, Merritt prides itself on establishing and maintaining client relationships. Every Merritt employee, in every aspect of Merritt's operations—including management, leasing, design, space planning, construction, and maintenance—is a business owner and a representative of the firm's commitment to meeting and exceeding client needs. With more than 60 locations, Merritt properties are strategically located near major transportation and service arteries to accommodate diverse customer needs. From Baltimore-based firms to national and international companies, Merritt works with customers to address their specific space requirements.

Product offerings range from Merritt's signature mansard-roof warehouse buildings to flex and state-of-the-art, Class A office buildings. Over the years, many of Merritt's customers have increased their space needs, and numerous build-to-suit buildings have been constructed for customers such as Procter & Gamble, Ford Motor Company, and Custom Direct, Inc.

Premier Properties throughout the Region

Several of the company's new property developments currently under construction include Merritt Owings Mills, a flex warehouse/office park; Columbia Corporate Park 100, a 26-acre, Class A office and mixed-use retail park, which is situated midway between Baltimore and Washington; and Beltway Business Community, an 87-acre, office/warehouse park with convenient access to Baltimore/Washington International Airport (BWI) and downtown Baltimore. In addition, three new office parks are under development in Loudoun County, northern Virginia.

The company's outstanding designs and service to the region have been recognized by a variety

COLUMBIA CORPORATE PARK, SITUATED MIDWAY BETWEEN BALTIMORE AND WASHINGTON, D.C., IS AN 88-ACRE OFFICE PARK COMPRISED OF CLASS A OFFICE BUILDINGS AND BUSINESS SUPPORT AND RETAIL SERVICE FACILITIES.

of organizations, including the National Association of Industrial and Office Properties (NAIOP) and the Associated Builders and Contractors (ABC). Leroy Merritt, chairman and CEO, has been recognized for his outstanding service to the commercial real estate community, having received the NAIOP's sixth annual Arnold Palmer Award in 1999.

Making the Community a Home for Everyone

In keeping with the firm's commitment to the concept of home, Merritt invests and partners with numerous charitable organizations in the Baltimore/ Washington region. An outstanding example of Merritt's community commitment is Exchange City, a project the firm undertook for Junior Achievement of Central Maryland. This make-believe city in miniature, located in Merritt flex space, is designed to help children learn about the economic and social intricacies of a community. Fifth graders throughout the region visit Exchange City, assuming adult jobs and responsibilities for the day.

Modeled after a flagship Junior Achievement program in Kansas City, Baltimore's Exchange City is now the fourth of its kind nationwide. Merritt provided the space and helped fund and construct the hands-on learning lab. Merritt's other charitable sponsorships include the Living Classrooms Foundation, a nonprofit organization operated for the benefit of providing hands-on education and job training with an emphasis on at-risk youth and groups from diverse backgrounds, and the Kennedy Krieger Institute, an organization dedicated to assisting children with special needs.

For more than three decades, Merritt Properties, LLC has been creating and managing homes for businesses, and the company looks forward to continued growth and support of its customers, employees, and community partners.

MERRITT DEVELOPS ITS PROPERTIES FOR THE LONG TERM AND IS COMMITTED TO MEETING AND EXCEEDING CUSTOMER NEEDS. PRODUCT OFFERINGS RANGE FROM MERRITT'S SIGNATURE MANSARD ROOF WAREHOUSE BUILDINGS (TOP) TO CLASS A OFFICE PARKS (BOTTOM LEFT) AND FLEX/WAREHOUSE BUILDINGS (BOTTOM RIGHT).

BALTIMORE

Profiles in Excellence

1970–1979

Maryland Environmental Service

Not many companies can show off an entire island as an example of their work. Then again, not many companies are as unique as the Maryland Environmental Service (MES), a hybrid of government agency and non-profit utility. MES combines the public sector's commitment to environmental protection with the private sector's efficiencies, flexibility, and responsiveness. Since 1984, on behalf of the Maryland Port Administration, MES has operated Hart-Miller Island, a 1,140-acre, man-made island that was created out of materials dredged from Chesapeake Bay and Baltimore's Inner Harbor. Out of dredged materials has risen a beautiful island, complete with parks, wetlands, and camping grounds.

The operation of a dredged material containment facility is just one of the many duties the some 500 employees of MES undertake. The business of MES is outdoors—providing water supply, wastewater purification, and solid and hazardous waste management services to municipalities, local governments, state agencies, private businesses, and consumers. With more than $52 million in annual revenues, the long arm of MES reaches to nearly every part of Maryland and the bay region. From projects as large as an 8 million-gallon-per-day wastewater treatment plant to those as small as a bag of Leafgro®, MES' own brand of soil conditioner, MES is reinventing ways of managing basic environmental matters. As the agency's annual report states: "We provide services that most profit-seeking businesses won't

THE MARYLAND ENVIRONMENTAL SERVICE (MES) BOARD OF DIRECTORS INCLUDES (SEATED, FROM LEFT) CATHERINE PIEPER STEVENSON; JAMES W. PECK, DIRECTOR AND CEO; (STANDING, FROM LEFT) JOSEPH SNEE; WILLIAM B.C. ADDISON; LAWRENCE SHUBNELL; LESLIE JACKSON JENKINS; KENNETH HOWARTH; AND JACK GULLO JR. NOT PICTURED IS DANIEL F. MCMULLEN JR.

ON BEHALF OF THE MARYLAND AVIATION ADMINISTRATION, MES IS RESPONSIBLE FOR THE COLLECTION AND RECOVERY OF DEICING FLUID APPLIED TO AIRPLANES DURING INCLEMENT WEATHER AT THE BALTIMORE-WASHINGTON INTERNATIONAL AIRPORT. MES RECOVERS 85 PERCENT OF THE DEICING FLUID APPLIED.

▼ KEITH E. HARVEY

and that many local government bodies can't."

Protecting Natural Resources

In 1970, when the Maryland General Assembly decided to create MES, its purpose was to provide environmental expertise to help local jurisdictions in their compliance with new and more stringent environmental regulations. MES is unique in that, although it is a state agency, it receives no operating funds directly from the state. The agency is totally self-supporting and its vision statement is clear: "MES commits itself to protecting and improving the environment for the citizens of Maryland by providing innovative, responsive, and cost-effective environmental management services to Maryland's local governments, state agencies, and private entities."

Chicken litter used to create energy; tire chips used as a leachate drainage and fluff layer in a landfill; two islands made into one dredged material containment facility, which also serves as a bird sanctuary and camping destination; and a program that recycles better than 85 percent of the glycol used

to deice planes—these are but a few of the innovative projects undertaken by MES on behalf of its clients. Where there is an environmental need, MES can devise an innovative solution.

Employees from a variety of disciplines make up MES, including engineers, scientists, lab technicians, geologists, certified operators, administrative professionals, a support staff, and a construction crew. The large staff also has the equipment to back up its work, including construction machinery, state-of-the-art computer networks, and laboratories. MES is proud to handle both large and small projects; contracts for a few hundred dollars receive the same careful attention as those that reach up to more than $1 million. The staff works around the clock as well, providing major maintenance and emergency repair for many facilities in the region.

The first clients for MES were municipal and state-owned water and wastewater treatment plants. Today, more than 160 water supply and wastewater treatment plants operate effectively because of MES' skilled staff and state-of-the-art technology. For existing plants, MES

▼ KEITH E. HARVEY

▲ KEITH E. HARVEY

is often called upon to improve the plant's efficiency or to bring it into greater compliance with changing government regulations. The agency has a 99.9 percent compliance record at its wastewater treatment facilities–a phenomenal record considering there are more than 700,000 permit limits it must meet. MES' engineers also design and build new water supply and wastewater plants.

When it comes to solid waste management, MES has long been a leader. While MES is well known for its Mid-Shore Regional Solid Waste Facility on the eastern shore, the agency is also a partner to other municipalities in providing innovative and complete recycling services. MES' Montgomery County Recycling Center is a model for the country. MES also runs the Used Oil Recycling Program, which has more than 170 collection locations. More than 6 million gallons of used oil have been collected through this program.

Yard waste, long the bane of many municipalities, has been transformed into a sought-after commodity by MES. Nearly 130,000 tons of yard waste are received by MES-managed composting facilities in Montgomery and Prince George's counties. Much of this yard waste is recycled into a product called Leafgro®, a soil conditioner so successful that, each year, demand far exceeds supply.

Receiving National Recognition

With such diverse tactics toward innovation, it is no surprise that MES has been nationally recognized. Recently, the National Recycling Coalition recognized the agency with the Outstanding Market Development Award. Next came an honor from the Solid Waste Association of North America: MES was given the Gold Award in Planning and Financial Management, as well as the Gold Award for Recycling Excellence. Two gold awards in one year was unprecedented. All three awards reflect the organization's ability to develop markets, provide comprehensive programs for recycling, and complete distinctive facility design and financing.

Through its community service, MES continues its unique path. A favorite is the annual playground project. Each year, members of the MES staff join together to take the day off and build one new playground. It is no surprise what MES chooses to use to make the new playgrounds—scrap tires. Tire swings, tire slides, a tire amphitheater, and a tire monster to climb on are just a few of the attractions at these popular playground sites. And, of course, the ground cover for the playgrounds is shredded tires. A soft landing for the kids, and for the community, too.

AT THE WESTERN BRANCH YARD WASTE COMPOSTING FACILITY, MES ACCEPTS MORE THAN 58,000 TONS OF YARD WASTE A YEAR AND TRANSFORMS IT INTO LEAFGRO®, A SOIL CONDITIONER THAT IS MARKETED TO THE LANDSCAPE AND NURSERY INDUSTRY, PROFESSIONAL GROUNDSKEEPERS, AND HOME OWNERS.

THE MONTGOMERY COUNTY RECYCLING CENTER, MANAGED BY MES, IS PART OF A COMPREHENSIVE SOLID WASTE PROGRAM THAT INCLUDES THE OPERATION, SORTING, PROCESSING, AND SALE OF RECYCLABLE MATERIALS (LEFT).

THE EFFLUENT FROM THE FREEDOM DISTRICT WASTEWATER FACILITY—A STATE-OF-THE-ART BIOLOGICAL NUTRIENT REMOVAL PLANT OPERATED BY MES—IS CRYSTAL CLEAR. THE FACILITY SERVES CARROLL COUNTY AND A NUMBER OF STATE INSTITUTIONS (RIGHT).

PricewaterhouseCoopers LLP

Around the world, the name PricewaterhouseCoopers LLP is synonymous with high-quality professional services. Major companies in nearly every industry across the board rely on PricewaterhouseCoopers for assurance and business advisory services, financial advice, tax and legal services,

management and human resources consulting, and business process outsourcing.

Baltimore is no exception, and is part of one of Pricewaterhouse-Coopers' most important regions. The Baltimore/Washington area practice is the second-largest practice in the firm's national network, and the third-largest practice in the world. Throughout the state of Maryland, the firm employs some 560 professionals, including 23 partners. In Baltimore alone, some 200 employees work at a downtown location, while a consulting services office of some 225 in nearby Linthicum serves companies in the area's burgeoning high-tech corridor.

PricewaterhouseCoopers was formed in 1998 by the merger of two legendary firms: Price Waterhouse and Coopers & Lybrand. Both of these firms trace their roots back more than 100 years, and both have enjoyed many individual successes along the way. Today, PricewaterhouseCoopers is one of the world's largest professional services organizations, with more than 160,000 partners and staff in 150 different countries and territories around the world. The firm's first Baltimore presence was established by Coopers & Lybrand in 1925, setting the stage for the region's major role in PricewaterhouseCoopers today.

consumer and industrial products, energy, and middle market services are the concentrations in Baltimore, allowing Pricewater-houseCoopers to maximize its resources and provide the best service to clients. The Baltimore office works with most of the city's leading financial institutions, such as T. Rowe Price, Legg Mason, and Allfirst. In the health care arena, PricewaterhouseCoopers' practice represents the interests of many of Baltimore's finest systems, including Johns Hopkins Health System and MedStar Health, Inc. These clients, and many others, have helped the firm establish leading local audit market share in nearly every category.

PricewaterhouseCoopers offers a wide range of services for its clients—from traditional accounting to forward-thinking change management. Assurance and business advisory services help clients with audits, systems, risk management, and transaction support. Among the firm's financial advisory service offerings are

Comprehensive Services: A Common Goal

PricewaterhouseCoopers focuses on five key industries, representing some of the region's major employers. Financial services, health care,

MELANIE VURGANOV

corporate finance, securities, litigation support, corporate recovery, valuation, and privatization services.

PricewaterhouseCoopers also offers corporate and individual tax consulting and compliance, as well as legal services. Clients can outsource key aspects of their business processes to the firm as well, including finance and accounting, procurement, and real estate. PricewaterhouseCoopers can even assist with human resources functions such as actuarial benefits and insurance, human resources outsourcing, and organizational effectiveness and development.

Many companies take advantage of PricewaterhouseCoopers' management consulting services, which include strategic change planning, process improvement, and technology solutions. While the range of its services is diverse, the firm's areas of expertise are all united around a common goal: to help clients operate their businesses more effectively, efficiently, and profitably.

◆◆◆◆◆◆◆◆◆◆◆◆◆◆◆◆◆◆◆◆◆◆

A Tradition of Service

In Baltimore and around the world, Pricewaterhouse-Coopers has long been an active corporate citizen, striving to give back to the communities where clients and employees live

and work. In the arts and cultural arena, PricewaterhouseCoopers sponsors the Baltimore Symphony Orchestra, National Aquarium, Enoch Pratt Free Library, Maryland Historical Society, and Citizens for the Arts in Maryland. The firm also supports a number of health and human services organizations, such as the Kennedy Krieger Institute, American Diabetes Association, Shore Health Pain Management Center, and Meals on Wheels of Central Maryland.

In addition, Pricewaterhouse-Coopers lends its support to well-known groups such as the Junior League of Baltimore, Junior Achievement of Central Maryland, and Boy Scouts of America, as well as smaller organizations such as the Students Sharing Coalition, a local youth leadership program; Caroline Center, an education and career resource for low-income women; and Literacy Works, Inc., which provides literacy programs to residents of Baltimore County.

Nationally, the firm is a partner with INROADS, Inc., a nonprofit group dedicated to developing and placing talented, diverse youth in business and industry. The program strives to prepare today's youth for corporate and community leadership in the future. In 2000, PricewaterhouseCoopers hired some 175 INROADS students nationwide, making the firm one of INROADS' top strategic partners.

MELANIE VURGANOV

The Baltimore offices participate in this program as part of the national partnership, and have retained several valuable INROADS employees.

The history, reputation, expertise, and service for which PricewaterhouseCoopers has become known make the firm the first choice of many of Baltimore's major corporations. Through its endeavors—both community and professional—the firm remains focused on quality and leadership. So whatever the question might be, PricewaterhouseCoopers LLP has the answer—and the experience, knowledge, and staff to support it.

CLOCKWISE FROM TOP LEFT: THE IMAGE OF A VESSEL HAS BEEN CHOSEN TO SYMBOLIZE THE INTERSECTION OF PEOPLE, KNOWLEDGE, AND WORLDS—THE THREE FUNDAMENTALS OF PRICEWATERHOUSECOOPERS' IDENTITY.

BALTIMORE IS PART OF ONE OF PRICEWATERHOUSECOOPERS' MOST IMPORTANT REGIONS.

PRATT STREET IS HOME TO MANY OF BALTIMORE'S LEADING FINANCIAL SERVICES ORGANIZATIONS AND MANY OF PRICEWATERHOUSECOOPERS' CLIENTS.

Through a series of strategic partnerships, Sinclair has diversified itself, with forays into the new media of the Internet and the broadcasting hardware industry. In 1999, SBG acquired an equity interest in Acrodyne Communications Inc., a leading manufacturer of transmitters and other television broadcast equipment, based in Pennsylvania. That same year, the company acquired a majority interest in G1440, Inc., an e-business solutions and applications provider, based in Columbia, Maryland.

Sinclair Ventures, SBG's wholly-owned venture arm, identifies opportunities where SBG's investment can have a demonstrable effect on the success of the company. Its primary investment focus is in Web content, Web infrastructure, and e-business solutions companies.

Investments attractive to Sinclair Ventures usually have a unique tie-in to the core television business. To date, Sinclair Ventures has made several strategic equity investments. These investments

strengthen Sinclair's position for the future and provide exciting new opportunities for the company.

From UHF broadcasting to digital television, the Sinclair name remains synonymous with innovation and excellence. Sinclair Broadcast Group has been a leader in television broadcasting and continues to lead the industry in new directions. Technology may be changing the face of broadcasting today, but Sinclair Broadcast Group is changing right along with it, ready to take on new challenges.

SBG HOSTS A VARIETY OF COMMUNITY SERVICE INITIATIVES. SINCE 1986, THE STATION HAS ORGANIZED THE CHAMPIONS OF COURAGE PROGRAM, WHICH SEEKS TO CELEBRATE POSITIVE ROLE MODELS—SUCH AS NAACP PRESIDENT KWEISI MFUME—IN THE BALTIMORE COMMUNITY. SBG ALSO ORGANIZES OPERATION PROM, A PROGRAM TO REDUCE PROM NIGHT DRINKING AND DRIVING.

The Maryland Science Center brings science out of the classroom and into the imaginations of thousands of children and adults each year. This interactive, state-of-the-art center is one of many family attractions along Baltimore's Inner Harbor, providing educational programming in an easy-to-understand, fun format, with exhibits that encourage visitors to touch, see, hear, and experience. The Maryland Science Center is consistently one of the area's most popular sites for locals and visitors alike.

A Dream Realized

The Maryland Science Center first opened its doors on June 13, 1976, realizing a dream long held by the Maryland Academy of Sciences. Today, the center includes three floors of interactive exhibits, the renowned Davis Planetarium, an IMAX® Theater, and a state-of-the-art rooftop observatory. More than 500,000 Marylanders and out-of-state visitors experience the center annually, and more than 250,000 schoolchildren and teachers participate in outreach programs each year.

Exhibits such as Chesapeake Bay, Beyond Numbers, the Hubble Space Telescope National Visitors Center, as well as compelling visiting exhibitions, delight visitors of all ages. The center's staff is internationally recognized for the quality of its presentations, creating original productions for planetariums worldwide, as well as for its own Davis Planetarium.

Another popular attraction is

the IMAX Theater, with its five-story-high screen and 38-speaker sound system. Both classic and cutting-edge IMAX 3-D films are shown in the theater, offering a spectacular visual experience. The Lightspeed Laser Theater offers another opportunity for amazing visuals, using laser technology to provide entertaining, educational presentations.

Reaching Out to Touch the Sky

Visitors can also check out Mother Nature's production in the sky at the Crosby-Ramsey Memorial Observatory, located on the center's roof. The completely refurbished observatory is computer controlled, allowing for the best views in the city, day or night. Outer space can also be explored at the center's newest exhibit, Outer Space Place, which introduces visitors to space travel, astronomy, the study of planets, and more. SpaceLink, a hands-on, multimedia space information center, is a popular feature in the OuterSpacePlace exhibit, as is the Hubble Space Telescope National Visitors Center.

The Maryland Science Center continues to cultivate interest in and understanding of science for all of the state's residents and out-of-town visitors. An important regional resource and national model for informal science education, the Maryland Science Center honors outstanding achievements in the fields of science and engineering. The center seeks to inspire young and old alike by encouraging careers in science and science-related fields, especially in those areas of particular importance to the state's economic well-being.

The Maryland Science Center— the dream of the Maryland Academy of Sciences—continues to shine brightly, touching the lives of children and adults, and helping them not only to be intrigued by science, but also to discover firsthand its awe-inspiring wonder.

CLOCKWISE FROM TOP: THE MARYLAND SCIENCE CENTER IS LOCATED AT BALTIMORE'S POPULAR INNER HARBOR.

LIVE DEMONSTRATIONS INTRODUCE THE CENTER'S VISITORS TO THE WONDERS OF EVERYDAY SCIENCE.

THE STARS COME OUT DURING THE DAY IN THE MARYLAND SCIENCE CENTER'S DAVIS PLANETARIUM.

THE CENTER'S POPULAR SCIENCE ARCADE OFFERS VISITORS A CHANCE TO GAIN NEW PERSPECTIVES ON THEIR WORLD.

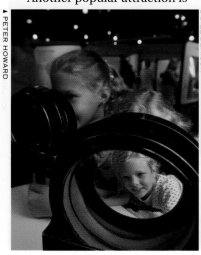

CITY LIGHTS HAS BEEN SERVING UP DELICIOUS SEAFOOD SINCE 1980 (TOP).

THE MILTON INN OFFERS AWARD-WINNING REGIONAL AMERICAN CUISINE WITH AN ELEGANT FLAIR (BOTTOM).

America (DiRoNa) award consecutively since 1993. The Brass Elephant is also a member of La Chaîne des Rôtisseurs, an international gastronomic society, and has hosted several Chaîne dinners.

◆◆◆◆◆◆◆◆◆◆◆◆◆◆◆◆◆◆◆◆◆◆◆◆
Casual Comfort at City Lights

In the heart of Baltimore's Inner Harbor, City Lights is an upscale, casual bistro serving regional seafood with flair. Located on the second floor of the landmark Harborplace center, City Lights features dramatic views of the Inner Harbor, National Aquarium, and other sights at one of Baltimore's most popular attractions. Both locals and tourists enjoy

lunch and dinner at City Lights seven days a week.

One of the original tenants of Harborplace, City Lights has been serving up delicious seafood specialties since 1980. The restaurant is known for its crab soup, which has been noted as the city's best in the Old Bay Crab Soup Stakes. In addition to seafood, the menu also offers a selection of soups, salads, sandwiches, and other entrées, including beef, chicken, and pasta dishes. Diners also enjoy an array of tempting desserts, as well as an extensive bar and wine list, to complement any meal.

City Lights is in an ideal location for visitors taking in the sights of Baltimore. Just a short walk from

Oriole Park at Camden Yards, the Convention Center, and the downtown business district, the restaurant is a favorite for business lunches and dinners. City Lights' outdoor seating is the perfect place to watch the sun set over the harbor and to enjoy a performance at the Inner Harbor amphitheater below.

◆◆◆◆◆◆◆◆◆◆◆◆◆◆◆◆◆◆◆◆◆◆◆◆
Award-Winning Food and Wine at the Milton Inn

Few structures in the Baltimore area enjoy as rich a history as the Milton Inn, and only a few restaurants in the region can be counted among the nation's best. But both are true of this Baltimore County restaurant, which is housed in a 240-year-old, fieldstone building and offers award-winning regional American cuisine with an elegant flair. The Milton Inn offers a fine-dining experience in an intimate, romantic atmosphere, making it one of Baltimore's favorite restaurants.

The Milton Inn was originally a coach stop, and it served travelers in this capacity for nearly 100 years. It was then purchased by John Emerson Lamb, who transformed it into Milton Academy, a school for boys. Lamb named his school after the poet John Milton, and the name has been associated with the building ever since. For 50 years, the Milton Academy educated young boys from the area. After the school's closing, the building became a private residence for some time. Then, it was reopened as a country inn in 1947. Over several decades, the Milton Inn developed a reputation for excellent food and service, as well as a charming ambience. Country Fare took over the restaurant in 1997, and has continued to build on the inn's already solid foundation.

Chef Brian Boston focuses on the quality of his ingredients and follows current food trends without being trendy. The menu features traditional items with an innovative twist. All sauces are prepared from reduction, a painstaking process that takes time, but produces the exceptional results the Milton Inn is known for. Diners can enjoy these creations for weekday lunches, which feature a fixed-price menu offering an appetizer, an entrée, and dessert. Dinner is also served seven nights a week. Guests can select from the à la carte menu or choose the chef's tasting menu, which is available Sunday through Friday. This fixed-price option offers a choice of appetizer, entrée, and dessert from a limited menu, including some of the restaurant's most popular specialties.

The Milton Inn has been consistently recognized as one of the finest restaurants in the region by international authorities like *Zagat's, Wine Spectator,* and DiRoNa. The inn's extensive wine cellar has won international acclaim, and has been a fixture in special wine-tasting dinners with local organizations and international culinary groups like La Chaîne des Rôtisseurs.

Old-World Service, New-World Atmosphere at REMOMO

Country Fare's newest restaurant is REMOMO, an Italian restaurant with an innovative blend of old and new. The restaurant serves up old-world food and traditional service in a sleek, modern atmosphere. Designed by noted San Francisco architectural firm Cass Calder Smith, the restaurant features curvy fixtures with dramatic colors and 60 feet of display kitchen open to the dining area. Operating partner Michael Dalesio and Chef Randy Stahl have created a vibrant place, where families and couples alike can enjoy excellent food in a casual, fun environment.

Stahl brings his years of experience as chef at the Brass Elephant to REMOMO, an example of Country Fare's partnership plan in action. The restaurant is located at Arundel Mills in Anne Arundel County, a $250 million center that features more than 200 specialty retailers, manufacturer's and retail outlets, off-price retailers, and dining and entertainment venues all under one roof.

The Country Fare Group offers something for everyone, from casual chic to sophisticated elegance. This unique group of restaurateurs has helped put Baltimore on the culinary map by providing some of the finest dining in the region. Whatever the future may bring, the Country Fare name will continue to be synonymous with quality in food, service, and management.

REMOMO SERVES UP OLD-WORLD FOOD AND TRADITIONAL SERVICE IN A SLEEK, MODERN ATMOSPHERE.

MRI Worldwide Baltimore/Timonium

MRI Worldwide Baltimore/Timonium has honored its 25th anniversary of staffing excellence with unparalleled client partnerships and a pledge to continue setting the highest standards for the recruiting industry. Since 1976, MRI has been a premier provider of innovative and intelligent staffing solutions throughout the United States and around the world.

"In the 21st century, unprecedented changes are transforming every aspect of the workplace—how companies hire and overall staffing practices," says Linda Burton, president and general manager. "Competition is furious, fueled by the onset of greater domestic growth and global expansion. The rising cost of conducting business, the blur of new technology, and the need to expand market share creates pressure that forces our client companies to fill their open positions faster than ever before. Therefore, it is imperative that they turn to us as the industry leader to solve their staffing challenges."

Founded by Ken Davis, the MRI team is part of the Management Recruiters International network. MRI is one of the world's largest and most successful executive search firms, with more than 1,000 offices in the United States and 32 countries. The Baltimore/Timonium office ranks in the top 1 percent of all MRI offices nationally, and has received the company president's Double Diamond award, a distinction shared by only 8 offices worldwide. The Baltimore/Timonium office stands out as an elite leader that delivers the results needed in today's highly competitive business world. "We are Baltimore's largest executive search firm, and we are very proud to be one of the most successful offices in the history of MRI," says Burton.

In any organization, strong leadership is the key to success. Burton and Davis have built MRI's Baltimore-area office into a team of more than 40 professionals, based on a strong foundation with emphasis on a client-focused approach, needs analysis, and consultative solutions. "We are a team of professionals who are experts at expeditiously identifying, qualifying, attracting, and delivering quality hires," says Burton.

Burton leads Baltimore's nationally recognized, award-winning team with state-of-the-art technology, unprecedented tenure, knowledge, leadership, and professionalism. Broad experience, expertise, and sound business solutions help MRI's clients adjust to the ever changing characteristics of the global workforce.

Says Burton, "We are very unique and literally can staff vertically from top to bottom, from high-level executives or mid-level managers through office support. That breadth of service ensures that we don't merely supply companies with employees. Instead, we enhance our services by identifying the clients' specific needs and—through continuous communication and progress reporting— ensure a proper and timely candidate/client match. These are the keys to our successful client partnerships."

CLOCKWISE FROM TOP LEFT:
LINDA BURTON IS PRESIDENT OF MRI WORLDWIDE BALTIMORE/TIMONIUM.

MRI'S INTERACTIVE TELEVIDEO NETWORK ALLOWS CLIENTS TO INTERVIEW LONG-DISTANCE CANDIDATES WITHOUT EVER LEAVING TOWN.

CERTIFIED SENIOR ACCOUNT MANAGER (CSAM) IS MRI'S INTERNATIONALLY RECOGNIZED DESIGNATION OF SPECIALIZED TRAINING AND DEMONSTRATED LEADERSHIP.

FOUNDER KEN DAVIS AND BURTON ARE INDUSTRY LEADERS WITH A CONSISTENT COMMITMENT TO EXCELLENCE.

THE BALTIMORE/TIMONIUM TEAM IS ONE OF THE MOST SUCCESSFUL AFFILIATES IN THE HISTORY OF THE MRI GLOBAL NETWORK OF MORE THAN 1,000 OFFICES ACROSS THE UNITED STATES AND 32 FOREIGN COUNTRIES.

Filling Both Permanent and Flexible Staffing Needs

No one has more experience in finding and placing the best people for available positions," Burton says. "Our client account teams manage the recruiting process through four focused and inclusive MRI divisions." Through these distinct divisions, MRI searches for individuals to fill professional and middle to upper management positions in the manufacturing, engineering, and high-tech industries. The Sales Consultants unit concentrates on hiring for sales, sales management, and marketing professionals, while MRI's CompuSearch team provides information technology specialists. Companies rely on MRI's OfficeMates5/DayStar division to find permanent and interim administrative, office support, and accounting and financial personnel.

Today's corporations demand alternatives to permanent placement in the new millennium. MRI's flexible staffing divisions have the systems, candidate networks, and national scope to meet any short-term staffing need, allowing the client to save recruiting, screening, and benefit costs. InterExec provides high-quality interim professional, technical, and managerial talent on an as-needed basis as an alternative to full-time employees or traditional management consultants. Salience trains, manages, and handles all payroll functions for temporary sales professionals to meet demands due to new product rollouts, sudden growth opportunities, or test markets. DayStar sources the best and brightest temporary/interim administrative and office support staff. It is due to the success of these systems that MRI has thousands of topflight performers on the job every day.

Managing the Most Important Asset

MRI commands state-of-the-art tools that assist clients in making the right decisions about their company's most important asset—its people. ConferView, MRI's interactive televideo network, enables a company to interview long-distance candidates without ever leaving town. SelecSys, MRI's proprietary, state-of-the-art personality assessment tool, helps to evaluate the potential fit of perspective employees. Humana, MRI's global staffing division, maintains locations in 32 countries and allows clients to fulfill their hiring needs worldwide. FAS Total Relocation Services takes the pain out of the relocation process by offering a complete range of reduced-cost, customized services, including comprehensive cost-of-living comparisons and moving, mortgage, travel, and financial services to ensure a smooth transition for new employees.

"Leave nothing to chance when selecting the right staffing partner," says Burton. Whatever a company's staffing needs, MRI Worldwide Baltimore/Timonium can fulfill them quickly and efficiently for a successful business partnership that lasts.

Ajilon

Quickness of motion, strength, and dexterity define the word "agility," and in naming Ajilon—the fast-moving information technology (IT) services corporation—that's just what the company's leaders had in mind. The firm has continually adapted to the demands of its clients, while maintaining its

central focus. As Ajilon's CEO Roy Haggerty puts it, "We want our customers to know that even as our firm grows phenomenally, it will remain client focused and flexible."

In the fast-paced world of technology, companies need employees who can make an immediate impact. Companies also want to minimize costs and to be prepared to scale down again after a project's completion. Ajilon's experienced team of technology staffers provides the perfect solution, providing additional staff with specialized skills on a temporary basis. "Ajilon IT expertise frees internal IT resources to pursue strategic initiatives," says Haggerty. The company can also manage IT services on an out-

sourcing basis, as well as assist with executive-level IT placement.

Among the many IT-related fields for which Ajilon can provide its unique expertise are management consulting, business analysis, integration and conversion management, installation, and implementation. In addition, qualified staff can assist with database design and maintenance; application development and support; network design, implementation, administration, and support; help desk support; telecommunications; and technical writing and documentation.

As the needs of the new economy diversify, Ajilon can assist clients with system transformation and e-business solutions, and provide the expertise to enable

businesses to enhance their e-commerce presence. The company's extensive network of specialists can even tackle software testing and quality assurance.

Each client receives a customized approach that is attuned to its unique needs, its available resources, and the solutions Ajilon can provide. This maximizes the end result for the client, providing the most effective and efficient solution that best utilizes its time and money.

A Proven Record of Success

While Ajilon has always prided itself on flexibility, agility has not always been part of its name. The company was established as

AJILON'S EXPERIENCED TEAM OF TECHNOLOGY STAFFERS PROVIDES THE PERFECT SOLUTION, PROVIDING ADDITIONAL STAFF WITH SPECIALIZED SKILLS ON A TEMPORARY BASIS.

Comp-u-Staff, back in 1978, as a three-person firm with offices in Towson, Maryland. In only four years, the business had grown to 35 employees and had opened an additional office in Harrisburg. In 1982, the company established an office in Washington, D.C., to serve its client base in the nation's capital.

The company continued to expand at a brisk pace, and it soon began to focus on strategic acquisitions. In 1990, Haggerty took the helm, and under his leadership, the firm has experienced phenomenal growth. Since 1990, the company's size has more than doubled.

As it attained a greater leadership position in the IT staffing industry, the company sought to establish a new corporate identity. In 1996, the corporation adopted the name Ajilon and hasn't looked back. Today, Ajilon is an industry leader of IT staffing services with more than 30 years' experience, $1.6 billion in revenues, and more than 15,000 employees worldwide. Ajilon has a network of more than 40 district offices across the country, as well as a number of international offices. The company's headquarters remains in Towson, where some 150 corporate-level employees provide support for the dynamic firm.

Distinguished Clients and Awards

From large multinational companies to midsize corporations to public employers, Ajilon serves a variety of clients. The company's clients represent a variety of industries, such as manufacturing, financial services, media and entertainment, health care, and transportation.

Whatever the industry, clients have reported high satisfaction with Ajilon's services. In a recent survey of more than 300 Ajilon customers, nearly 100 percent said they would turn to the company again to solve IT challenges. GTE Corporation, a major client, awarded the company its Supplier of Excellence award, and the Chrysler Corporation has honored Ajilon with its Quality Excellence Award. This type of recognition from clients is a testament to the company's reputation as an industry leader.

The key to Ajilon's success is its people; its team of experienced, knowledgeable staff is an invaluable asset to the firm. Ajilon strives to pass along that success to its employees through excellent compensation and benefits programs.

A Helping Hand

Through the company's 30-plus years in Baltimore, Ajilon has remained committed to the community. The company regularly supports the Susan G. Komen Breast Cancer Foundation's Race for the Cure, as well as other events and organizations supporting breast cancer research and education. The company also supports United Cerebral Palsy (UCP) through donations of time, talent, and resources.

In 1998, Baltimore County recognized Ajilon for its pro bono work in developing an automated patient record system for the county's Women's Cancer Protection Program (WCPP), which provides free medical services to underprivileged women.

Ajilon has successfully navigated the volatile world of high technology and emerged the leader. As technology and business continue to evolve, the company is poised to adapt to the changing environment, providing clients with its trademark agility. Ajilon's record of success and its focus on growth and development will ensure the firm's continued leadership for years to come.

THE KEY TO AJILON'S SUCCESS IS ITS PEOPLE; ITS TEAM OF EXPERIENCED, KNOWLEDGEABLE STAFF IS AN INVALUABLE ASSET TO THE FIRM.

Wills & Associates, Inc.

Wills & Associates, Inc. is one of the mid-Atlantic region's leading public relations firms, specializing in media relations, government and business relations, fund-raising, and institutional development. The firm also provides comprehensive writing and editorial services, crisis communications, and special events planning. Whether for traditional clients in the financial industry or emerging businesses in the technology sector, Wills & Associates applies a thorough knowledge of public relations principles and a personal, consultative approach that makes the company stand out among many larger firms.

Wills & Associates was founded in 1978 by George Wills. A former White House Fellow at the Office of Management and Budget and director of public relations at Johns Hopkins University, he later spent many years in management at public relations giant Hill and Knowlton before starting his own firm. Wills' experience in government relations and his connections in Washington, D.C., served the firm well. Over the years, Wills & Associates has worked with the auto industry on safety belt legislation; the American Medical Association on malpractice insurance issues; and the region's electric utilities, railroads, and financial institutions on communications strategy. The company has also consulted on initiatives to develop new business enterprises in Russia. Wills & Associates built a solid reputation with traditional public relations clients, forging specialties in the fields of public policy and finance, and the firm continues to build on that foundation.

WILLS & ASSOCIATES, INC. PRIDES ITSELF ON A PERSONALIZED, COLLABORATIVE, AND STRATEGIC APPROACH TO SUPPORT CLIENTS' PUBLIC RELATIONS NEEDS.

THE PUBLIC RELATIONS FIRM OF WILLS & ASSOCIATES, FOUNDED BY GEORGE WILLS (LEFT) AND CURRENTLY RUN BY PRESIDENT AND CHIEF OPERATING OFFICER BRADFORD WILLS, HAS BEEN LOCATED IN DOWNTOWN BALTIMORE FOR MORE THAN 20 YEARS. THE FIRM ALSO HAS OFFICES IN BETHESDA, TO STRENGTHEN ITS TIES TO THE WASHINGTON, D.C., AREA.

Growing with the Technology Sector

George Wills' son, Bradford C. Wills, joined the firm in 1993, translating his knowledge of the technology and telecom sectors to expand the firm's client mix. Today, technology and telecommunications clients—in such areas as wireless, Internet, e-commerce, and broadband—make up more than half of Wills & Associates' business. The father-son partnership views these markets as significant growth areas for the firm's future. Clients like Telecorp PCS, Westell Technologies, and Metapath Software International appreciate Wills & Associates' sound knowledge of public relations, as well as the company's understanding of new economy needs. "Tech and telecom companies have the same public relations needs as brick-and-mortar enterprises," says Bradford Wills. "They just want it faster." Wills & Associates expects to continue to grow its presence in the technology sector, and to continue to evolve the firm to meet business's changing demands.

Wills & Associates provides a low-key, thoughtful alternative in the hyperkinetic world of public relations. Much of that is due to the firm's smaller size, which allows for the development of close relationships with clients. "The large PR firms are a very different animal," says George Wills. "Our size allows us to focus on targeted projects and offer more personalized, collaborative, strategic consultation." Clients appreciate this approach, as evidenced by the stability of the company's client list. This stands in contrast to the regular turnover seen in larger firms, demonstrating the strength of Wills & Associates' client relationships.

Solid Family Leadership

In 2000, Bradford Wills was named president and chief operating officer of the firm, with George Wills assuming the role of chairman and chief executive officer. The change recognizes the exciting new direction of the firm, and solidifies the strong family relationship in its leadership. The firm has also opened an office in Bethesda, further strengthening its ties in the Washington, D.C., area.

For more than 20 years, Wills & Associates, Inc. has provided sound advice and targeted solutions to hundreds of institutions and corporations throughout the United States and abroad. Now, the firm's leadership looks toward the future with anticipation, fully prepared for the challenges over the next horizon.

GKV

When people like the ads, people buy the stuff. This simple state-

National Aquarium

world-class aquatic museum dedicated to education and conservation,

Bob Ward Companies

Great Blacks In Wax Museum Inc.

As educators and members of the African-American community, husband-and-wife team Dr. Elmer Martin and Dr. Joanne Martin recognized the lack of positive role models for African-Americans and the lack of education on African-American history and achievement. In 1983, they had the idea of

creating a museum to chronicle and celebrate the history and accomplishments of African-Americans, an endeavor that became their lives' work.

Out of the Martins' idea, Great Blacks In Wax Museum Inc. was born. They felt the more visual medium of wax would best capture the imaginations of young people, and they couldn't have been more correct. The museum quickly outgrew its first location on Saratoga Street in Baltimore, and moved to the Oliver neighborhood in 1988, where it remains today. Though still growing, the museum occupies nearly 30,000 square feet of space in several renovated buildings along North Avenue.

Each year, attendance figures at Great Blacks In Wax Museum increase; in 1999 alone, the museum hosted more than 229,000 visitors. Although the museum is a treasured part of Baltimore's historical community, 54 percent of visitors come from out of state, and most of its Maryland visitors live outside the city.

VISITORS TO THE GREAT BLACKS IN WAX MUSEUM ARE DRAWN BY THE LIFESIZE, LIFELIKE WAX FIGURES, WHICH HIGHLIGHT HISTORIC AND CONTEMPORARY PERSONALITIES OF AFRICAN ANCESTRY.

Heroes and Heroines throughout History

Visitors are drawn by the lifesize, lifelike wax figures, which highlight historic and contemporary personalities of African ancestry. One of the most powerful exhibits is a replica of a 19th-century slave ship, which depicts the horror of captivity for passengers as they began life as American slaves. But the museum also celebrates many accomplishments through the centuries. Wax figures clad in historic attire portray the struggles, achievements, and contributions of African peoples worldwide. Highlights include ancient Africa, as well as the North American colonial period, antebellum and postbellum periods, Reconstruction, Harlem renaissance, civil rights era, and present times.

Among the figures included in the museum are the writer Richard Wright and the athlete Jesse Owens, as well as African freedom fighters Stephen Biko, Winnie Mandela, and Nelson Mandela. Other exhibits feature outstanding Marylanders like Eubie Blake, Billie Holiday, Dr. Benjamin Carson, and Kweisi Mfume, as well as superlative educators, labor movement leaders, and modern civil rights era heroes.

Expansion plans are under way to provide more space for the museum's exhibits and educational programs. The plans call for classrooms, a library, a theater, an auditorium, and restaurant and retail space, as well as a fun, educational

area for younger children. The Martins hope to fill the new space with exhibits featuring African-American leaders in science and technology, leaders in spirituality and religion, and winners of international awards like the Pulitzer and Nobel prizes.

More Than a Museum

Over the years, Great Blacks In Wax has become much more than a museum to the Baltimore area. The Martins are active in the Oliver Community Association and the Historic East Baltimore Community Action Coalition, and have been a catalyst for revitalization efforts in the area. The museum has also become a de facto community center, offering educational programs, internships, and fellowships for area residents.

The Martins embarked on this project with several objectives: to stimulate interest in African-American history, motivate young people to achieve, dispel notions of racial superiority and inferiority, and work with other organizations to improve the status of African-Americans. Some 20 years later, the objectives are the same, but it is clear that much has been accomplished along the way.

When five Maryland-based real estate companies merged in 1984 to form O'Conor, Piper & Flynn (OPF), it was big news. *The Wall Street Journal* called it the nation's largest real estate merger to date. The new entity immediately became a major real estate player in Baltimore.

Continuing to provide comprehensive, cutting-edge services, OPF operates more than 47 offices, with approximately 2,100 sales associates stretching from Delaware to the eastern shore, across the state of Maryland to south central Pennsylvania, and into West Virginia.

Success Breeds Success

OPF's initial success did not go unnoticed. In 1998, NRT Incorporated, now the world's largest owner of residential real estate firms, acquired OPF. The company took on one of NRT's international brands, ERA, becoming the largest broker in the ERA network. The next year, NRT Mid-Atlantic Inc. (NRTMA) broke off from O'Conor, Piper & Flynn ERA (OPF/ERA) to service not only OPF/ERA but also Pardoe Real Estate ERA in Washington, D.C., suburban Maryland, and Virginia; and Jack Gaughen Realtor ERA in the Harrisburg region.

Industry Leader

Representing an impressive network of national mortgage investors who offer everything from the smallest government-backed loan to conventional loans in excess of $1 million, OPF/ERA's clients receive the best rates with ERA Mortgage's guarantee to beat any lender's price or pay the client. All OPF/ERA associates shared in the Most Valuable Partnership award from Cendant Mortgage, reflecting the firm's solid relationship with its mortgage partner.

From vacation rentals to multi-million-dollar homes, OPF/ERA's beach rentals and investment properties run the gamut. The company's professionals provide more than 25,000 families with beach rentals annually.

NRTMA Relocation helps clients buy, sell, or rent a home anywhere in the world. The firm's relocation team has been awarded the Cendant Mobility Broker Services Gold Circle of Excellence and Five Star Circle of Excellence awards, and has received a 98 percent customer satisfaction rating.

NRT Mid-Atlantic Title Services provides comprehensive services at competitive rates, backed by full-time attorneys who guide OPF/ERA clients through the legal aspects of closing on a home. Stellar service has made OPF/ERA a major player in the insurance industry for nearly a quarter of a century. Additionally, the company's customers enjoy special values thanks to numerous affiliations with companies such as Budget Truck Rental, ADT Home Security Systems, and Ramada Hotels.

OPF/ERA offers unparalleled service to its clients. The firm's full-time Home Service Center handles the details of moving—utility connections, newspaper subscriptions, change-of-address paperwork, locksmith services, and other necessities. Customer Care counselors arrange for storage facilities, moving services, and contractors, or whatever home services the client needs.

OPF/ERA has become a leader in technology, using a communications network spanning three states. Its Web site, www.opf.com, features more than 6,000 homes for sale, and offers agents, buyers, and sellers information at their convenience. OPF/ERA associates can access information from anywhere, allowing quicker response to client needs.

Civic and Community Partners

Committed to their communities, OPF/ERA offices sponsor community days, children's safety days, and other worthwhile causes. Annual events benefit Toys for Tots, Habitat for Humanity, and the Susan G. Komen Breast Cancer Foundation. Among other charitable causes, the corporation supports House with a Heart and United Way, in addition to real-time closed captioning for the hearing impaired on WJZ-TV newscasts.

OPF/ERA takes great pride in its many achievements. Since its earliest days, O'Conor, Piper & Flynn ERA has been changing the way people buy and sell homes. Continuing its growth, the company is poised for leadership into the future.

CLOCKWISE FROM TOP LEFT: O'CONOR, PIPER & FLYNN ERA (OPF/ERA) SALES ASSOCIATES ARE CONSTANTLY IN TOUCH WITH CLIENTS DURING THE BUYING AND SELLING PROCESS.

JOHN EVANS SERVES AS PRESIDENT OF OPF/ERA.

OPF/ERA IS IN THE BUSINESS OF HELPING FAMILIES ACHIEVE THE AMERICAN DREAM.

STUART ZOLOTOROW

Tremont Suite Hotels

Since 1983, the staff at Tremont Suite Hotels has been greeting visitors and natives alike to Baltimore. Guests at both the Tremont Hotel and the Tremont Plaza are welcomed in grand style at these all-suite hotels, where luxury and convenience come together. ◆ Both properties are owned and managed by

William C. Smith & Co., a Washington, D.C.-based real estate development firm. Chris Smith—son of the founder and now chief executive officer of the company—came to Baltimore in the 1970s and urged his father to become part of the renaissance there. In the early 1980s, Chris Smith decided to convert an old apartment building into the city's first all-suite hotel. It was that idea that led to the opening of the Tremont Hotel in 1983 and the Tremont Plaza just one year later.

Since 1983, the staff at Tremont Suite Hotels has been greeting visitors and natives alike to Baltimore. Guests at both the Tremont Hotel and the Tremont Plaza are welcomed in grand style at these all-suite hotels, where luxury and convenience come together.

Elegance and Style with Conveniences of Home

Smith got the name Tremont from a 19th-century Boston hotel, known for its elegance and style. He aimed to capture that lost grace in his new hotels, while offering guests the best of modern conveniences and services. The company spent $3.5 million in the conversion of the 1964 apartment building into the Tremont Hotel, complete with a marble foyer, antiques, and fine artwork. Another $17 million was spent to convert the Tremont Plaza, making the pair two of Baltimore's most elegant hotels.

DAVE ADLER

The Tremont Plaza features 230 suites of various sizes, from the spacious, two-bedroom Chairman suites to the comfortable, deluxe studio suites. The Tremont Hotel offers 58 suites, including four on the luxurious penthouse level.

Suites at both properties provide separate living and bedroom areas, with queen-sized beds and comfortable furnishings. But the most unique feature is the fully equipped kitchen.

Guests can put that kitchen to good use by utilizing the hotels' free grocery shopping delivery service. It's just one of many thoughtful touches that makes both Tremont hotels feel like a home away from home. Complimentary newspaper delivery, daily shoe shine service, plush terry robes in each room, and complete concierge services are some of the hotels' other amenities. For the hotels'

DAVE ADLER

many business travelers, there is a complete on-site business center, plus voice mail and dataports in every suite.

Baltimore's Hollywood Connection

The Tremont hotels' special features have made them popular spots for Baltimore's visiting film crews and stars. The hotels have hosted more than 40 movie and television productions, including the cast and crew of *Homicide: Life on the Street*, *Runaway Bride*, and *Liberty Heights*. Baltimore has been a popular filming location in recent years, and both properties are uniquely suited to meeting the demanding requirements of production companies. Two upper floors of the Tremont Plaza have been converted into a production suite, complete with a film editing room and a screening

room. This unique feature cements the Tremont Plaza's place as Baltimore's Hollywood connection.

All of the Tremont's guests, celebrities or not, enjoy the properties' convenient locations in downtown Baltimore. The Tremont Hotel and the Tremont Plaza are only a few blocks apart, and both are close to the Convention Center, the Inner Harbor, Camden Yards, and the city's business centers. Historic Mount Vernon is a short walk, and the National Aquarium and Harborplace shopping are also within walking distance.

Many of the city's finest restaurants are close by as well— some even right within the hotels' four walls. The Tremont Plaza features Tug's Bar & Grille for casual American fare, as well as the Plaza Deli, renowned for its gourmet

sandwiches, salads, and homemade soups. Voted Best of Baltimore for many years, the Plaza Deli is also a favorite with visiting film crews and stars. For fine dining, the Tremont Hotel offers gourmet fare at the 8 East Restaurant, and drinks, light fare, and entertainment at Celebrities Lounge.

Today, both hotels are again undergoing multimillion-dollar renovation projects. In addition to renovating the Tremont Plaza's 230 suites and the Tremont Hotel's 58 suites, the project also entails the development of a banquet facility at the Masonic Temple Building on North Charles Street. This location will be a welcome addition to the more than 10,000 square feet of function space currently available at the Tremont Plaza in its 11 function rooms.

Tremont Suites' Hometown Team

More than 200 residents of Baltimore are employed at the Tremont Suite Hotels, and many have been part of the team since the hotel opened its doors more than 15 years ago. The commitment of its associates is part of what makes the Tremont Suites' experience a special one. "Legendary guest service is our goal, and our associates are the key to making that goal a reality," says Helma O'Keefe, general manager. That exceptional service breeds loyalty among Tremont's clientele, many of whom visit the hotel every time they come to Baltimore.

Tremont Suite Hotels is committed to its home city, and demonstrates that commitment through its contributions to many civic and charitable organizations. The company is active in the Historic Charles Street Association, and associates regularly donate their time and resources to the Maryland Food Bank and the South Baltimore Learning Center. Tremont Suites goes the extra step to help those in need; when a fire at the nearby Charles Towers apartment building left residents homeless, the hotels opened their doors to the displaced tenants and assisted the Red Cross in its relief efforts. For the businessperson, the tourist, or the Hollywood star, the Tremont Plaza and the Tremont Hotel are ready to serve.

SUITES AT BOTH PROPERTIES PROVIDE SEPARATE LIVING AND BEDROOM AREAS, WITH QUEEN-SIZED BEDS AND COMFORTABLE FURNISHINGS.

THE TREMONT PLAZA FEATURES TUG'S BAR & GRILLE FOR CASUAL AMERICAN FARE.

Comcast Cable Communications, Inc.

Comcast Cable Communications, Inc. is helping Baltimore establish its position on the cusp of technological innovation, building a web of high-speed information systems within the city. Dedicated to providing first-class cable and communications services, Comcast has been growing and evolving within the Baltimore County area since 1984.

Comcast traces its roots back to 1963, when three men teamed up to bring cable television to Tupelo, Mississippi. They saw that a bright future lay in store for television, and, with only 1,200 households, helped to begin the cable television revolution. The company soon took off, making its first public stock offering in 1972 and establishing itself in major markets across the country. Today, Comcast is the nation's third-largest cable provider, reporting more than $5 billion in revenue in 1998, and serving some 5.5 million customers through its consolidated and affiliated cable operations.

The company has grown dramatically, both in the size of its customer base and in the scope of its operations. Comcast is actively involved in cable programming content as a managing partner of QVC and the controlling partner of E! Entertainment Television. The firm also offers other telecommunications services across the coun-

try, such as cellular phone service and high-speed cable Internet access.

Growing in Baltimore

Comcast came to Baltimore in 1984 with the acquisition of Caltec, then Baltimore County's cable provider. Since this acquisition, the company has increased cable coverage to more than 340,000.

In 1995, Comcast began an initiative to replace coaxial cable with fiber optics to give the people of Baltimore better service and reception, and also to provide a platform for the firm's cable modem service, Comcast@Home. Baltimore County was chosen by Comcast to be the first market for Comcast@Home, a high-speed Internet service that delivers the information superhighway 100 times faster than conventional modems.

According to Doug Sansom, vice president and general manager of Comcast's Baltimore Metropolitan Area Systems, the company's goal is that Comcast customers in the Baltimore metropolitan area should always have state-of-the-art telecommunications services at their fingertips. "The company's credo states that we will be the one to look to first for the communications products and services that connect people to what's important in their lives," says Sansom.

Comcast is committed to providing the cutting edge of technology to the communities it serves, and Baltimore is a shining example of this service. The success of

Comcast@Home in Baltimore made the Baltimore metropolitan area system an ideal site to receive Comcast Digital Cable when it was launched in 1998. One of the first successful attempts at marketing interactive programming, Comcast Digital Cable offers 200 channels of programming with a crystal-clear digital picture and CD-quality sound, maximizing the value of home entertainment centers with premium movie channels like HBO, Cinemax, and Showtime.

Comcast Digital Cable's interactive programming guide allows users to browse schedules much like a computer database, putting programming information at the tips of the customer's fingers. All of this information is provided without needing a special television or lengthy installation process.

Innovative Community Contributions

Since coming to Baltimore, Comcast has made it a priority to better the community. According to the *Baltimore Business Journal*, Comcast was Baltimore's single-largest corporate philanthropist of 1999, contributing more than $8.5 million to various nonprofit, education, civic, and charitable organizations.

In addition, Comcast launched its own Student Achievement Awards in 1992, committing to award a $1,000 scholarship to one student in every Baltimore, Howard, and Harford county school each year. The company has contributed some $200,000 to this program in schools across Maryland in the past eight years, and has helped approximately 200 county scholarship students manage the cost of a college education.

The company regularly donates airtime as well, valued in the millions of dollars, for public service announcements and segments promoting awareness of nonprofit and charitable organizations. Time is given for interviews with local elected officials to help keep Baltimore-area residents informed about local politics.

Through its High Speed Education Connection program, Comcast brings the educational power of the Internet to schools in Baltimore, Howard, and Harford counties. Comcast has wired more than 200 schools in these counties with the Comcast@Home service, paying for the cost of installation in full and providing the access free of charge.

Comcast also created and manages OnlineSchoolyard.com, an award-winning K-12 site designed to help students find educational sites and information. Sansom believes it is Comcast's duty to provide for the educational needs of the community going into the next millennium. "Students will still be able to look to us first

for the educational resources that will give them an added advantage in the technology-driven economy and eliminate the digital divide in the Baltimore metropolitan area," says Sansom.

For more than 30 years, Comcast's businesses have grown and evolved, placing the company in a position of leadership in today's high-technology communications industry. Now, in the Baltimore area, Comcast is putting its expertise to work, making an unparalleled network of information accessible to its subscribers. In the coming years, Comcast expects to see its growth continue in Baltimore, as more people embrace the convenience and excellence of the company's digital cable and high-speed Internet services.

COMCAST AND ITS EMPLOYEES TAKE AN ACTIVE ROLE IN THEIR COMMUNITIES.

TODAY, COMCAST CUSTOMERS ARE ENJOYING THE BEST IN INFORMATION, EDUCATION, AND ENTERTAINMENT SERVICES: COMCAST DIGITAL CABLE AND COMCAST@HOME.

Gr8 is anything but typical, and by design, defies traditional advertising agency categorizations. The integrated communications agency combines marketing, design, and technology strategies to strengthen corporate and product branding, build customer relationships, improve productivity, and manage valuable business and customer information for its clients. All of these skills come together into the unique package that is Gr8, a pioneering local company that is having an international impact.

Craig Ziegler, president and chief executive officer, has been a trailblazer since 1985, when he opened Graffito, a local graphic design studio that introduced Baltimore to the cutting edge. As the first studio in the mid-Atlantic region to embrace computer-aided design (CAD), Graffito became synonymous with striking, powerful imagery created through the latest in computer technology. When Graffito began to recognize the potential of new media technologies, it launched Active8, a multimedia arm focused on exploiting the capabilities of 3-D graphics and interactive media. In 1993, the two companies were combined to form Gr8, enabling the united agency to integrate and expand its client service offerings, as well as gain a position as an industry leader.

A Leader in Interactive Marketing

Gr8 has attracted widespread attention as an industry leader today, as it continues its pioneering ways. The agency has been named one of the top 100 interactive agencies in the country by AdweekOnline, and has received more than 750 national and international awards of excellence, including seven 1999 WebAwards from the Web Marketing Association, *Internet* magazine's Best of the Internet award, *Marketing Computers* magazine's Golden ICON award, and multiple ADDY awards.

A big part of Gr8's success is due to the agency's unique ability to meld marketing, design, and technology ideas. Left-brained and right-brained talent work together through a defined, collaborative process to identify clients' business objectives, apply creative insight, and deliver effective ideas. Major clients like the Library of Congress, Sylvan Learning Centers, National Gallery of Art, Smithsonian Institution, Baltimore Ravens, Greater Baltimore Alliance, Office of the Mayor, Baltimore City, and TradePower are happy with the results and keep coming back to Gr8.

Addressing Traditional Needs in Nontraditional Ways

Gr8 addresses the traditional communications needs of businesses in nontraditional ways. The agency applies cutting-edge visual design to standard communications vehicles like marketing brochures, collateral materials, annual reports, and signage, as well as developing innovative presentation media, like portable presentations, kiosks, video walls, and interactive theaters. Gr8 also helps clients develop highly visual and interactive Internet, intranet, and extranet environments to powerfully showcase their products and services, while delivering efficient communications and operational benefits.

In Gr8's in-house digital editing suite, the firm's staff creates the latest in video development and

Gr8 partners include (from left) Morton Jackson, chief creative officer; Craig Ziegler, president and chief executive officer; and Arthur Balter, chief marketing officer.

▲ ED WHITMAN

animation for a variety of client uses, including training, trade shows, and direct marketing. The agency even supports clients' public relations efforts, including trade show promotion and media cultivation. All of these services tie into Gr8's core competencies, which lie in helping clients strengthen their brand, increase market awareness, improve productivity of marketing and sales teams, and increase sales cycle efficiency.

Ziegler credits the Gr8 team for the agency's consistent quality and innovation. "Whether they are marketers, designers, or technologists, our employees are creative people, and we treat them as such," says Ziegler. This supportive attitude contributes to the agency's very low staff turnover, even in highly competitive employment markets. Gr8 strives to provide an environment and culture that spark creativity, encourage intellectual growth, and provide a comfortable level of autonomy. And employees respond.

Partnerships with NASA and HP Broaden Skills

Never one to rest on its laurels, Gr8 also actively pursues opportunities to participate in innovative partnerships that broaden its reach and scope of experience. Currently, the agency is part of an alliance with NASA, Georgetown University, University of Maryland Baltimore County, and Incube8, working to improve the way people communicate, handle commerce,

and share knowledge. Gr8 takes the initiative and researches such areas as ontology, artificial intelligence, reactive media, and broadband and mobile communications. The agency is also an HP Business Partner, working on collaborative projects to integrate future technologies into the daily business environment.

As a corporate citizen of Baltimore for more than 15 years, Gr8 is committed to the city and its future. Ziegler is an active leader of Baltimore's technology community, sitting on the board of the Greater Baltimore Technology Council and serving on the advisory board for the NASA Incubator Program at Baltimore's Emerging Technology Center. He is also a member of the Greater Baltimore Branding Initiative, an 18-month-long effort directed by the Greater Baltimore Alliance. This collaborative endeavor of business, community, and government leaders is charting a visionary and focused brand for the Greater Baltimore area to actively shape the region's economic development position for the new century. Ziegler also sits on the advisory board for the University of Baltimore's doctoral program in publications design, and he is a popular speaker who addresses students, entrepreneurs,

and business leaders on integrated marketing and Web-centric business processes.

Inside Gr8's offices, commitment to education and outreach continues, as the agency supports a variety of programs that give back to the community. One example is Building STEPS, a two-year college preparatory program designed to expose inner-city students to science- and technology-based professions. A participant in Building STEPS, Gr8 hosts groups of students, and provides them real-world insight into design and development.

Whatever the medium or the message, Gr8 demonstrates its typical style—one of innovative design, extreme effectiveness, and uncompromising quality.

CLOCKWISE FROM TOP LEFT: GR8'S INVITING RECEPTION AREA IS A PRELUDE TO THE DYNAMIC WORK SPACES WITHIN.

GR8'S WORK SPACE EMBRACES A CREATIVE COLLISION OF ASSORTED TEXTURES, COLORS, AND INDUSTRIAL MATERIALS.

LARGE, OPEN WORK SPACES ALLOW GR8 EMPLOYEES THE ULTIMATE FREEDOM TO COLLABORATE AND BE CREATIVE.

GR8'S WEB SITE HAS WON SEVERAL NATIONAL AND INTERNATIONAL AWARD COMPETITIONS, INCLUDING THE ADDYs, NEW YORK FESTIVALS, AND THE WEB MARKETING ASSOCIATION'S WEBAWARDS.

Kaiser Permanente Mid-Atlantic

Since 1945, the Kaiser Permanente name has been synonymous nationwide with quality health care that is accessible and affordable for working people. And since 1980, families in the mid-Atlantic region have been entrusting the Kaiser Permanente doctors and nurses with their health care. ◆ In the

Greater Baltimore-Washington area, Kaiser Permanente Mid-Atlantic States cares for nearly 550,000 members through 24 community medical centers and a network of community-based physicians, including many Johns Hopkins providers. Kaiser Permanente's Baltimore-area medical centers are located in downtown Baltimore, Severna Park, Towson, White Marsh, and Woodlawn. The organization also has partnerships with area hospitals, such as St. Agnes HealthCare and the Greater Baltimore Medical Center. In addition to primary and specialty care, some Kaiser Permanente centers offer ambulatory surgery, lab, X-ray, and on-site pharmacy services.

Quality Care within Easy Reach

Nationally, Kaiser Permanente is the oldest and largest not-for-profit HMO, with 8 million members across the country and a presence in 11 states and the District of Columbia. One reason for this success is the way Kaiser Permanente practices medicine. The organization remains committed to maintaining the independence of its doctors and other medical professionals who will help make decisions on patient care. In keeping with this philosophy, Kaiser Permanente separates the administrative and insurance functions from medical care. In fact, that division of duties is the genesis of its name. Kaiser Permanente is a working partnership of two organizations: the not-for-profit Kaiser Foundation Health Plan of the Mid-Atlantic States, Inc. and the Mid-Atlantic Permanente Medical Group. The structure allows the organization

AT THE CITY PLAZA MEDICAL CENTER, LOCATED IN DOWNTOWN BALTIMORE, KAISER PERMANENTE MID-ATLANTIC MEMBERS ARE CARED FOR BY THE PHYSICIANS OF THE MID-ATLANTIC PERMANENTE MEDICAL GROUP WHO INCLUDE (FROM LEFT) REBECCA E. BYRD, M.D., INTERNAL MEDICINE; RICHARD DIETRICH, M.D., CHIEF OF PEDIATRICS/BALTIMORE; AND JEFFREY DUNBAR, M.D., INTERNAL MEDICINE.

to offer quality medical care, while providing its members with efficient, competitive rates and services.

Kaiser Permanente recently launched Kaiser Permanente Online, a confidential, interactive, members-only Web site. By logging on to www.kponline.org, members can consult with nurses and pharmacists, access drug and health encyclopedias, locate information about health education classes, and receive customized health assessments. A call center provides additional resources, and strives to provide fast responses to calls about appointments, lab results, and benefits. Through the call center, members can be connected to customer service representatives and registered nurses who can make appointments, take messages, and provide medical advice.

In keeping with its commitment to health maintenance, Kaiser Permanente has established many preventive care programs for its members. The Be Well health education program offers a variety of courses on common health issues, including programs on stress management, weight loss, prenatal care, and diabetes management. In addition, each patient receives comprehensive preventive guidelines, which provide a timetable for regular checkups, immunizations, and other appropriate tests.

The organization's efforts have been recognized by industry authorities and in the national media. Kaiser Permanente is fully accredited by the National Committee

for Quality Assurance. And *U.S. News & World Report* placed Kaiser Permanente on its honor roll of all HMOs, giving the organization the only top, four-star rating in the mid-Atlantic region in September of 1998 and November of 1999.

Reaching Out to the Community

In addition to its medical mission, Kaiser Permanente is committed to its social mission: to improve the communities it serves. Through its community relations department, Kaiser Permanente implements a number of strategies to bring health information, care, and support to those in need.

Each year in the Baltimore-Washington area, Kaiser Permanente provides millions of dollars to help uninsured lower-income families and children receive health care attention. In conjunction with local jurisdictions, hospitals, and nonprofit organizations, Kaiser Permanente provided aid to more than 4,000 people in 1999. Through a unique partnership with Baltimore County, Kaiser Permanente also helps provide quality, affordable health care to uninsured working adults through Partners Health Insurance Program (PARTNERSH.I.P.). This innovative program received the Baltimore County 2000 Bridge Builder Award. The county also presented Kaiser Permanente with its 2000 Child Health Promotion Award for the organization's efforts to improve children's health in the region.

Through contributions and sponsorships, Kaiser Permanente supports many health education organizations and events throughout the year. The company has generously given to the Baltimore Hadassah chapter's Check It Out program, a breast cancer awareness program that has reached more than 32,000 high school girls. The organization's Community Health Impact Grants help local groups pursue new strategies and expand their services. These grants have benefited diverse organizations such as Family Tree, a mental health outreach program for teens; Helping Up Mission, a shelter for homeless men; Healthcare for the Homeless, a free health clinic; and Providence Adult Daycare Center.

Kaiser Permanente's employees regularly participate in a number of local fund-raising events, including the HERO-AIDSWALK, Susan G. Komen Foundation's Race for the Cure, and the Johns Hopkins Children's Center radiothon T-shirt sale. Organizing these efforts are the community service committees at each Kaiser Permanente medical center, which also identify opportunities in their neighborhoods and recruit volunteers from local staff.

Kaiser Permanente Mid-Atlantic holds fast to its mission. In the competitive world of managed health care, the company shines through as a leading provider of quality health care that is both affordable and accessible.

KAISER PERMANENTE'S BALTIMORE LEADERS INCLUDE ROBERT L. WILLIAMS (LEFT), EXECUTIVE DIRECTOR AND VICE PRESIDENT BALTIMORE AND REGIONAL MEDICAL OPERATIONS, AND ROBERT KRITZLER, M.D., AREA MEDICAL DIRECTOR.

SUPER WEEVIL IS ONE OF THE VIBRANT CHARACTERS OF *Professor Bodywise's Traveling Menagerie*, A PLAY THAT BRINGS HEALTH AND SAFETY MESSAGES TO SCHOOLS AND COMMUNITY GROUPS AS PART OF KAISER PERMANENTE'S FREE EDUCATIONAL THEATRE PROGRAM.

BALTIMORE

Profiles in Excellence

1986–1995

Booz · Allen & Hamilton Inc.

All around the world, Booz·Allen & Hamilton Inc. helps its clients achieve and sustain success. That is the goal of this leading global management and technology consulting firm, which has been guiding the world's leaders since World War I. With more than 90 offices on six continents, Booz·Allen is truly an international firm, but its deep roots in government and national security give the company a strong presence in the Baltimore-Washington region where some 5,000 employees live and work. Booz·Allen has 10 offices in Maryland alone, including Baltimore, Annapolis Junction, Rockville, and Linthicum.

Booz·Allen is committed to providing its clients more than answers: the firm helps Fortune 500 stalwarts, federal and state government agencies, and new economy start-ups achieve their mission and deliver their purpose. Known across the globe as a practical strategist, Booz·Allen combines strategy and implementation for innovative, holistic solutions that endure over time and successfully rise to the challenges of the new economy.

Making an Impact on the World

Booz·Allen Maryland employees contribute to many exciting projects that have a profound impact on the world. At the Seabrook , Maryland, office, Booz·Allen associates work with officials at NASA's Goddard Space Flight Center, helping ensure the success of NASA missions through effective project management and strategic planning. Booz·Allen communications engineers work hand in hand with NASA managers to meet the communications needs of space stations and the space shuttle. At the National Business Park office, Booz·Allen consults on a variety of strategies, systems, and technology outsourcing issues for the National Security Agency. The firm provides this agency with solutions to emerging challenges such as information assurance and global digitization.

Moving west to the Rockville office, the Federal Drug Administration (FDA) and the Department of Health and Human Services (HHS) are major Booz·Allen clients. The firm supports FDA and HHS in protecting the American public through the regulation of food, cosmetics, and drugs. And in Baltimore, the firm has worked extensively with the Maryland Transit Administration, providing engineering consulting for such transportation projects as the light-rail system and the bus network. Booz·Allen managed all the engineering, quality assurance, warranty management, and acceptance testing for Baltimore's light-rail, ensuring that the system was running effectively before the opening of Oriole Park at Camden Yards. Other Booz·Allen clients in Maryland include the Environmental Protection Agency, the Department of Defense, and the Department of Energy.

Helping Clients Make History

The firm was originally founded in 1914 in Chicago, when Ed Booz started a new profession—management consulting. By 1943, the firm was known as Booz·Allen & Hamilton, and through the 1940s it worked closely with military and civilian leaders to help the country prepare for war and, later, for peace. Booz·Allen played a role in many of the major historical developments of the 1950s and 1960s, including the development of television, air travel, and satellite communications. The next few decades brought explosive growth, as the firm consulted about the formation of the National Football League, the turnaround of Chrysler Corporation, and strategic repositioning for the AT&T

THE ACTIVE INVOLVEMENT OF BOOZ·ALLEN & HAMILTON INC. EMPLOYEES IN VOLUNTEER AND COMMUNITY SERVICE ACTIVITIES DISTINGUISHES THE FIRM'S COMMUNITY RELATIONS PROGRAM. AS PART OF THE CHRISTMAS IN APRIL PROGRAM, BOOZ·ALLEN EMPLOYEES REHABILITATE HOUSES FOR THE POOR AND ELDERLY IN CITIES ACROSS THE UNITED STATES.

divetiture. Today, Booz·Allen is a privately held corporation with more than 10,000 employees worldwide, who make history each day through their efforts.

Booz·Allen's employees enjoy this challenging setting, and they are rewarded with excellent compensation and benefits, as well as a highly supportive work environment. The firm makes employee recognition and appreciation a priority, and sponsors a host of programs to foster a sense of community and achievement among its associates. One example is the Values in Practice (VIP) Award, one of Booz·Allen's highest honors, which recognizes staff for outstanding demonstration of the firm's core values. Winners—and a guest—receive an all-expenses-paid land or cruise vacation, as well as a commemorative gift. Other award programs recognize employees who perform above and beyond the call of duty, going the extra mile for a client or coworker. Employees also enjoy quarterly celebrations—such as a Mardi Gras party, a crab feast, and a family day at a local amusement park—which provide fun, social opportunities to relax and celebrate the team's many achievements.

Making a Difference in the Community

The company's generous spirit carries over into the community as well, where Booz·Allen regularly sponsors and supports a variety of events and organizations. Both at a corporate and at an individual employee level, Booz·Allen supports such organizations as the Special Olympics, Boys and Girls Clubs, Arthritis Foundation, Whitman Walker AIDS Clinic, and American Cancer Society. Booz·Allen's employees also volunteer for Everybody Wins, a mentoring and reading program for children, and So Others Might Eat (SOME), a shelter and soup kitchen. The firm has also performed pro bono consulting for a number of nonprofit organizations, including the Smithsonian Institution, Nature Conservancy, Children's Hospital, and Wolf Trap, America's National Park for the Performing Arts. Booz·Allen's employees are encouraged to donate their time and use their professional skills to benefit worthy causes.

Booz·Allen is also committed to preparing the next generation of experts in the national security field. As a sponsor of the National Security Scholarship Program, Booz·Allen contributes to a generous scholarship fund and provides internship and cooperative work opportunities for eligible students. The scholarship program, founded by Mark Gerencser, Booz·Allen vice president, is provided through the Independent College Fund of Maryland, and also involves the participation of many other leading companies in the national security field.

Achieving and sustaining success is the goal at Booz·Allen & Hamilton Inc.—not only for the firm's clients, but for its employees and its community as well. All three groups reach that goal at Booz·Allen, where employees make history and make a difference.

Magco Inc.

Mark Gaulin has built Magco Inc. from the ground up. Gaulin founded the commercial and industrial roofing company from his home in 1987, and, since that time, the company has raised the roof on the roofing industry. From innovative new products to progressive organization, Gaulin and Magco have changed the face of commercial roofing.

Magco began growing as soon as it opened for business, and Gaulin hasn't looked back since. The company has outgrown several facilities, and will soon move to a brand-new, 30,000-square-foot building in Jessup, Maryland, which should accommodate the company's needs for some time. Magco's consistent growth and success have been fueled by the company's unwavering commitment to quality, performance, and safety—elements that have propelled the business to the top of the industrial and commercial roofing industry.

Comprehensive Capabilities, Professional Service

In its first six years of business, Magco concentrated on establishing its reputation in the region. Today, that reputation is rock solid, based on the company's comprehensive capabilities and professional service. Magco can manage a wide range of roofing projects, including roof recovery, tear off, new construction, deck replacement, and plaza deck renovations. The firm's trained staff—authorized by all major manufacturers—is qualified to handle all roofing systems, including EPDM, built-up roofing (BUR), modified, single-ply, and metal. In addition, Magco focuses on completing projects on schedule and under budget, a professional touch that clients appreciate. Sophisticated computerized reporting and management practices help keep Magco on top of millions of square feet of roofing projects, producing satisfied customers throughout the region.

Those customers have given Magco a variety of projects, from shopping malls and airports to office buildings and hospitals. Currently, Magco's work can be seen on many high-profile facilities in the Baltimore area, such as Johns Hopkins Hospital, Baltimore Convention Center, Villa Julie College, IKEA at White Marsh, National Aquarium, and PSINet Stadium, home of the NFL's Baltimore Ravens, winner of Super Bowl XXXV.

MetFab Revolutionizes Roofing Industry

In 1993, Gaulin expanded in a new direction, with the introduction of MetFab, a metal manufacturing company. MetFab's most prominent product is a steel architectural roofing and wall system, which is available in a variety of styles and colors. MetFab also produces steel roofing shingles, which are relatively new to the industry, and offer many advantages over traditional materials. Steel shingles are exceptionally durable, energy efficient, environmentally friendly, and significantly lighter than asphalt shingles.

In addition to shingles, MetFab produces eight different architectural metal panel profiles, as well as coping, fascia, gravel stops, wall panels, and cornices. Customized pieces can even be developed to meet exact specifications. All MetFab materials carry a 20-year

MAGCO INC.'S HOME OFFICE IS LOCATED IN JESSUP, MARYLAND.

warranty against chalking, cracking, and color fading, and MetFab steel shingles claim the best warranty in the business with 50 years' coverage on both material and replacement labor. MetFab's headquarters is also located in Jessup, and Gaulin expects this innovative product to experience significant growth in the future.

New Vision for Commercial Roofing Nationwide

In 2000, Gaulin took on yet another challenge. As a founder of TECTA America Corp., a nationwide consortium of commercial roofing contractors, he helped start a revolution in the industry. For the first time, property managers and owners can enjoy continuity of service for all the roofs under their care. TECTA can provide one point of contact and then distribute projects to its certified members across the country. Also, TECTA can handle all aspects of commercial roofing for clients, including maintenance and repair, disaster recovery, reroofing and restoration, and new roof planning and installation. All TECTA members must meet high standards for quality, service, and business practices, ensuring a positive experience for the client. Currently, Magco is one of 10 companies that make up TECTA, offering commercial roofing services from coast to coast.

Magco is also an active member of more traditional roofing trade associations, such as the Associated Roofing Contractors of Maryland and the National Roofing Contractors Association. The company is a sponsor of the Roofing Industry Alliance for Progress as well.

Giving Back to the Community

The roofing industry isn't the only group that benefits from Magco's time and talents; the company also regularly supports a number of local organizations and causes through pro bono work and donations of labor and materials. At the Earth Conservation Corps Center in Washington, D.C., Magco donated labor to help develop a green roof to reduce storm water runoff into the Anacostia River. The unique project involved waterproofing the entire, 3,000-square-foot roof surface, which was then covered by three inches of soil and plant life. For its involvement in this innovative project, Magco was nominated for the National Roofing

Contractor Association's 2001 Gold Circle Award for service to the community. In 1993, the company was recognized as Howard County's Outstanding Volunteer Group for its Roof Raising Project benefiting Ellicott Enterprises. Magco has also supported the Grant-a-Wish Foundation program at Johns Hopkins Hospital, and donated materials and labor for reroofing at the Hospice of the Chesapeake.

Since its inception, Magco Inc. has been a leader and an innovator in the commercial roofing field. With many successes under its belt, the company continues to forge ahead and raise the bar in its industry.

SOME OF MAGCO'S MOST NOTABLE PROJECTS INCLUDE THE BALTIMORE CONVENTION CENTER (LEFT), AND THE BROADMOOR COOPERATIVE APARTMENTS (TOP RIGHT) AND TILDEN GARDENS (BOTTOM RIGHT) IN WASHINGTON, D.C.

not everyone can work for RDA. The Timonium, Maryland-based software engineering firm hires about one of every 15 candidates it interviews, after a lengthy, multitiered selection process. That's what it takes to build the type of team RDA values—a highly experienced, committed team that can work collaboratively with clients on complex projects. It's not an easy task, but it is one that RDA does exceptionally well, as evidenced by the company's status as a leader in its industry.

Getting Down to Business

RDA's tag line says it all: "Custom software solutions that mean business." The software engineering firm delivers just that to companies in a variety of industries. "In the crowded e-business field, RDA stands out as a straightforward company that avoids the hype and gets down to creating business solutions that work," says R. Donald Awalt, founding chairman and CEO. "We are more than con-sultants to our clients—we partner with them and serve as an extension of their information technology and internal business teams." RDA's highly experienced software engineers and project managers provide clients with reliable, secure, easily integrated systems that are designed to accommodate future growth and change without costly modifications. Ultimately, these systems help companies improve efficiency, increase profits, and reduce costs, providing a solid return on the technology investment.

Major national and international companies like Pfizer, Sallie Mae, and UPS turn to RDA to help them solve complex business problems. For one recent project, RDA developed a system for NASD Regulation, a subsidiary of the National Association of Securities Dealers, to keep track of some 5,600 NASD member firms and 500,000 securities industry employees. This new data management system allowed NASD to successfully input its 1 millionth filing in record-breaking time. Its collaborative approach and focused dedication to finding a solution made RDA successful in this case, and in many others the company undertakes each year.

Profitable Growth since Day One

Awalt's commitment to the company's high standards reflects the fact that his name is riding on them—literally. RDA takes its name from Awalt's initials, symbolizing the company's roots as a one-man operation. After years of experience at top technology companies like Texas Instruments, Muse Software, and General Instrument Corporation, Awalt decided to go it alone in 1988. But he wasn't alone for long, and soon the company was up and running. From day one, RDA was profitable, and now, more than 13 years later, the company's growth and success are impressive.

Today, RDA employs close to 300 people at its headquarters just north of Baltimore, and at its satellite offices in Atlanta, Chicago, Philadelphia, northern Virginia, and Bethesda. The company is exploring opportunities for further expansion, and is looking for ways to bring its technology solutions to more businesses nationwide. In 2000, RDA's annual sales exceeded $49 million.

Not every software engineering firm can deliver solutions like RDA does. In a highly competitive industry filled with new entrants, RDA distinguishes itself as an experienced, focused performer that means business.

R. DONALD AWALT IS FOUNDING CHAIRMAN AND CEO OF RDA.

◄ ERIC STOCKLIN

Rock Spring Village is a premier assisted living facility that has been a part of the Harford County community for more than 10 years. At its opening in 1989, Rock Spring Village was the largest freestanding assisted living facility in Maryland. Nestled in tranquil surroundings, the one-story building offers a variety of living solutions to its residents, from private rooms to spacious two-room suites and shared accommodations. Convenient living on one level includes neighborhood lounges and kitchens; crafts and entertainment rooms; a large restaurant-style dining room and private dining facilities; and an aviary, an aquarium, and many gardens.

The Best of Old and New

Rock Spring Village offers a variety of services for the comfort and convenience of residents. Independence and privacy are the watchwords of the facility's around-the-clock professional staff. Residents enjoy three home-cooked meals each day in the comfortable dining room, featuring a choice of entrées and accompaniments brought to the table by friendly servers.

Personalized assistance makes the tasks of daily living a little bit easier. Staff provide assistance on an individualized basis, ensuring privacy and dignity. Cleaning, linen, and laundry services are provided, and an on-site beauty/barbershop provides the extra touch once a week.

Residents enjoy a variety of social and recreational programs tailored to their interests and needs. The social calendar includes exercise, crafts, bingo, community excursions, movies, card games, and many other enjoyable activities. Residents can even take advantage of regularly scheduled transportation services for shopping, physician visits, and social activities.

Rock Spring Village offers its residents the comfort of nurses around the clock, and nurses and professional assistants are actively involved in monitoring the well-being of each resident.

Professional dietitians are available to ensure that special dietary needs are identified, and customized menus are provided as needed. In addition, housekeeping, dining, and maintenance professionals are always on the job, maintaining the highest standards of cleanliness, comfort, and safety.

A Part of the Community

But Rock Spring Village is more than just a building; it is a community of residents, staff, and families, as well as an active part of the greater community. For 10 years, its staff and residents have participated in the Magic Me program with South Hampton Middle school, bringing seniors and youngsters together for mutual learning and sharing. The facility also hosts an Alzheimer's family support group, and participates annually in the Memory Walk to raise funds for Alzheimer's research. The staff at Rock Spring Village work actively with many other community organizations, including Mothers Against Drunk Driving, Pets on Wheels, and Harford County's Annual Caregivers Conference. And Rock Spring Village's semiannual celebrations bring residents, families, and community members together for a variety of events, including old-fashioned ice-cream socials, antique car rallies, food, and fellowship.

Since its opening, Rock Spring Village has seen its surrounding community change from a tranquil, rural community to a thriving suburban metro area. Through it all, Rock Spring Village has retained its tranquil, homelike ambience, while keeping up with the improvements and advances in assisted living and senior care. Excellence never goes out of style, and the staff at Rock Spring Village are committed to carrying their old-fashioned, high-quality standards well into the new millennium.

ROCK SPRING VILLAGE IS A PREMIER ASSISTED LIVING FACILITY THAT HAS BEEN A PART OF THE HARFORD COUNTY COMMUNITY FOR MORE THAN 10 YEARS.

Rifkin, Livingston, Levitan & Silver, LLC

The law firm of Rifkin, Livingston, Levitan & Silver, LLC (RLLS) brings together some of the most experienced legal professionals in the state of Maryland. The members of the firm and its partners boast an impressive record of service to the state and in the practice of law. Since its founding in 1989, RLLS has established itself as the largest government relations and government contracts law firm in Maryland. In addition to its government and administrative law focus, RLLS has built a solid reputation in corporate law and litigation, making it one of the premier full-service law firms in the region.

Each of RLLS' partners enjoyed years of success in the public and private sectors before uniting to create the firm. Alan M. Rifkin was former Maryland Governor William Donald Schaefer's first chief legislative officer, and Rifkin previously served as counsel to the Maryland Senate. While serving in Schaefer's cabinet, Rifkin spearheaded the authorization of the Camden Yards sports complex, now the home of the Baltimore Orioles and Ravens, and was widely credited with many of the Schaefer administration's early successes. Scott A. Livingston was an assistant attorney general with the Maryland Department of Transportation and the author of *Contracting with the State of Maryland*, a widely quoted reference in the area of procurement law. Former Senator Laurence Levitan served as chairman of the Maryland Senate's Budget and Taxation Committee for 16 years. Former Judge Edgar P. Silver served in the General Assembly of Maryland before his appointment to the Circuit Court of Baltimore, where he served for more than 20 years, while Joel D. Rozner served as Governor Parris Glendening's chief of staff during Glendening's tenure as Prince George's County executive. Rozner also was the county's people's zoning counsel. Michael V. Johansen was counsel to the Maryland Senate's Budget and Taxation Committee before joining the firm.

This powerful combination of partners, joined by a team of experienced attorneys and staff, provides the firm's clients with professional, top-quality legal advice and guidance.

Navigating the Maze of Government Laws, Regulations, and Contracts

With its wealth of experience in governmental affairs, administrative law, government contracts, and litigation, RLLS has helped a wide variety of clients navigate the complex maze of government laws, regulations, and processes. On the government relations side of the firm's practice, attorneys regularly lobby and monitor legislative activities, draft legislation and testimony, prepare witnesses for hearings, and organize grassroots support.

On the administrative and contract law side of the firm, RLLS' attorneys represent a wide variety of corporations and institutions at the local, state, and federal levels. Included in this division of the firm is RLLS' Sports and Corporate Practice Area, which provides a wide range of legal services to various professional sports franchises, including negotiations with rights holders, matters relating to uniform players contracts, lease and contract issues, and trademark protections.

RLLS' attorneys are also active in the area of state procurement law and state contracting—helping clients develop bids and proposals, draft and negotiate subcontracts, comply with all applicable regulations, submit bid protests, and arbitrate disputes.

Legal Solutions for Businesses

For more than a decade, RLLS has represented a vast array of corporations, institutions, sports franchises, and individuals with the singular goal of assisting its clients in achieving successful and practical solutions to business objectives. Whether solutions involve governmental action or judicial resolution, RLLS has gained a well-earned reputation for success.

THE FOUNDING PARTNERS OF RIFKIN, LIVINGSTON, LEVITAN & SILVER, LLC (RLLS) INCLUDE (FROM LEFT) MICHAEL JOHANSEN, SCOTT LIVINGSTON, EDGAR SILVER, ALAN RIFKIN, JOEL ROZNER, AND LAURENCE LEVITAN.

▲ LISA MASSON

Commitment to Baltimore

Although RLLS maintains offices in the state's capital in Annapolis and in Greenbelt, the firm's headquarters is located in Baltimore, demonstrating RLLS' strong commitment to the city. According to Rifkin, "We chose to locate in Baltimore because we believe the city is the central economic engine for the state."

RLLS has contributed to Baltimore's success in a number of ways, both as a corporate entity and through the individual efforts of its partners and associates. Rifkin serves on the board of directors of the Baltimore Symphony Orchestra, Babe Ruth Museum, and Loyola College, while Levitan is the founder of the state's CEO Roundtable. Silver has been recognized by countless civic and charitable organizations for his generous service over the years, and Rozner serves on various local chambers of commerce. The firm is also active in various regional economic development forums and local chambers of commerce, supporting activism among its employees.

The firm of Rifkin, Livingston, Levitan & Silver, LLC shines among the region's best and brightest, from its well-known partners to its newest associates. An unbeatable combination of integrity, experience, and ethical professionalism makes RLLS one of the most well-respected law firms in Maryland and beyond.

WITH ITS WEALTH OF EXPERIENCE IN GOVERNMENTAL AFFAIRS, ADMINISTRATIVE LAW, GOVERNMENT CONTRACTS, AND LITIGATION, RLLS HAS HELPED A WIDE VARIETY OF CLIENTS NAVIGATE THE COMPLEX MAZE OF GOVERNMENT LAWS, REGULATIONS, AND PROCESSES.

Among the firm's clients are some of the area's most prominent companies. RLLS has served as outside counsel for the Baltimore Orioles and the Maryland Jockey Club, the parent organization for Pimlico Racetrack and the Preakness. RLLS also frequently represents national and international organizations that conduct business in Maryland, such as Accenture, Sverdrup Civil, Hertz Corporation, Circuit City/CARMAX, Washington Area New Automobile Dealers Association, Maryland Association of Realtors, American General Corporation, The Zamoiski Co., HCR-ManorCare, Suburban Hospital, Giant Food, and many others.

RLLS HAS SERVED AS OUTSIDE COUNSEL FOR THE BALTIMORE ORIOLES AND THE MARYLAND JOCKEY CLUB, THE PARENT ORGANIZATION FOR PIMLICO RACETRACK AND THE PREAKNESS.

Greater Baltimore Technology Council

Increasingly, the Baltimore area is becoming known as a gold mine for growing high-tech companies, with a wealth of resources and infrastructure in place. A whole host of emerging and established technology companies; a network of service providers and prospective investors; world-class universities and

research laboratories; and supportive federal, state, and local government agencies make the Greater Baltimore region an emerging hot spot in the technology community.

Greater Baltimore Technology Council (GBTC) is a nonprofit organization that serves as a catalyst for the region's high-tech growth. Despite its short life, the organization has made an impressive impact, much like the companies that it supports. Originally a part of the Greater Baltimore Committee, the council was formed in 1990 to examine and address the needs of the area's emerging high-tech sector. After the industry took off in the late 1990s, the council spun off as an independent entity in

1999. Today, GBTC is funded by its membership, the Maryland Department of Business and Economic Development, and the nonprofit Abell Foundation.

According to Penny Lewandowski, GBTC executive director, "The future is here." Of course, she doesn't mean that in a general, visceral sort of way. Lewandowski means that in the Greater Baltimore area today, GBTC is cultivating and nurturing the future for even brighter possibilities.

Fueling the Fire

GBTC fuels the fire by helping companies harness available resources. The council provides opportunities for networking within the community so local movers and shakers can share ideas and information, cultivate new business and markets, nurture new talent and entrepreneurship, and promote the industry and the region. Through GBTC, the high-tech industry also gains a more powerful voice with local and national legislatures, ensuring that their thoughts are heard and their interests are served.

The council also sounds the bullhorn for the technology community, making sure business

leaders in the state and across the country know about the high-tech excitement and energy in Baltimore. Through GBTC's marketing efforts, new resources and businesses are drawn to the region, and media attention is focused on Baltimore's vibrant technology community and the dynamic companies that compose it.

Immersion in the Community

GBTC is truly immersed in the technology community, having set up shop in the Emerging Technology Center (ETC), a technology incubator at the renovated Can Company complex in Baltimore's Canton neighborhood. There, many of the region's newest and most promising companies are growing by leaps and bounds. GBTC's presence at ETC allows a unique window into the defining culture of the high-tech world, and provides the council with unparalleled understanding of the issues critical to its members.

If technology has birthed the new economy, then GBTC is the new nonprofit. Discarding the conventions of yesterday, GBTC moves at the lightning-fast speed of the industry it serves, constantly evolving and adapting to the fluid needs of its membership.

Studies have shown that environmental design impacts mood, healing, and overall well-being. Those issues are extremely important in hospital and senior living facilities—locations historically associated with drab, institutional interiors. Hyde Incorporated Interior Design is dedicated to changing this norm, focusing its expertise and ingenuity on improving the quality of design and transforming the healing environments within these long-overlooked health care institutions. With this goal in mind, the firm is building a distinguished reputation in this exciting design field.

Strong Foundations and Professionalism

The firm's founder, Andrea V. Hyde, ASID, built her reputation over the past 21 years, working with many well-respected Maryland architectural firms. Her love of and exposure to commercial design and construction has served her well, gaining experience and establishing her own commercial interior design firm in 1993. Since then, Hyde Interior Design has grown steadily based on its commitment to design excellence, a solid reputation, repeat business, and the referrals of its many satisfied customers. Hyde's goal is to continue to grow her clientele, both regionally and nationally, and to become recognized as an expert, innovator, and advocate for the growing international movement to improve the design of health care environments.

Hyde Interior Design currently employs eight degreed designers, and is poised to add additional designers to support its growing clientele. Because of the dynamic and competitive nature of the health care field, designers at Hyde Interior Design are continuously trained in leading-edge technology, design trends, and methodologies.

Teams of Expertise

The firm's business structure has three distinct teams of expertise, focusing on separate project types: senior living, health care, and multidisciplinary corporate design.

Today's seniors want function and service in attractive, home-like settings that are considerate to their physical limitations. Hyde's senior living team provides that and more through careful and creative collaboration from concept through opening. The firm works with some of the country's top senior living developers, including Genesis Eldercare, Marriott Health Services, and Erickson Retirement Communities.

The hospital health care team has designed many large, high-profile inpatient and outpatient projects for LifeBridge Health, MedStar Health, Inova Health, Adventist Health, Mercy Medical Center, University of Maryland Medical Systems, and Mt. Washington Pediatric Hospital. The firm's work at Mt. Washington's Rosenberg Center earned it the Best Healthcare Design Award 2000, awarded by ASID Maryland and the *Daily Record*.

Research shows that good interior design is good business; increasing employees' efficiency, effectiveness, morale, and workplace satisfaction. Although Hyde Interior Design specializes in health care design, the company's corporate design team provides creative strategic facility programming, planning, and design for its clients, including Coca-Cola Enterprises, *The Baltimore Sun*, UMBC, The Chapman Company, VIPS, Celera Genomics Corporation, The U.S. Air Force, and The U.S. Courts.

For nearly 10 years, Hyde Interior Design has been building a reputation for excellence in the design community. Its functional, efficient, and beautiful designs have satisfied a wide range of clients, and delighted countless others who live, visit, and work within them everyday.

HYDE INCORPORATED INTERIOR DESIGN IS A FIRM WITH A STRONG BACKGROUND IN HEALTH CARE AND CORPORATE DESIGN.

Gilden Integrated

While a company's capabilities and its focus on efficiency and quality are paramount in today's fast-paced world, its location matters less and less. That's how Gilden Integrated, the Baltimore-based advertising agency, has managed to usurp Madison Avenue and land national high-tech accounts. Gilden Integrated bills itself as The Ad Agency Digitally Remastered, and the company is growing quite rapidly.

After many years of work as creative director at several advertising firms, Baltimore native Jack Gilden recognized a need in advertising. The new economy created by the high-tech sector was developing at unprecedented speeds, and traditional advertising agencies were not focused on the tech sector. Plus, the needs of these new companies did not fit into standard advertising molds. Gilden decided to take advantage of this opportunity, and created Gilden in 1995 to serve that unique market.

Based in Baltimore, Gilden focused on national accounts from day one. Nextel, Aether Systems, Integrated Data Communications, Cambrian, HireFuze.com, and Legg Mason Funds soon joined forces with Gilden. Today, Gilden's clients are found at the top of industry segment lists, and the firm is sought out by dynamic technology businesses that desire the creativity, strategy, and experience that its team brings to the table.

Challenging Tradition

Urgency is critical when dealing with the high-tech clients that dominate Gilden's portfolio. With these clients, the Gilden team steps outside the traditional advertising mind-set and takes on a consultative role, advising the client on strategy, research, planning, branding, and positioning. In fact, Gilden has taken many companies through the many stages of growth—from businesses with five employees to companies with several thousand. The firm's thorough knowledge of advertising, graphic design, public relations, market research, and media planning provides businesses with a unified approach to their marketing needs.

Each aspect of the firm's offerings reflects the fast-paced, dynamic feel that makes Gilden distinctive. Its branding and strategic planning work has supported companies that have raised billions. Gilden's award-winning creative work has sparked debate and discussion in the *Wall Street Journal*, *Computer World* magazine, and several leading advertising publications. The company's bigger, faster, "Magnum PR" approach to public relations has catapulted firms from obscurity to market leader. Gilden's Web and interactive development capabilities maximize the effectiveness of these media, and integrate the new approaches into a balanced marketing strategy.

All this knowledge and experience doesn't weigh Gilden down; on the contrary, the firm prides itself on its ability to keep up with the rate of change in the technology sector. This is a definite advantage in an industry that doesn't fit comfortably into traditional advertising slots, and where speed to market is everything. Gilden's mastery of the technology life cycle has fueled its growth, and promises to serve the firm well into the future.

That growth has been extraordinary, as Gilden has brought its fresh approach to more and more clients. The agency's team is filled with award-winning writers and designers, all of whom share a commitment to Gilden's new definition of agency.

Honoring the Past, Moving toward the Future

To reflect the comprehensive services it offers, the agency recently changed its name to Gilden Integrated. And the company has relocated its offices as well; Gilden's steady growth necessitated a move from its original location to

JACK GILDEN, PRESIDENT OF GILDEN INTEGRATED, SAYS THE AGENCY STEPS OUTSIDE THE TRADITIONAL ADVERTISING MIND-SET WHEN DEALING WITH TECHNOLOGY BUSINESSES.

a renovated landmark in the city's Hampden community. Gilden himself has roots in Hampden, and welcomed the opportunity to rescue a 100-year-old church that had been damaged by fire. The massive structure, with stone walls and beautiful stained glass, now houses the 12,000-square-foot headquarters of Gilden Integrated. Inside the historic architecture are the agency's state-of-the-art technology and modern office facilities. The renovation was roundly praised by city officials and civic leaders, who lauded Gilden's commitment to the city and its architecture.

Gilden has demonstrated its commitment to the community in many other ways. The agency gives generously of its time and resources to a number of organizations in Baltimore. In 2000, the company donated an unprecedented $1.2 million in cash, services, and in-kind gifts to the University of Maryland School of Nursing, including work on an aggressive media campaign to encourage a new generation of nurses. Other local pro bono work includes consulting services with Turn Around, a resource for domestic violence victims; the annual Jones Falls Valley celebration; and the Hampden Village Main Street Organization and annual community celebra-

tions, including the city's only Christmas parade.

Gilden Integrated makes an impact, both for its clients and for the community. Whether rehabbing an old church or redefining the advertising agency for state-of-the-art companies, the Baltimore firm attacks the task with energy and enthusiasm.

Profiles in Excellence 1996-2001

Absolute Quality Inc.

Stephen Muirhead felt so strongly about the reputation of his company that he spelled it right out in the name: Absolute Quality (AQ). That's the only acceptable standard at the Hunt Valley company, which provides comprehensive testing and technical customer support to clients in software development, hardware manufacturing, e-business, and the interactive entertainment industry. From the start, AQ has lived up to its name, and today is one of the world leaders in this cutting-edge field.

As technology has taken off, software publishers, e-business merchants, and hardware manufacturers are under increasing pressure to get products to market quickly. In addition, users have higher expectations for quick, reliable, and accessible technical support. Muirhead recognized those realities, and founded AQ in 1996 to fill a unique need. Though the company originally focused exclusively on the testing of multimedia and multiple-player computer games, AQ soon branched out to provide technical customer support and testing for a variety of clients.

Today, AQ still works with many of the leading companies in the interactive entertainment industry,

STEPHEN MUIRHEAD IS THE FOUNDER OF ABSOLUTE QUALITY INC. (AQ).

but the company also serves the testing and support needs of a variety of clients. Whether it is providing technical support for a company's internal sales management system or testing the stability and security of a new e-commerce Web site, AQ applies the same attention to detail and commitment to excellence. Through thorough testing before a release and com-

prehensive customer support afterwards, AQ can save clients time and money by reducing production delays and minimizing support needs.

Comprehensive Testing at All Stages

Before a successful launch, new technology requires thorough testing to ensure functionality and quality. AQ's experienced team of testers applies rigorous techniques to any product, simulating real-life situations and tracking performance. Complete and thorough testing helps clients improve the quality, stability, and reliability of its products, and reduce support costs after release. For games, AQ can provide complete testing on PlayStation, Game Boy, and Nintendo 64 consoles, as well as multiplayer testing on both PCs and Macs. The company's Web site testing capabilities are extensive, with attention to load and stress, functionality,

AQ IS HEADQUARTERED IN HUNT VALLEY.

performance, e-commerce, and security. AQ can even provide testing services for multilingual software and sites, assessing localization and translation functionality in 10 languages.

During the testing and beyond, AQ's staff and clients can track problems through the company's proprietary bug reporting and tracking program, Bug City. This one-of-a-kind program, developed by AQ staff in 1998, allows clients to view bug reporting for their products 24 hours a day, seven days a week at no charge. This systematic approach allows clients to identify trends, isolate variables, and, ultimately, fix problems more quickly and effectively.

Support Options to Fit Every Need

Even with AQ's exhaustive testing, end users still experience the occasional problem, or just have a question that they need answered. AQ can handle that for clients, as well, through the firm's seamless customer care programs that give end users a variety of options. Through on-line Web chat support, users can ask questions and immediately receive answers. Customer service representatives (CSRs) can even

utilize collaborative Web browsing capabilities to "push" desired information to site visitors. All e-mail inquiries are answered within 24 hours, and e-mail support responses remain branded with a client's domain name for seamless service. Live telephone support, interactive voice response systems, and fax-back and call-back support are also available, providing an option to fit nearly every user's needs. All support interactions are tracked in a database and reported to clients regularly, reflecting the frequency and length of AQ's support personnel interactions.

To provide the very best in customer service and product knowledge, all AQ staff go through a rigorous training program. Absolute Quality University (AQU) provides new employees with an intensive, two-week training curriculum on the required core competencies. But the learning doesn't stop there; all employees undergo ongoing skills enhancement training and quality assurance training, to ensure nothing less than absolute quality.

AQ's clients come from diverse industries, but all share a need for high-quality, cost-effective testing and technical support. Hasbro Interactive, Activision, Hewlett-

Packard, Gamespy.com, Hunter Douglas, LEGO New Media, and Scholastic all utilize AQ's services, making the company a leading provider of testing and support services in the market. According to one industry report, AQ has tested or supported well over half of the top 20 PC titles in the United States, including seven out of the top 10.

That accomplishment was reached after only four years in business, a testament to the company's explosive growth. In its first year, AQ had only 17 employees and 10 clients. Today, its employees number more than 200 and its revenues reach close to $10 million. In 1999, AQ opened offices in Alameda and Glasgow, expanding its reach on the West Coast and in Europe. AQ doesn't intend to slow down anytime soon; recently acquired venture capital funding will be used to help the privately owned company expand its operations centers and open new markets to its services.

The future is sure to bring change and continued growth for this dynamic company, as it evolves to take advantage of new opportunities. But one thing's sure to stay the same: AQ's commitment to absolute quality for its clients and end users.

Aether Systems Inc.

Aether Systems Inc. describes its business as "wireless solutions for a portable planet," a phrase that accurately represents both the company's expertise and the fast-paced industry it thrives in. As technology continues to evolve at an amazing speed, businesses and consumers want

to remain in touch without being tied down. Aether meets these needs through its array of wireless data services, systems, and software, providing solutions for a wide variety of end users.

Since its inception in Baltimore in 1996, Aether has been among those at the front of the wireless data curve. The company's initial focus was on the financial services industry, a market that remains a major part of Aether's business today. One of Aether's first ventures was Reuters MarketClip, the first service that provided real-time stock quotes through a wireless communication device. Before the introduction of MarketClip, stock quote information was subject to a 20-minute delay, which can be an eternity in today's fast-paced financial markets. Today, Aether helps major financial institutions like Morgan Stanley Dean Witter (MSDW), Merrill Lynch, E*Trade, and Charles Schwab provide their customers with real-time wireless trading and financial services applications.

Through Aether products like MSDW's TradeRunner and Schwab's PocketBroker, customers can use handheld wireless devices like personal digital assistants

(PDA), Web-enabled telephones, and two-way pagers to access all the same services available on-line. Aether is now one of the world's leading providers of customized wireless financial data products.

After succeeding in the financial services field, Aether aggressively expanded its business through internal growth and a series of strategic acquisitions. Today, Aether also provides wireless communications solutions to industries including health care, transportation/logistics, mobile government, and sales force automation for a variety of businesses.

Setting the Industry Standard

Wireless communication offers many exciting possibilities in the health care field, providing instant communication of critical patient and treatment information, and simplifying the storage and retrieval of patient data. Emergency medical technicians, doctors, and hospitals utilize two-way wireless messaging for valuable communications, while similar devices could be used to collect data from participants in clinical trials. Doctors can submit prescriptions via a wireless device, reducing errors and speeding delivery of important medicines. There are many potential uses for wireless communications in the health care field, all of which will streamline procedures and allow health care workers more time for quality patient care.

Many corporations find that Aether's solutions improve the efficiency of their delivery and transportation departments, and sales departments benefit from wireless communications as well. Aether's sales tools include a high-end wireless notification and response system that bridges the gap between Web site consumers

AETHER SYSTEMS INC. HAS BEEN HEADQUARTERED IN BALTIMORE SINCE ITS FOUNDING IN 1996.

AETHER INTUITIVE WIRELESS APPLICATIONS GIVE USERS THE FREEDOM TO MANAGE FINANCIAL ACCOUNTS, RETRIEVE E-MAIL, AND MORE—FROM VIRTUALLY ANYWHERE.

CEO, was honored as KPMG's Technology Entrepreneur of the Year for the Greater Washington, D.C., area. Oros has also been a finalist for Ernst & Young's Entrepreneur of the Year award. In addition, *Mobile Computing* magazine named Oros its Person of the Year for 2000.

Since its founding, Aether Systems has grown from a small start-up to an international company and market leader. The company operates more than 20 offices throughout the United States and worldwide, and employs more than 1,400 people around the world. With its winning combination of innovative solutions and cutting-edge technology, Aether's future looks bright. As society becomes increasingly mobile and information-driven, Aether will continue to be at the head of the pack, providing the tools to take communications to the next level.

and retailers. Sales agents are notified when consumers express interest in an item on their Web site, making the product a natural application for auto sales, real estate, and insurance.

The company has also established a successful Wireless Commerce division, developing a wireless commerce portal that will deliver applications including wireless bill paying, proof of payment, wireless proof of sale, and other transactions. Aether's work in this area allows users to view and pay bills and make person-to-person payments via PDAs, Web-enabled telephones, and pagers.

Diverse Interests

During its rapid growth, Aether established several affiliated companies to pursue specific niches within the wireless communications realm. Through a partnership with Reuters, Aether formed Sila Communications to offer its wireless data systems in Europe. Aether is also an investor in Inciscent, Inc., which focuses on the communication needs of the small-business and home office market, providing wireless e-mail, two-way wireless data, and Internet access to this growing segment. Together, Aether and 3Com Corporation were initial investors in OmniSky Corporation, providing wireless e-mail, Internet access, and other electronic transactions for consumers.

Education is another area that can benefit greatly from wireless

applications, and Aether is addressing this market through a joint venture, MindSurf. Aether formed MindSurf with Baltimore-based Sylvan Learning Systems Inc. to bring the power of mobile computing to kindergarten-through-grade-12 education. The MindSurf vision brings low-cost wireless handheld devices to students, providing unique opportunities for student learning and improved parent-teacher communication.

Aether's meteoric rise has been noted by leading business organizations both regionally and nationally. In 2000, David S. Oros, Aether's founder, chairman, and

Every minute of every day, the task at hand for the team of professionals at G1440 is to develop Internet strategy and services for a diverse—and growing—set of clients. G1440 is truly a complete e-solutions provider, able to manage every step of the process from analysis and develop-

ment to hosting and maintenance.

G1440 originally was founded by Larry Fiorino in 1998 under the name NETFanatics. With Maryland-based Sinclair Broadcast Group as a majority shareholder in the company, the company benefits from solid financial backing and strong business resources. After two years of steady growth, the firm took off in 2000, completing two strategic acquisitions to expand its scope of capabilities and reach. The company then changed its name to reflect its growth and the depth of its service.

Today, G1440 has more than 100 employees and offices in Columbia, Maryland; Baltimore; and San Francisco. The company is well on its way to attaining its goal of being an international e-solutions powerhouse, combining the best in design with the best in technology.

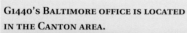

G1440's BALTIMORE OFFICE IS LOCATED IN THE CANTON AREA.

◆◆◆◆◆◆◆◆◆◆◆◆◆◆◆◆◆◆◆◆
A Solutions Powerhouse

The acquisition of Baltimore-based Impreza Design in 2000 was a turning point for G1440, as Impreza's expertise in on-line marketing and advertising rounded out the firm's skills in back-end Web development. "Together, Impreza and G1440 can offer a true full-service approach to Web development," says Matt Goddard, Impreza's co-founder and president of G1440's Baltimore office. "We now are able to offer a fully integrated product that capitalizes on the assets of both companies."

Goddard co-founded Impreza in 1996 with partner David Taub, and led the company to become one of the top Web development specialists in the Baltimore/Washington area. With a potent combination of training in financial management and marketing, Goddard provides a unique set of skills that help clients translate business goals into marketing strategies, while Taub's art direction makes this happen. Through the years, Impreza has helped clients as noteworthy as Cellular One, Comcast Online Communications, Engenia Software, the University of Maryland, and ViaCast realize their goals through technology.

In addition to the company's design capabilities, Impreza also brought with it an impressive

collection of proprietary methodologies in graphical user interface (GUI) design, which helps clients optimize their profit-making potential. The value revenue model is a strategic planning tool that helps clients determine exactly why users visit their site and identify revenue streams that deliver value. Another GUI tool, critical path charting, enables designers to create the optimal navigation system for any Web site. Through the systems path exercise, a client's organizational processes and sales process are mapped out, providing information that can help designers improve the sales process, and raise revenue or lower costs. These systematic approaches demonstrate the firm's understanding of the unique challenges of Web design, successfully combining the aesthetic elements and functional requirements needed to realize e-business objectives.

The G1440 Difference

G1440 strives to combine the best in graphic design with the most scalable, robust engineering architecture. This one-of-a-kind, full-service approach makes G1440 an industry leader, redefining the implementation of e-business initiatives. Major clients like Starbucks, MileOne, Reel.com, Intuit, ViaCast, and Esurance have turned to the firm again and again to help them optimize their Web presence. With the newly expanded capabilities of G1440, the firm can extend its reach even further, bringing its unique brand of Web development and strategy to e-businesses around the world.

While Impreza has joined the G1440 family, Goddard and Taub still maintain a strong commitment to the Baltimore area. Since Impreza's founding, this team has been a major force in Baltimore's technology community and plans to continue in that role. He serves as a board member of the Greater Baltimore Technology Council, and was the brains behind the council's Baltimore Tech Leaders billboard campaign highlighting emerging high-tech companies in the region.

G1440 also is a major supporter of the city's Live Where You Work program, offering employees discounted rent at a renovated row house near its offices in the city's Canton section. In addition, the company invested in Canton by

becoming involved in a joint venture to renovate a 15,000-square-foot commercial space in the neighborhood. The transformed space became G1440's Baltimore office in 2001, adding to Canton's growing community of dynamic high-tech companies along the harbor.

Through its combination of insightful design and engineering expertise, G1440 creates an even more powerful force in the world of e-solutions, and further strengthens the region's stature as a high-tech hotbed. The company's contributions to the area and to the industry will impact both entities for generations to come.

Meridian Medical Technologies, Inc.

Meridian Medical Technologies, Inc. is a technology-based health care company that designs, develops, and produces a broad range of automatic injectors, prefilled syringes, cardiopulmonary diagnostic and monitoring products, and other innovative health care devices. A world leader in auto-injector technology in critical market segments, Meridian is aggressively developing new auto-injector opportunities and is actively leveraging its unique proprietary technology in cardiopulmonary diagnostics. Meridian operates in two segments: Pharmaceutical Systems and Cardiopulmonary Systems.

Every product developed and produced by Meridian is designed to save lives through early intervention health care and emergency medical treatment. Quality of life is enhanced by all of the company's products, and continued research to save both lives and health care dollars is an ongoing objective.

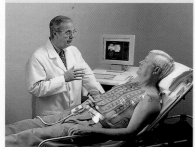

A Diverse Product Line

The Pharmaceutical Systems business serves the commercial and government markets with lifesaving products based on the company's technology leadership in auto-injectors (penlike, spring-loaded, prefilled devices) that allow patients to self-administer injectable medications quickly and easily. The Commercial Business unit produces the EpiPen™ auto-injector, the leading product for the emergency treatment of allergic reactions to bee stings, insect bites, foods, and drugs. The company also provides contract research and development, and performs pharmaceutical manufacturing for pharmaceutical and biotechnology companies in areas such as pain management, oncology, and growth hormones.

The Government Business unit serves the global market with auto-injectors containing nerve agent antidotes and other medications for the immediate protection of military and civilian populations. While current products are primarily for military personnel, they are now available to state and local emergency preparedness organizations for anti-terrorism, natural disaster, and industrial accident programs.

With heart disease the number one killer in the United States, and current electrocardiogram (ECG) technology able to diagnose only 46 percent of heart attack victims, there is much opportunity for progress. Meridian's Cardiopulmonary Systems business offers exciting new technology that can help physicians rapidly diagnose problems within the heart's electrical system. The innovative PRIME ECG™ system uses 80 leads instead of the traditional 12 to provide cardiologists and emergency physicians a clear window to the electrical performance of the heart, which can provide earlier and more accurate diagnosis of heart attacks and other problems. Rather than a traditional ECG pattern, proprietary software translates information into easily interpreted, full-color, diagnostic images resulting in saved lives and better outcomes for patients. The PRIME ECG system has been approved for sale in Europe, and is currently undergoing clinical trials for submission to the U.S. Food and Drug Administration. In 2000, this exciting new technology was awarded Millennium Product status in the United Kingdom, endorsed by Prime Minister Tony Blair to recognize innovation and creativity in the marketplace.

Giving Back to the Community

Meridian maintains its corporate headquarters in Columbia, Maryland, with complete sterile pharmaceutical manufacturing and packaging capabilities in St. Louis. Meridian's Northern Ireland facility provides research, development, and manufacturing for the PRIME ECG and other cardiopulmonary products. The company makes lasting contributions to each of these locations through the dedication of time, talent, and financial resources.

In Maryland, Meridian Medical Technologies, Inc. actively supports the Food Allergy Network—and other food allergy awareness campaigns—to help educate the public about the very real danger of food allergies. The company is also involved with Hammond High School in Columbia, providing various kinds of support for students preparing to enter the workforce or those who are college bound. Meridian also supports the local chapter of the Easter Seals, American Cancer Society, Howard County Chamber of Commerce, and University of Maryland Baltimore Campus Research Park.

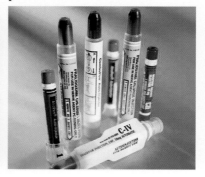

Sierra Military Health Services, Inc. (SMHS) was launched in 1996, soon after the United States began introducing a managed care approach for its military health care coverage. That program, called TRICARE, delivers managed care health benefits to active duty and retired military personnel and their depen-

dents in 11 regions throughout the country. SMHS is the prime contractor for TRICARE in the Department of Defense's Region 1, which stretches from Maine through northern Virginia, including the entire Washington, D.C., area.

In total, SMHS serves nearly 1 million people in Region 1. Through local partnerships, SMHS offers a wide range of health care services, including primary and preventive care, behavioral health services, network management, pharmacy benefits, and health care advice and education for TRICARE beneficiaries. The company also handles claims processing, credentialing, and utilization management reporting for its clients, ensuring cost-effective, efficient care that maintains the highest standards.

Based in Baltimore

With Baltimore as its headquarters, SMHS is well positioned to service Region 1, and the company benefits from easy access to Washington, D.C. SMHS' Baltimore offices house the firm's operations, government affairs, medical affairs, information systems, contract compliance, and finance departments, as well as the beneficiary services hub, which assists ben-

eficiaries with processing enrollments, scheduling appointments, and coordinating referrals, in addition to responding to general questions about the TRICARE program.

In addition to its Baltimore presence, SMHS also maintains TRICARE service centers (TSCs) in or near each of the 32 military treatment facilities in Region 1. These administrative offices are staffed with managers, customer service representatives, health care coordinators, and other personnel to help beneficiaries obtain health care services, enroll in the TRICARE program, and find answers to their TRICARE questions. Through its innovative TRICARE Ombudsman Program (TOP), SMHS also provides a dedicated primary customer service source at each TSC throughout the region, to work face-to-face with walk-in customers on their TRICARE issues.

SHAREing with the Community

While the company serves a diverse region spanning the Northeast and the mid-Atlantic states, SMHS is also a strong corporate citizen of Baltimore and supports a variety of organizations and

causes in the city. Many SMHS employees participate in the Sierra's Helpful and Responsive Employees (SHARE) program. This group encourages volunteerism among employees and provides valuable assistance to a variety of community organizations and projects. In Baltimore, the company regularly supports the Juvenile Diabetes Research Foundation, United Way, and Toys for Tots. SMHS is a valuable member of Baltimore City Community College's (BCCC) advisory board, and the company has provided financial support for the BCCC Foundation's Call Center Training scholarship program. Additionally, SMHS has provided sponsorship of the city's annual Fourth of July celebration.

In 2000, the president of SMHS, David R. Nelson, was chosen as Ernst & Young's Entrepreneur of the Year in the health care/life sciences category. This award represents the success of SMHS' mission, which is to raise the standards of excellence and exceed the expectations of its customers, employees, and partners. Through its commitment to quality, service, and choice, Sierra Military Health Services is helping the country's armed forces remain fit, healthy, and ready to serve.

SIERRA MILITARY HEALTH SERVICES, INC. (SMHS) PRESIDENT DAVID R. NELSON AND HIS SON, BRIAN ROBERT, KICK OFF THE JUVENILE DIABETES RESEARCH FOUNDATION'S 2000 WALK TO CURE DIABETES AT THE BALTIMORE ZOO (TOP).

SMHS OFFERS A RANGE OF SERVICES AND PROFESSIONAL OPPORTUNITIES IN BALTIMORE, FROM CLINICAL POSITIONS AND CUSTOMER SERVICE TO INFORMATION TECHNOLOGY (BOTTOM LEFT AND RIGHT).

Network Technologies Group, Inc.

Companies demand lightning-fast access to information, fueled by the demands of the new economy. Since 1998, Network Technologies Group, Inc. (NTG) has helped hundreds of companies access their information faster and better. Today, NTG engineers, installs, and maintains high-tech, bandwidth-intensive communications systems for a variety of clients across the country, helping companies realize a quicker ramp up to the information superhighway.

NTG offers an end-to-end solution for cable television and communication companies, providing a full array of outside plant construction and engineering services, structured wire services, and enterprise voice and data network services. The company is a member of the Association of General Contractors, and its highly skilled staff is experienced in every aspect of engineering, as well as in both aerial and underground construction. NTG provides customized solutions for each project, working with the client to determine the most efficient and cost-effective approach. Virtually every campus-wide structural wiring component can be engineered and installed by NTG, including specialized paging, multimedia cabling, certified shielded and unshielded twisted pair cables, and wireless and fiber-optic networks. As communication technology capabilities have evolved, NTG has remained at the forefront of planning and implementing both traditional and nontraditional voice and data communications platforms.

Today, NTG is responsible for more than 4,000 miles of aerial and underground fiber projects in Maryland, Virginia, and Delaware, making the company one of the biggest players in the region.

Meeting Increasing Demands with Explosive Growth

Through sound management and a commitment to excellence, NTG has experienced record growth since its inception. Originally founded by Victor Giordani, chief operating officer; Michele Tobin, chief executive officer; and Dan Welsh, executive vice president, NTG now employs nearly 400 people and expects to maintain this pace of growth as it continues to expand operations nationally.

Growing demands for increased bandwidth and an increasing

trend toward outsourcing in the cable television and communications industries have provided an opportunity for advancement, and NTG has responded aggressively. Investors have recognized an opportunity with NTG and have backed the company's growth with substantial venture capital. The company's investors include Abell Venture Fund, the venture capital arm of the Abell Foundation; Spring Capital Partners L.P., a Baltimore-based firm; and Mercantile-Safe Deposit and Trust Company. This funding has allowed NTG to hire the employees and purchase the additional equipment necessary to serve the firm's growing customer base quickly and efficiently.

Revenues have multiplied steadily; in its second year, NTG more than tripled in size. NTG ended 2001 with revenues of $23 million. An additional $10 million in growth is expected for the year 2002.

Diverse Experience with Major Clients

NTG has served a wide range of clients, from the U.S Department of the Interior to the Howard County School District. At the University of Maryland-College Park, working with Comcast Cable Communications, NTG surveyed, designed, and installed for the entire campus community the construction of 4,320 dedicated lines and a total of 9,100 outlets. Of only a three-

month duration, this project included construction of pathway and riser cabling on interiors, as well as between buildings, that consisted of both high and low rises. Outside plant construction on the project involved 4.5 miles of underground placing. For Adelphia Cable in Louden County, Virginia, NTG installed a 680-mile ring of fiber over land, along with both aerial and underground new construction.

Cambrian Communications asked NTG to engineer and build an 11-mile quad duct system through high-visibility areas of Baltimore County. A significant portion of the work included state-of-the-art outside plant construction, including "trenchless" technology techniques. The company has also worked with such international companies as Federal Express, Corvis, Allied Riser, and Ciena.

NTG's founders made a conscious decision to set up shop in Baltimore, and the company remains committed to the economic health of the city. "One of the primary goals from our inception has been to assist in rebuilding the employment base of the city of Baltimore," says Tobin. "Our business experiences in Baltimore have been incredibly rewarding." In the beginning, the company set a three-year goal of creating 150 city-based jobs, and exceeded that number quickly. Today, the NTG headquarters remains in Baltimore's Fells Point neighbor-

hood, and satellite offices have been established in Sterling, Virginia, and Glendale, Maryland, with a location in Delaware planned during 2001.

Growing with the City

NTG further demonstrates its commitment to the city through its participation in civic and public works programs to benefit the region and its residents. The company is an active member of the Greater Baltimore Technology Council, and all of its executives are engaged with multiple charitable organizations in the Greater Baltimore region. NTG also actively recruits employees from the region's vocational schools and the Empower Baltimore and Strive programs, all of which help provide specific skill training for residents seeking employment.

In 2000, Network Technologies Group, Inc. was named on the dbusiness.com 50 to Watch list for hot growth companies in its market. The dbusiness.com list focuses on relatively unknown small- to mid-cap companies that are having a significant impact on the economy. NTG certainly fits that mold, but it is doubtful that the company will be unknown for long. With its impressive customer list, its sound management, and a strong position in a growing industry, the firm is poised for even greater things in the future.

NTG'S ENGINEERING DEPARTMENT USES STATE-OF-THE-ART SOFTWARE AND EQUIPMENT TO PROVIDE CUSTOMERS A QUALITY PRODUCT ON PROJECTS SUCH AS LONG-HAUL DUCT AND FIBER PLACEMENT, CAMPUS-WIDE CONSTRUCTION, AND STRUCTURED WIRING FOR ELECTRICAL, VOICE, AND DATA.

kforce

High tech and high touch—that's what kforce, a Web-based specialty staffing service, delivers to organizations and individuals around the world each day. Through its groundbreaking approach, kforce, one of the leading full-service staffing, consulting, and training companies in North America,

has reinvented professional staffing. Now the best of traditional and on-line staffing models are available from one affordable, convenient, and accessible source.

Technology has changed the way the world works, and professional staffing is no exception. The Internet has become a major tool for job seekers and employers, who enjoy its privacy, convenience, and efficiency. However, choosing a new position or employee is still a very personal decision, and many candidates and organizations still desire that human contact. kforce offers the best of both worlds, combining the convenience and capabilities of the Internet with the personalized service only a real live person can provide.

Benefits for Job Seekers

At kforce, job seekers find a whole host of resources, from general career management information to tips targeted to their situation. Once the free registration process is complete, job seekers can create a personal profile, indicating their needs and preferences, and attach a résumé and other pertinent information. Registered users can also search the site's job database, which includes a wide range of temporary, contract, and permanent positions. Job seekers can also indicate one of kforce's specialty areas, which include information technology, finance and accounting, human resources, engineering,

pharmaceutical, health care, legal, scientific, insurance, investments, and e-solutions consulting. Job seekers that specify one of these areas are assigned a recruiting specialist, who has extensive background in the specialty area and knowledge of the local market.

For those who need more guidance, there is a whole host of resources available at kforce, including information on self-assessment, marketing and packaging, interviewing, conducting a job search, and conduct on the job. Job seekers can even take advantage of on-line tools like Homefair.com™ Calculator and Salary Wizard™, which allow users to make educated relocation decisions and compare salaries for

KFORCE OFFERS THE BEST OF BOTH WORLDS, COMBINING THE CONVENIENCE AND CAPABILITIES OF THE INTERNET WITH THE PERSONALIZED SERVICE ONLY A REAL LIVE PERSON CAN PROVIDE.

comparable jobs in different locations.

Benefits for Employers

Employers benefit from kforce's services as well, which can help them shorten their hiring cycle and enjoy a higher offer-to-hire ratio. Organizations choose a level of membership based on their needs, which allows them to post a specified number of positions each year and search the kforce database for qualified candidates. Some organizations utilize the services of a recruiting specialist, who can help match qualified candidates with open positions. Employers can take advantage of on-line resources as well, with special informational sections on recruitment, legal issues, interviewing strategies, and retention and development. Candidates for each position are prescreened, interviewed, and tested before being submitted to member employers, saving companies time and money.

Another advantage of the kforce approach is its understanding of a variety of markets through its local office network. With more than 2,000 recruiting specialists in 44 domestic markets and one international market, kforce serves many of the most desirable employment venues. The company's local recruiters understand regional employment issues, and can help both job seekers and organizations find just the right fit.

Education Services

Through its Education Services division, kforce offers a variety of training options designed to meet the needs of individuals and employers in a range of markets. The on-line e-learning community provides mentored classes with live chats and interaction with certified instructors, a convenient alternative for many busy professionals. Students can even purchase training materials on-line, making new skills even more accessible. kforce also designs custom training programs to meet an organization's specific objectives, and can coordinate education outsourcing at an employer's site, via the Internet, or at kforce's training facilities. In addition, kforce offers public training for Microsoft, Lotus, and Novell products at its training centers.

The KnowledgeForce Resource

kforce today represents the combined strength and resources of a number of leading specialty staffing organizations across the country. Originally founded as Romac & Associates, the company has continued a pattern of growth and innovation designed to enhance customer service and ensure effective results by uniting with firms offering the experience, expertise, and resources the clients require. Over the years, top firms such as Source EDP, Source Finance, UQ Solutions, SCI, PCS, Science Solution, CRE, Bayshore, and CEIM have joined kforce. Romac further strengthened its position in 1998 by merging with Source Services Corporation, one of the industry's outstanding leaders. In 1999, the company launched kforce.com, a groundbreaking on-line career management and recruiting resource for career-motivated professionals and the organizations that seek them.

kforce.com is derived from Romac's long-held tag line: The KnowledgeForce Resource. The name acknowledges the company's decades of experience in the professional staffing field, while still speaking the language of the new economy. It is another example of kforce's successful melding of the tried and true with the new and innovative. This approach has served the company well, as it also serves the needs of job seekers and employers around the globe.

THROUGH ITS GROUNDBREAKING APPROACH, KFORCE, ONE OF THE LEADING FULL-SERVICE STAFFING, CONSULTING, AND TRAINING COMPANIES IN NORTH AMERICA, HAS REINVENTED PROFESSIONAL STAFFING.

Network Security Wizards

While wizards and dragons are typically associated with ancient tales, Network Security Wizards (NSW) shows that such things are anything but primeval. In fact, NSW is on the cutting edge of technology, with its Dragon line of network intrusion detection tools. ◆ As the world

becomes increasingly dependent on computers, it also becomes increasingly vulnerable to high-tech attack. Whether a low-level prank or a sophisticated scheme, the effects of computer crime can cost businesses millions of dollars and untold complications.

Ron Gula recognized this. His experience in the U.S. Air Force and at the National Security Agency, combined with years of network security work at several high-tech companies, gave him a unique understanding of these challenges. While several intrusion detection systems (IDSs) were on the market, none of them performed up to Gula's expectations. He believed he could build a better IDS, one that would include all the features he was looking for as a user. So in early 1999, Gula established Network Security Wizards with his own savings,

and introduced his own IDS, the Dragon Sensor.

Best-of-Breed Intrusion Detection

The Dragon Sensor quickly became popular among security professionals and Internet service providers. A network monitor, the Dragon Sensor watches live network packets, looking for unusual activity. It can detect signs of computer crime, network attack, network misuse, or anomalies, and it responds very quickly, making it a natural fit for high-bandwidth networks. If an event occurs, the Dragon Sensor can send e-mail messages and pages to alert administrators, taking action to stop the event. The system even automatically records details of the event for future forensic analysis. Typically, Dragon Sensors are deployed on stand-

alone systems in front of firewalls or at key network choke points.

NSW quickly followed the Dragon Sensor introduction with the launch of Dragon Squire, its host monitoring system. The Dragon Squire looks at system logs for evidence of malicious or suspicious application activity in real time, monitoring key system files for evidence of tampering. Dragon Squire has been tuned to prevent high load levels and to minimize any negative impact to a server's performance. Besides being an excellent system security tool, Dragon Squire can also analyze firewall logs, router events, and just about anything that can speak SNMP or SYSLOG.

NSW also offers the Dragon Server, which facilitates the secure management of all Dragon Sensors and Dragon Squires. Dragon Server can aggregate all alerts into one central database so that disparate attack information can be correlated. The system also includes a variety of reporting and analysis tools, as well as the ability to customize alerts via e-mail, SNMP, or SYSLOG messages.

Complete Services Support

In addition to its Dragon line, NSW also offers a full range of direct services to help clients get the most out of the company's IDS tools. The firm offers regular training classes at its Columbia, Maryland, offices, as well as complete installation, configuration, and support of its Dragon equipment and software. The NSW team can provide clients with monthly Dragon Squire and Dragon Sensor log reviews, presenting an expert interpretation of detected network activity. Through partnerships with a variety of network security service providers, NSW can even offer 24-hour monitoring of multiple Dragon Sensors.

NETWORK SECURITY WIZARDS (NSW) IS PART OF ENTERASYS NETWORKS.

Committed to quality, NSW continually evaluates and improves its products and services, adding new technology and features to keep one step ahead of the ever evolving threats to network security. New versions and upgrades of the Dragon line are released regularly, and the NSW team is forever on the lookout for ways to improve its IDS products.

Cabletron's Enterasys Networks

NSW's whirlwind first year was capped off with an impressive distinction: in 2000, the Dragon Sensor tool won the Network Computing Well-Connected Award in the category of enterprise security intrusion detection. The buzz soon attracted investors, and later that year, Enterasys Networks acquired NSW. Enterasys falls under the umbrella of holding company Cabletron, a Standard and Poor's 500 index company that owns several of the most innovative organizations in the telecommunications and networking industry. NSW is proud to join this distinguished family, and is confident that its best-of-breed products will make a significant impact for Enterasys.

"The intrusion detection marketplace is growing at 39 percent yearly, and spending in the enterprise portion of the market is expected to reach more than $500 million by 2003," says

Gula. "This makes the addition of NSW and its award-winning IDS product lines a natural for Enterasys, and it gives the company a vital component in the building of an industry-leading enterprise network security portfolio."

Gula should know. He has become an in-demand expert in the network security field,

speaking frequently at industry events and contributing articles for publication on related topics. Now, with the backing of a large corporation behind the company, the sky is the limit for Network Security Wizards. On its own, the firm revolutionized the IDS field. Now, as part of Enterasys Networks, the sky is the limit for NSW.

NSW's DRAGON LINE OF NETWORK INTRUSION DETECTION TOOLS CAN SAVE COMPANIES FROM COSTLY COMPUTER CRIME.

Radisson Plaza Hotel Baltimore Inner Harbor

Located in what was once the Lord Baltimore Hotel—a downtown landmark since 1928—the Radisson Plaza Hotel Baltimore Inner Harbor offers both business and vacation travelers alike modern-day conveniences in an old-world atmosphere. ◆ Originally commissioned in 1925 by hotel owner and businessman Harry Busick, the Lord Baltimore was designed by New York architect William Lee Stoddard. Constructed in fewer than eight months, the hotel opened for business on December 30, 1928, with Maryland Governor Albert C. Richie being the first to sign the guest register.

Under the management of the Busick family, the Lord Baltimore became not only a prime location for travelers, but also a social hot spot for Baltimore's elite. The hotel's ballrooms were host to countless conferences, wedding receptions, debutante balls, dinner dances, and holiday parties.

The hotel has changed hands several times since its opening. In 1960, the Busicks sold the hotel to the New York-based Weissberg hotel chain. In 1969, Baltimore lawyer and sportsman Zanvly Krieger purchased the hotel, and began major renovations that required the closing of the hotel until it could be reopened in 1973. In 1984, businessman Saul

THE RADISSON PLAZA HOTEL BALTIMORE INNER HARBOR'S ELEGANT GUEST ROOMS FEATURE A WIDE RANGE OF MODERN CONVENIENCES.

Palmutter purchased the hotel and began renovations to restore the hotel's original charm, while modernizing its services. Completed in 1985, the hotel opened its doors under the management of Brookshire Hotels. The hotel became part of the Radisson hotel family in 1990.

Modern Conveniences in an Old-World Atmosphere

Today's Radisson Plaza Hotel features all of the modern conveniences today's patrons require. The hotel's 424 elegantly decorated guest rooms—including two two-bedroom Crown Suites, two one-bedroom Crown Suites, and 16 Parlor Suites—feature such amenities as coffeemakers, electronic locks, two-line telephones with voice mail and built-in data ports, cable television, pay-per-view movies, irons and ironing boards, and a complimentary copy of USA Today delivered to the door each morning. In addition, guests can request hair dryers, Turkish-style bathrobes, and scales.

To complement its in-room amenities, the Radisson Plaza Hotel offers its guests a variety of other services, including room service, safe deposit boxes for storing valuables, valet parking, and concierge service. Guests looking to stretch their legs can utilize the hotel's fitness center, which features a whirlpool, a sauna, stationary bicycles, stair

machines, weight machines, and free weights.

A Wealth of Dining Delights

Whether they are looking for a light snack or a delicious full-course meal, guests and visitors to the Radisson Plaza Hotel will find a dining choice to please any palate. The Lord Baltimore Grille, located in the hotel's lower lobby level, is the hotel's signature restaurant. The grill is open for breakfast, lunch, and dinner, and features sumptuous breakfast and lunch buffets, as well as a complete à la carte menu. Guests dine in casual elegance while overlooking the splendor of the hotel's decor.

For guests on the go, the Deli offers either dine-in or carryout convenience for breakfast and lunch. A popular meeting place for both lifelong Baltimoreans and visitors, the Lobby Lounge serves cocktails and appetizers in a casual, yet elegant, setting.

A One-Stop Shop for Meetings and Conventions

The Radisson Plaza Hotel's convention and meeting facilities are second to none in the Baltimore area. As it was in 1928, the hotel is today a popular location for business meetings, conventions, wedding receptions, and social gatherings. With 21,000 square feet of dividable meeting and banquet facilities, the hotel can host groups as small as 10 or as large as 800. The Radisson Plaza Hotel also features two elegantly decorated ballrooms and a 125-seat amphitheater. The hotel offers complete catering services in all of its meeting and convention spaces, and state-of-the-art audiovisual equipment is available to make any event a success.

Steeped in tradition, yet committed to the modern luxuries of a 21st-century hotel, the Radisson Plaza Hotel Baltimore Inner Harbor maintains the legacy of the Lord Baltimore with elegant style. Dedicated to ever-improving service and facilities, the hotel continues to rewrite that legacy with each new guest who passes through its doors.

THE INTERIOR OF THE RADISSON PLAZA HOTEL REFLECTS ITS HISTORY AS A BALTIMORE LANDMARK.

THE RADISSON PLAZA HOTEL'S CONVENTION AND MEETING FACILITIES ARE SECOND TO NONE IN THE BALTIMORE AREA. AS IT WAS IN 1928, THE HOTEL IS TODAY A POPULAR LOCATION FOR BUSINESS MEETINGS, CONVENTIONS, WEDDING RECEPTIONS, AND SOCIAL GATHERINGS.

Towery Publishing, Inc.

Beginning as a small publisher of local newspapers in the 1930s, Towery Publishing, Inc. today produces a wide range of community-oriented materials, including books (Urban Tapestry Series), business directories, magazines, and Internet publications. Building on its long heritage of excellence, the company has become global in scope, with cities from San Diego to Sydney represented by Towery products. In all its endeavors, this Memphis-based company strives to be synonymous with service, utility, and quality.

A Diversity of Community-Based Products

Over the years, Towery has become the largest producer of published materials for North American chambers of commerce. From membership directories that enhance business-to-business communication to visitor and relocation guides tailored to reflect the unique qualities of the communities they cover, the company's chamber-oriented materials offer comprehensive information on dozens of topics, including housing, education, leisure activities, health care, and local government.

In 1990, Towery launched the Urban Tapestry Series, an award-winning collection of oversized, hardbound photojournals detailing the people, history, culture, environment, and commerce of various metropolitan areas. These coffee-table books highlight a community through three basic elements: an introductory essay by a noted local individual, an exquisite collection of four-color photographs, and profiles of the companies and organizations that animate the area's business life.

To date, nearly 90 Urban Tapestry Series editions have been published in cities around the world, from New York to Vancouver to Sydney. Authors of the books' introductory essays include two former U.S. Presidents—Gerald Ford (Grand Rapids) and Jimmy Carter (Atlanta); boxing great Muhammad Ali (Louisville); Canadian journalist Peter C. Newman (Vancouver); two network newscasters—CBS anchor Dan Rather (Austin) and ABC anchor Hugh Downs (Phoenix); NBC sportscaster Bob Costas; record-breaking quarterback Steve Young (San Francisco); best-selling mystery author Robert B. Parker (Boston), American Movie Classics host Nick Clooney (Cincinnati); former Texas first lady Nellie Connally (Houston); and former New York City Mayor Ed Koch (New York).

To maintain hands-on quality in all of its periodicals and books, Towery has long used the latest production methods available. The company was the first production environment in the United States to combine desktop publishing with color separations and image scanning to produce finished film suitable for burning plates for four-color printing. Today, Towery relies on state-of-the-art digital prepress services to produce more than 8,000 pages each year, containing well over 30,000 high-quality color images.

An Internet Pioneer

By combining its long-standing expertise in community-oriented published materials with advanced production capabilities, a global

▼ STEVE DAVIS

TOWERY PUBLISHING PRESIDENT AND CEO J. ROBERT TOWERY HAS EXPANDED THE BUSINESS HIS PARENTS STARTED IN THE 1930S TO INCLUDE A GROWING ARRAY OF TRADITIONAL AND ELECTRONIC PUBLISHED MATERIALS, AS WELL AS INTERNET AND MULTIMEDIA SERVICES, THAT ARE MARKETED LOCALLY, NATIONALLY, AND INTERNATIONALLY.

JONATHAN POSTAL ▲

Towery began the trajectory on which it continues today, creating community-oriented materials that are often produced in conjunction with chambers of commerce and other business organizations.

Despite the decades of change, Towery himself follows a long-standing family philosophy of unmatched service and unflinching quality. That approach extends throughout the entire organization to include more than 120 employees at the Memphis headquarters, and more than 40 sales, marketing, and editorial staff traveling to and working in a growing list of client cities. All of its products, and more information about the company, are featured on the Internet at www.towery.com.

In summing up his company's steady growth, Towery restates the essential formula that has driven the business since its first pages were published: "The creative energies of our staff drive us toward innovation and invention. Our people make the highest possible demands on themselves, so I know that our future is secure if the ingredients for success remain a focus on service and quality."

sales force, and extensive data management capabilities, Towery has emerged as a significant provider of Internet-based city information. In keeping with its overall focus on community resources, the company's Internet efforts represent a natural step in the evolution of the business.

The primary product lines within the Internet division are the introCity™ sites. Towery's introCity sites introduce newcomers, visitors, and longtime residents to every facet of a particular community, while simultaneously placing the local chamber of commerce at the forefront of the city's Internet activity. The sites include newcomer information, calendars, photos, citywide business listings with everything from nightlife to shopping to family fun, and on-line maps pinpointing the exact location of businesses, schools, attractions, and much more.

Decades of Publishing Expertise

In 1972, current President and CEO J. Robert Towery succeeded his parents in managing the printing and publishing business they had founded nearly four decades earlier. Soon there-

after, he expanded the scope of the company's published materials to include *Memphis* magazine and other successful regional and national publications. In 1985, after selling its locally focused assets,

Photographers

Originally headquartered in London, **ALLSPORT** has expanded to include offices in New York and Los Angeles. Its pictures have appeared in every major publication in the world, and the best of its portfolio has been displayed at elite photographic exhibitions at the Royal Photographic Society and the Olympic Museum in Lausanne.

Owner of Highlight Photography and author/photographer of *Racing is Everything*, a book exploring NASCAR and IndyCar competitions, **STEVE BAKER** photographs images on assignment for selected clients. He is an internationally published photographer, contributing to more than 250 publications, and his corporate clients include Mobil Oil, Eastman Kodak, the U.S. Olympic Committee, the National Museum of Sports, and Budweiser.

Many of the photographs appearing in *Baltimore: Life in the City* were taken by current and former staff photographers at the **BALTIMORE SUN**. Since 1904, the newspaper's professional photojournalists have documented the city as it has grown and developed from day to day, paying a fitting tribute to its people and places.

JEFFREY F. BILL is a freelance photographer. His principal client is the Baltimore Zoo, and he is the assistant director of news photography at the *Baltimore Sun*.

Contributing to such exhibitions as *Works by Contemporary Maryland Artists 2000, Artscape, and Carroll Visions*, **GREGORY W. BLANK** has had several single-artist shows at the Carroll County Arts Council and has participated in two group showings at the C. Alden Phelps Gallery. His images have appeared in *Guidepost* and *Covenant Companion*, and he won top prizes in the Carroll County Tourism Photography Contest and the Life around Baltimore calendar contest.

DAVE BOARMAN JR. is originally from the Baltimore area and enjoys landscape, nature, and sports photography.

Originally from Chicago, **SCOTT BOEHM** owns Boehm Photographic and specializes in photography and graphic design.

After working for newspapers in Virginia, North Carolina, and Chicago for 12 years, **ROB BROWN** began his freelance career in Baltimore in 1996. He specializes in editorial, sports, and travel photography and has earned dozens of awards for news photography.

A freelance photographer, **MARSHALL CLARKE** specializes in documentary, portrait, black-and-white, and color landscape photography. His images were exhibited at the *Photography 2000* show at Stage Gallery in New York.

LEE FOSTER, a veteran travel writer and photographer, has had his work published in major travel magazines and newspapers. He maintains a stock library that features images of more than 250 destinations around the world.

Owner and sole propietor of Photopia Studios, **MICHELLE GIENOW** was the winner of the Maryland Society of Professional Journalists' Feature Photographer of the Year for 1997, 1998, and 1999. Her images have appeared in such publications as the *Baltimore Sun, Baltimore City Paper, New York Times, Boston Globe*, and *Christian Science Monitor*.

JOSHUA DUDLEY GREER specializes in fine art, portrait, and architecture photography. He is currently attending Maryland Institute College of Art in Baltimore.

MARK HAMILTON, manager of the Picture People photography studio, specializes in artwork, stock, weddings, and glamour photography. His images have appeared in magazines and corporate advertisements.

Originally from North Carolina, **ROB HOLMES** specializes in commercial photography and animation and owns HolmeZart/NVision Animation. His images have been published in *Good Housekeeping, Esquire*, and *Vanity Fair*.

A self-taught photographer, **ROBERT HOUSTON** owns Bob Houston Ltd. and specializes in photojournalism and people, nature, creative, and editorial photography. His work was shown at the Smithsonian, and he is the recipient of an award from Eastman Kodak.

OSWALDO JIMENEZ, originally from Ecuador, has lived in the Baltimore area for almost 25 years.

Once an aerospace photojournalist for NASA, **DENNIS KEIM** now owns dk-studio and specializes in corporate and editorial photography. His travel and editorial photography have been featured in local, regional, and national publications, and his lifestyle photography has appeared in three books: *Huntsville—Where Technology Meets Tradition, Huntsville—A Timeless Portrait*, and *To the Edge of the Universe*.

After studying art in his native Ireland, **JAMES LEMASS** moved to Cambridge, Massachusetts, in 1987. His specialties include people and travel photography, and his photographs have appeared in several other Towery publications.

Before his death in August 2000, **MIKE McGOVERN** owned Mike McGovern Photography and specialized in landscape, portrait, editorial, corporate, and institutional collage photography. He did a great deal of portrait work of the people of Baltimore, and his images have been featured in more than 15 exhibitions and various local and national magazines.

GREG PEASE, a Baltimore-based photographer specializing in business and industry, and owner of Greg Pease Photography, began his career as a commercial photographer in 1974 and has won numerous awards for his work. His images have been published in books, magazines, and advertisements worldwide, and he has contributed to several Towery publications.

Owner and president of James Scherlis Photography, **JAMES SCHERLIS** specializes in editorial/ feature, performing arts, weather, nature, and stock photography. He has served as the official photographer for the National Symphony/

Kennedy Center; the Peabody Conservatory of Music; and the Library of Congress, Music Division. He has contributed to several Towery publications.

A Vietnam veteran, **RON SCHRAMM** has photographed all areas of Chicago and has images in the new Midway Airport Terminal. He is a member of the Chicago Convention & Tourism Bureau and the American Society of Media Photographers.

TONY SWEET is widely published in print and electronic media. He lectures, conducts workshops, and produces fine art prints, and he contributes frequently to *Shutterbug* magazine and Nikon's consumer Web site.

As the owner of Michael Townsend Photography, **MICHAEL TOWNSEND** specializes in travel, nature, and cultural imagery photography from

46 states and 40 countries. With 88,000 original images on file, he has been published in *Newsweek, Atlantic Monthly, Money & Seattle,* and other publications.

Originally from Taiwan, **SONG S. WANG** specializes in landscapes, cityscapes, and macrophotography. His awards include honorable mention and first place in Photoworkshop.com's Assignments #9 and #10 respectively. His images represent part of his documentation of his time spent in Baltimore.

A retired actor, **ROBERT WOOD** achieves success in the artistic community through his writing, music, and photography.

For further information about the photographers appearing in *Baltimore: Life in the City,* please contact Towery Publishing.

© GREG PEASE PHOTOGRAPHY

TOWERY PUBLISHING, INC.
THE TOWERY BUILDING, 1835 UNION AVENUE, MEMPHIS, TN 38104
WWW.TOWERY.COM

PUBLISHER: J. Robert Towery EXECUTIVE PUBLISHER: Jenny McDowell SALES MANAGER: Dawn Park-Donegan MARKETING DIRECTOR: Carol Culpepper PROJECT DIRECTORS: Theresa Adkins, Kelly Crew, Chris Watson EXECUTIVE EDITOR: David B. Dawson MANAGING EDITOR: Lynn Conlee SENIOR EDITORS: Carlisle Hacker, Brian L. Johnston PROJECT EDITOR/CAPTION WRITER: Danna M. Greenfield EDITORS: Jay Adkins, Stephen M. Deusner, Rebecca E. Farabough, Ginny Reeves, Sabrina Schroeder PROFILE WRITER: Jennifer Taylor Arnold CREATIVE DIRECTOR: Brian Groppe PHOTOGRAPHY EDITOR: Jonathan Postal PHOTOGRAPHIC CONSULTANT: Thomas Graves PROFILE DESIGNERS: Rebekah Barnhardt, Laurie Beck, Glen Marshall PRODUCTION MANAGER: Brenda Pattat PHOTOGRAPHY COORDINATOR: Robin Lankford PRODUCTION ASSISTANTS: Robert Barnett, Loretta Lane, Robert Parrish DIGITAL COLOR SUPERVISOR: Darin Ipema DIGITAL COLOR TECHNICIANS: Eric Friedl, Mark Svetz DIGITAL SCANNING TECHNICIAN: Brad Long PRINT COORDINATOR: Beverly Timmons
(Printed in Korea)

© GREG PEASE PHOTOGRAPHY

LIBRARY OF CONGRESS CATALOGING-IN-PUBLICATION DATA

Baltimore : life in the city / introduction by Barry Levinson ; art direction by Karen Geary ; sponsored by the Greater Baltimore Alliance.
    p. cm. — (Urban tapestry series)
  Includes index.
  ISBN 1-881096-96-3 (alk. paper)
    1. Baltimore (Md.)–Civilization. 2. Baltimore (Md.)–Pictorial works. 3. Baltimore (Md.)–Economic conditions. 4. Business enterprises–Maryland–Baltimore. I. Levinson, Barry. II. Greater Baltimore Alliance. III. Series.

F189.B15 B33 2001
975.2'6–DC21

2001025706

Index of Profiles

© GREG PEASE PHOTOGRAPHY